The Solo Traveler

To BRIDGET:
to wonderful fellow
traveler

The Solo Traveler

A SHOESTRING GUIDE TO GEOGRAPHIC AND PERSONAL JOURNEYS

George Harris

ISBN-13: **9780692746639**
ISBN-10: **0692746633**
Library of Congress Control Number: 2016910356
Lunchpail Productions, Thousand Oaks, CA

To Rita, my bride of all these years, who was the pot of gold at the end of the rainbow of this journey.

Contents

Intro to the Introduction

I REALLY AM NOT SURE whom this book is intended for. What happened was that one day in our church, the pastor had asked me to tell the congregation a little about myself so they would know more about me—one of their Sunday-school teachers and church elders. (By the way, a church elder in a Protestant church is one who goes to endless meetings to figure out what additional committees need to be formed in order to have more meetings.) I figured that the congregation might be interested in hearing about my travels through Europe and Africa, back when I was in my twenties, and how I had rededicated my life to following God during those years.

After my testimony, a bunch of church members came up to me and said, "That was one of the most interesting stories I've ever heard. If you ever write a book about it, I will read it." It was really that simple.

However, to just launch into the story of my trek through foreign lands without any kind of context didn't seem to make sense. As they sing in *The Sound of Music*, "Nothing comes from nothing." So, I started thinking back to the time in my life when I first got interested in traveling. The more I looked back, the more I realized that my geographical travels were always connected with a soulful sojourn. So, as Mr. Portokalos in *My Big Fat Greek Wedding* says, "And there you go!" I started tying the two journeys together, which makes the book a better read, as most people like travelogues, whether they are physical or spiritual.

I have kept a journal since I was sixteen, writing about the day's activities and my thoughts about them on almost a daily basis. As I wrote down the episodes from my life that appear in these pages—particularly my travels—I was surprised how few of these events actually came from my diary; so many of them have just been impressed in my memory. I have told many of these stories countless times, usually to my daughters when they were younger and needed something to quiet them down. A story promised to a child is one of the few guaranteed ways to get immediate obedience!

I have tried to write these stories as factually as my memory allows, but many of the names in this book have been changed so that, in this day of computers and identity ubiquity, no one will feel stalked, attacked, or slighted.

Most people spend more time planning a two-week vacation than they do planning the direction of their lives. We go about our day doing things just because we think we're supposed to without questioning the basic ideas behind them. Why do I do this? Why do I go to this church but not to that religious service? Is it because I grew up that way?

I decided early on to figure out this thing called "life," and I invite you to travel with me.

I write this book, as one person told me, "as one beggar telling another beggar where to get bread." Please take it as it is intended—as a sharing of a meal.

Introduction

IT IS A PECULIAR FEELING, limply waiting to die—especially when you are at the supposed prime of life at twenty-five. But there is no denying it; here I am in the middle of Nowhere, Africa, weak, sick as a dog, and lying in a chicken coop made of mud and wire, with clucking fowls walking over me and giving me an occasional peck for good measure. Outside the coop, a handful of young boys periodically come by to look at me, laugh at me, and try to steal the remaining few earthly belongings that are in my day pack. As I spend my third day in this Saharan purgatory, I reserve all of my strength to simply endure another day, tolerate the chickens, and fend off the young thieves. I'm too weak to get up, too sick to hold down any food or drink, and have absolutely no idea how to get out of this forgotten section of Mali and return to a semblance of civilization, so I can make it to a hospital and possibly recover.

Recover. Will I? Will someone find me before I die? And if I die, how long will it take before someone from my family back in the United States finds out? Let's face it. If I die here, the first thing that will be stolen from me will be my passport. That should make a lot of money for someone in the black market. During this two-year excursion, I had sent my parents a letter every week, and had even numbered them so they would know if the mail system was awry. It would probably take about a month or two for them to realize the letters had ceased. Could they then trace my steps from my last letter and figure out that my remaining moments were in the Dogon cliffs of Mali? The infinitesimal chance of that occurring was quite depressing, but with little else to do, I would pass the time playing out various dismal scenarios of grief for my family. It's quite frightening what you can think about when there are no distractions—just you and God, alone, for five days, struggling to survive.

Survive. Would someone eventually find me before I died?

When you are alone, I mean *really* alone, you have a lot of time to think about your life. Usually, with all of the distractions of society like work, TV, smartphones, books, radio, and—above all—people, you have plenty of ways to prevent yourself from thinking about your identity, your life, and its meaning. Socrates once said, though, that the unexamined life is one not worth living.

Well, in this situation, I have a lot of time to examine and think. When there are no distractions, the thinking goes deeper and deeper into the recesses of your mind. You start thinking about your entire life. And it's not a flashback but a slow rewind—with plenty of time to reflect and dwell on all of the details and all of the motives behind your actions. You have time to look more deeply into your selfish desires and what you have *really* done with your life.

Mixed with this intense introspection is my meditation on a verse in the Bible. I'm too weak to hold up a book to read anything or even to write in my journal (which—I mentioned before—I have faithfully done since I was sixteen). All I have the strength to do is to lie still, review my life, and pass the slow, lethargic, hot, and undulating day by repeating—over and over again— a verse written by a very wise man almost three thousand years ago:

> But those who trust in the Lord shall renew their strength
> They will take their wings and fly like eagles
> They will walk and not grow tired
> They will run and not grow weary. (Isaiah 40:31)

Over and over—from the rising of the early, blistering sunrise, to the relieving dusk—I pass the oppressive hours with this verse as I pass in and out of consciousness. Alternatively, I mull over this verse and wonder about how little I've trusted in this God during my life—let alone known in any intimate detail. My two-and-a-half-year journey through the United States, Canada, Europe, the Middle East, and Africa was supposed to answer my questions about God's existence, truth, and my place in His picture—as well as His place in mine. Instead, I've ended up sick to my stomach and shaking like a leaf, with the closing chapter of my life frighteningly and apparently at hand.

How did I end up like this? More important, how and why did I even start on this trek?

CHAPTER 1

My Big Fat Greek Church

I TRULY BELIEVE, WITH ALL my heart, that we are all born with an inherent knowledge of our Creator. Only through a constant assault from people who have given up on life can we begin to doubt this obvious fact that stares at us every single moment. As the great band leader Duke Ellington once said, "Being able to say, 'God is dead' disproves the statement."

I can't recall a single moment in my life when I didn't realize this great God existed. I remember being about four years old and standing in the middle of my neighborhood on a windy day with my friend Marc Johnson. We tried to figure out why it would be so windy on this day, and with our scientific and analytical minds, we decided that it was God's way of trying to introduce Himself to us. So, we extended our hands and shook hands with this Creator of weather. It was very reassuring that someone like Marc, a guy three years older than I, was there to share and validate that moment with me.

That was why I liked going to church so much. I liked the fact that other people, all different ages and sizes, came to this place to talk about and learn about God. I grew up being baptized as a Greek Orthodox, going to a Greek Orthodox church, and being a second-generation Greek American. I just took it for granted that most of what was going on in church should not be understandable by anyone in attendance. My biggest surprise at church was when the priest would say the same words my dad would utter under his breath when he was really mad about something, but the priest seemed to be singing the words out loud. Was this the priest's way of showing anger? My older sister Kathy and I would look at each other in bewilderment as Father Kezios

1

would solemnly chant the words that, just yesterday, our father had put to an entirely different use.

While all of the stuff that I didn't understand was going on during the church service, I would look around and be awed by all of the pictures and stained-glass windows. There were pictures of men with deep, stern, detached, and detailed expressions on their faces whose feet seemed to be levitating off the ground. They were each doing something I didn't understand or holding an object that didn't make sense, but it must have seemed important to them. I always thought it was very cool that I could go to church and see a picture of a guy on a horse killing a dragon. Mostly, the people held their arms halfway up, as if giving some kind of secret signal with their hands. Each man had words written in Greek either on a book or under his levitating feet, keeping the secret code intact. What were these esoteric words, and who were these mysterious men? They seemed very serious and intent.

After the mysterious beginning of the service, Father Kezios would come down from the steps of the altar and gently talk with us kids, who had been herded into the front while the parents stayed in the rear of the church. It seemed peculiar that this man, who just a few moments ago was intensely chanting while swinging incense back and forth in a hypnotic fashion, could so quickly change temperaments and talk to us like a regular guy. Each week, he would tell us some interesting story from the Bible. It usually ended with "obey your parents," "obey God," or "start giving to the church." After four years of this, I think we started to get the message.

After he had given a variation of one of the three thematic lessons, Father Kezios would dismiss us to go to our Sunday-school lesson. Being a fairly new church, we didn't actually have classrooms to go to. Kids my age (about six years old) met in a room next to the kitchen, which at a Greek church is the choice spot. You're allowed to inhale the first smells of all the great food and pastries that were being made for the people after church. Between the smells of the incense, candles, and food, my olfactory nerves were overloaded by the time church let out. Who says church isn't sensual?

The only Sunday-school lesson I remember at that old church was when the teacher put up one of those flannel boards in front of the kitchen cupboard. On it was a cutout of dirt. The teacher—a kind lady who was someone's mom—when you are in first grade, everyone looks old!—started putting up little flannel emblems of seeds on the flannel ground. All but one of the seeds had a miserable-looking facial expression. The flannel seeds were placed on various parts of the ground: one where the soil was pretty rocky, cracked, and parched; one by the side of the road; and the last miserable-looking seed amid some thorny-looking bushes. The teacher explained how these seeds were God's word, and that one was crushed by the side of the road by Satan and another was put on rough soil that prevented the seed from developing root—like someone who keeps on disobeying God and gives into the temptation to sin. (What was sin? Basically disobeying any of the three major pillars of discussion that Father Kezios constantly referred to.) The last miserable seed was entangled within the thornbush because it was trapped by the ways of the world that were against God's ways. I must say, all of these three seeds looked extremely miserable.

But the teacher had one last seed, and she placed this smiling and cheerful seed into a part of the flannel dirt that was rich and brown. This seed, she said, would grow into a big tree and bear much fruit. Almost as if on cue, the sun started shining through the kitchen/classroom window, right onto that happy seed. Right then and there, I knew I wanted to be a seed like that—useful to God.

What was even more amazing was when the teacher told me that Jesus taught this story around two thousand years ago. I thought, "Hey, Jesus can really speak to me! This guy is great. I like him!" It really boggled my little six-year-old mind that this guy, Jesus, who is either pictured as a baby or agonizingly hanging on a cross actually was able to take the time to tell some stories. He really existed and did things!

I'm sure that I learned other things during my Sunday-school years, but nothing really made an impression on me until a year or two later when we had a substitute teacher. Our classroom had moved out of the kitchen by then. (I definitely missed the smells, but such are the ebbs and flows of life.) We were now transferred to the storage room, which was filled with papers, boxes, and various pieces of equipment. Well, there we all were, and an older girl came walking in. She must have been in junior high or high school. All I know for sure was she looked smart and wasn't a parent. (Some mom must have been sick, and heaven forbid if a father ever taught. That option was simply out of the equation.) She seemed really confident and self-assured, and she didn't even have any flannel boards to help her teach us. She just sat herself down in a chair facing us, put her hands on her knees, and calmly declared, "Today, I am going to talk to you about heaven."

For the rest of the class, she gave the most vivid, intriguing, inspiring, and glorious description of this eternal home—no drawings, no paintings, and no role-playing games, just a detail-by-detail depiction of bliss, joy, peace, and health. And the best part was that we would be able to share heaven with all of our friends—not only our friends, but with people from throughout history.

Well, this thought just overwhelmed me. Being an all-American boy, I loved playing baseball and army. For me, the possibility of actually being able to see ballplayers like Lou Gehrig, Babe Ruth, and Christy Mathewson— as well as meeting army heroes like George Washington, Abe Lincoln, and Ulysses S. Grant—was just too good to be true. And to be with them forever! What is *forever* to a kid? It was long enough to make me want to go there; that's for sure!

This girl's guided tour of heaven made the hour-long Sunday-school class go by in a flash. I, along with all of the other kids, was completely disappointed that the class had to end. We wanted more; we had no idea that anything could be that good!

Next week, to our surprise, the girl came back to teach again! We were overjoyed. This time, she asked us what we wanted to learn that week. We all answered in unison, "Heaven!" She was overwhelmed, and she said she had already told us everything she knew. "Tell us again!" And so she did, going over every detail she had covered before for the second time. What did we care? No one else had told us about heaven before. We simply sat back in our tiny chairs and basked in the balm this girl offered us. It was at that time, right then and there in front of all of my snot-nosed witnesses, I knew I wanted to get to the place she described. I felt like I had some secret power and knowledge. Could life really be that good? How could I ever be unhappy or miserable again, knowing that this was what I had to look forward to? I felt set for life!

CHAPTER 2

Sunday-School Confidential

WHAT WAS PECULIAR ABOUT THIS whole thing about God, Jesus, and heaven, was that not many of the people I knew—particularly the ones at my church—seemed that excited about this stuff. Whenever the priest came to visit our classroom, I felt that he was checking up on us more than anything else. He had this long black robe (or was it a cape like some action character?) that flowed behind him as he walked. The chains and sashes under his cloak, as well as the decorated cap surrounding his bearded face—a face that had a stern seriousness—gave hints of some villainous character. He didn't appear to me to be that deeply interested in us or our lives; whenever he entered, it seemed like one of those inspection scenes that I had seen in an old World War II movie, with the Gestapo agent skillfully walking around the room, checking for any slip or deviation from what he expected. I half expected to see him don a white glove and go around the room, looking for dust. It didn't help my fear of the priest when I noticed that, at the church, there was a bathroom for boys, for girls, and one for "clergy." That made the priest seem like he was from another planet in my opinion. What was the big secret?

It also bothered me that all of my Sunday-school teachers were women. Now, I have nothing personally against women; in fact, most of these teachers were wonderful, funny, and tender-hearted ladies. But I had to ask myself, weren't there any men who were smart enough to teach about Jesus, or were they only qualified to sell doughnuts after church?

By the fifth grade, I had reached the point that I was getting bored and discouraged at church. I mean, after going every week for my whole conscious life, I'd heard just about every story from the Bible that needed to be taught. I used to sit in the back row of Sunday school with my friend Nick Lidis and just crack jokes the whole hour. The teacher, Mrs. Matzukas, would get frustrated and angry with our lack of decorum, and she would try to get us to behave by keeping us off balance with questions from her lesson. Having been properly trained in the Orthodox tradition, however, I had learned that answering "Jesus" or "the Trinity" to any question thrown at me usually silenced the critics. I remember numerous episodes of impressing Nick with my ability to answer Mrs. Matzukas's intricate theological demands while simultaneously drawing army characters on my notebook.

By this time, I had been with all of these same Greek kids for my entire childhood. The peculiar aspect of my relationship with these kids was that I would only see them on Sundays. No Greek kids went to my school or lived in my neighborhood. In fact, there was only one time I visited the home of a Greek kid that I knew from the church. He was one of the weirdest and most intense kids I'd ever come across, so that didn't exactly draw me into the Greek youth culture. Besides, there's something completely unnatural about being friends with a kid because your parents tell you, "He's Greek." I grew up in a neighborhood that consisted of mostly first-generation European Jews and Germans. (In retrospect, I wonder what kind of conversations these German and Jewish families had at neighborhood get-togethers, since this was not so long after World War II!) Going to church was like getting together a group of people who have absolutely nothing in common except an attraction for lamb kebobs. After a lifetime of this, I was getting quite bored with anyone who had olive skin and one big eyebrow. Going to church seemed like a stupid reason to miss Sunday-morning football games on TV.

All of this changed once I reached the sixth grade. Yes, I was still stuck in a small room with the same collection of Greek faces I'd known my whole life and who had become my Sunday wallpaper. And, true, I felt like I had learned everything about being Greek Orthodox that one needed to learn in order to be qualified to go to the adult church service and be properly bored out of one's mind listening to a service in a language that I didn't even understand. But an essential lesson I learned the first day in sixth-grade Sunday school was one I've kept to this day: just when you think you've come to the end of your rope, God always comes, at just the right time, and brings someone into your life to guide you along the difficult path. Little did I know when I sat down in that classroom that afternoon that would I see Christianity, and God, differently—in ways that have stayed with me the rest of my life.

We waited—9:59 a.m., 10:00 a.m., 10:05 a.m.—still no teacher on this first day of class. What is going on in here? Have we finally been forgotten? We're all just standing around in our classroom, waiting for some new teacher to show up. Suddenly, bursting in like a whirlwind, is this adult guy (maybe thirty years old!) who is completely out of breath and is carrying a stack of papers that are flying in every direction. While late and appearing completely unorganized, he's got this great optimistic look in his eye and a smile on his face. Mustachioed, wearing a white dress shirt, his sleeves rolled up and supported by garters like I'd seen in old Westerns, with hair bursting out of his collar like a burning bush, and big, broad shoulders like a fullback, this guy obviously isn't an ordinary Sunday-school teacher. First of all, he's male. Second, he *looks* like a male! Everyone in the class is simply dumbfounded.

"Hi! I'm Mr. Floor, and I'm your teacher this year," he exclaims enthusiastically. "First thing we're going to do is rearrange these desks so that they make one big table. We're all going to face each other here." Shocked and stunned by this coup d'etat, we willingly submit to this restructuring of our lives. We each take seats—I sit next to Nick—with Mr. Floor at the head of the table.

"I am here to teach you, but I'm also here to learn from you," he opens. "You've been taught a lot already, I'm sure. I want your opinion on things, and I want to know why you think that way. For instance, why are you at church today?" he asks the class.

No one knows what to say. The silence is oppressive. I'm sitting there thinking, "Should I answer 'Jesus' or 'the Trinity'?" I finally offer my best shot: "Jesus."

"What do you mean by that?" He quickly peruses the class roster on a clipboard. "What's your name...George?" I am stymied for an answer. I think about trying "the Trinity," but I know that would not suffice. Within the first five minutes of this class, my entire arsenal of theological knowledge has become obsolete! No one had ever gone into depth about anything in church before, but before we know it, we are all participating in an incredibly stimulating and enjoyable discussion on some fantastic subjects. As the incredibly short hour comes to a close, Mr. Floor states, "From now on we will have discussions like this on topics for you to learn about."

As I leave that classroom with Nick, I am thrilled by the inspiring lesson, the give-and-take-style discussions, and by Mr. Floor himself. My head is spinning…a real man, fun, and enthusiastically teaching us about God. What is he, a failure at something and having to do this instead of jail time? He said he was an accountant. Did he do something illegal, and now he has been banished to a sixth-grade class for restitution? The rumors were flying.

That whole year flew by like magic. It was the first time I actually felt that someone was concerned about my opinion and growth in spiritual matters. I couldn't wait to get to church and share my thoughts with Mr. Floor.

The most amazing part of the entire Sunday-school year was yet to come, though. One Sunday while we were sitting in our class, having a lively discussion over some subject, Father Kezios barged into our classroom like a storm trooper. Goateed, with cape flying in the background, hands cupped as he paced the floor, he looked like the Grand Inquisitor. A hushed silence overtook the classroom as we wondered among ourselves what had brought the priest into our midst. "Someone here must have done something really bad," was all I could think, and we were all going to get punished for it. Quick, what excuses could I think up?

No, it was nothing like that. In his condescending voice, he invited us to take part in the annual Christmas play. "I've heard so many wonderful things about your class, and I would like to have you youngsters do a live performance of the Nativity scene for our adults in a few weeks." To us kids, this sounded more like a threat than an honor. We sat in silent bewilderment as Father Kezios exited like a whirlwind, as dramatically as he had entered. Whoosh! All that was missing was the cry of a raven.

"Well, kids," said Mr. Floor, as he tucked his pile of notepads into his folder, "I guess we need to figure out who is going to be in town Christmas week, so we can hand out these parts. Looking for volunteers for this opus." Floor found no takers. Not to be discouraged and immediately taking charge, he assigned me the role of Joseph, Nick the part of baby Jesus (since he was the shortest boy in the class), and Lisa Navrides as the Virgin Mary. Lisa was a natural pick for this role, as she had never—and I mean *never*—missed a Sunday at church her entire life. Our church gave out medals for going to church if one missed fewer than three times a year. Lisa had never missed a day since I had first known her in kindergarten. Her blouse was filled with these ribbons and medals, making her look like a World War I veteran. Even more amazing was the fact that she had never spoken a word the entire six years we had gone to Sunday school. I wouldn't have recognized her voice if my life depended on it. An entire life of church in abject silence…Maybe she was training to be one of those Carmelite nuns, was all I could think. So, it was me, Nick, and silent Lisa as the holy family, with the various supporting roles of shepherds, angels, and wise men passed out among the rest of the kids.

Rehearsals were a blast. Instead of sitting in a classroom, we rehearsed and worked out our roles as we assembled the stage for the Nativity scene. Painting, assembling, and drawing, mixed with memorizing lines and cues for the show of shows was a fun time of working together. I got to know Mr. Floor even better as I saw him dive into this labor with obvious enthusiasm. By the week before the show, we were all set and ready to go.

All except for one problem. A major problem. As we were getting dressed for the presentation for our parents that Sunday morning, just a few hours before the *big show*, Father Kezios comes into our room to deliver the horrifying news to us: Lisa Navrides, who hadn't missed a day of Sunday school *ever*, had gotten the flu the day before and was unable to attend. It was like being told Cal Ripken was going to take a day off from the ball game. The Nativity scene without Mary? There was simply no way! Everyone looked stunned. What were we going to do? As the saying went (and Father Kezios sternly emphasized), "The show must go on!" Unfettered and optimistic, Mr. Floor simply turned to all of the girls who were in our class and calmly explained the situation to them. The part was relatively easy; there were barely two lines worth memorizing. All they had to do was make an entrance, stare at the baby Jesus (or Nick in this case), say the lines, and stare out at the adoring parents. He made the offer sound so reasonable, so simple, and so rewarding that it seemed impossible to turn down.

Unfortunately, he was dealing with hyper-self-conscious eleven-year-old Greek girls who wouldn't be caught dead doing anything that even hinted of not looking absolutely cool. The thought of possibly missing a line at such short notice, wearing clothes that might not fit right, or missing a cue was just too much for the self-conscious pubescents to risk. With his offer rejected by his students, Mr. Floor started scrambling for substitutes. Looking around for parents or other students proved fruitless, and the clock was impatiently ticking away, closer and closer to the time of performance.

I felt so sorry for Mr. Floor. He had put intense effort into this class and project, only to have us students let him down. He looked discouraged but not disheartened. Suddenly, his eyes lit up with inspiration. Pulling me aside, he confided in me, "George, what do you think if I play the part?"

Stunned beyond belief, I looked at Mr. Floor and froze. Then Nick smiled and said, "It will be a Christmas no one will ever forget."

Explaining the situation to Father Kezios, we not only got the OK, but for the first time in my life, I saw a priest laugh. I felt like I was watching a stained-glass window come to life!

A GREEK ORTHODOX NATIVITY

Being on the stage with Nick, as the baby Jesus, and my other friends, as the shepherds, we played our parts with proper sixth-grade sobriety. When Mr. Floor burst out onto the stage as Mary, with his hairy chest exploding out of the first-century dress and his broad shoulders taking the seams to their absolute limits, I thought the walls were going to collapse at the intensity of laughter. The sight of a thirty-year-old mustachioed accountant playing the blessed Virgin is one of both glory and irreverence that I cherish to this day. Knowing that Mr. Floor gave up all sense of decorum and sacrificed himself for our project was the first poignant example of real Christlike love I had ever seen. I had met a real Christian man.

CHAPTER 3

Don't Know Much about Theology

I STUMBLED INTO JUNIOR HIGH, and as with any kid trying to find his own identity, I struggled along trying to find out how to fit in socially and scholastically. Two deeply influential episodes occurred within the confines of those adolescent school walls that have been embedded in my mind.

The first one occurred during my world-history class, led by a dowager of a lady named Mrs. Alpin. She was hunched, thin, and frail, yet her appearance contrasted with an attractively razor-sharp wit and an alluringly eloquent way of delivering material that sparked in me a still-present interest in history.

During one class period, the discussion and lecture turned to the first century of Christianity. One kid in our class, Kenny, raised his hand and said something about the Bible and Christianity. I have no recollection of his exact statement, but I do remember Mrs. Alpin's response. She quietly turned to him and pointedly asked, "Sir (she always called us male students "sir," and we loved it!), have you read the Bible cover to cover?"

Kenny, surprised by the question, replied that he hadn't. Seriously and calmly, she looked him right in the eye, with a firm glaze of conviction, and replied, "Never bring up religion if you don't know what you're talking about." Then she turned away from him to segue into another topic. I was dumbfounded by her directness and by the simplicity and profundity of her comment. She was absolutely right: I needed to know a lot more about topics like religion before I started getting into those types of discussions.

That concept was really reinforced during an after-school discussion among some students in one of my classes. I had missed my English class that day. When I saw two of the girls from that class, Karen and Nancy, sitting on the lawn and chatting, I thought I'd find out what had occurred in my absence. Well, they were in deep discussion about the guest speaker. It seems that a Jesus freak came to the class and spoke about the life of Jesus and the need for believing that he was God in the flesh. They were kind of mocking both the speaker and Jesus, and at one point, Nancy said, "Wasn't Jesus's mother a prostitute, anyway?" I flashed back to Mrs. Alpin's comment and realized that, when it came to religion, people, in spite of our self-acclaimed knowledge, are completely ignorant about spiritual things.

I was confronted by my own ignorance and weakness just a short time later. During a lunch break, I saw a bunch of my friends sitting and eating in a circle, hanging out with each other on the lawn. I strode over to check out the scene and realized that two of my friends, Marty and Mike, were into a serious discussion. As soon as I sat down, Mike looked me in the eye and asked me, "Do you think I'm going to hell?" His look was a combination of bewilderment and incredulity.

I glanced over to Marty, who had a Bible in his hand and fervently said to us, "The Bible says that if you don't ask Jesus to forgive your sins, you're going to hell."

I felt like I was in the crossfire at Bull Run, and I hadn't even opened my lunch pail! I don't remember exactly what I said, but it was something that was a combination of humor and avoidance. I essentially chickened out of the discussion because I realized, at that very moment, that what I believed could have an incredible impact on people, and I wasn't sure I was even confident enough in my beliefs to stand up and say, "When it comes to my faith, I'd rather please God than my friends." Once again, I saw my lack of religious knowledge to be a hindrance to me. Mrs. Alpin had struck again!

Because of my ambiguous attitude toward religious things—and the fact that I had seen firsthand what tensions religious differences can create—during the first part of my teenage years, I looked at church as either simply an interference to my watching football games on TV or a means of helping my favorite football team (Oakland Raiders) win a game through prayer and petition. Most of my life was wrapped up in sports, and our neighborhood was filled with guys my age actively pursuing the meaning of life through playing various sports through the seasons. At the local parks, or in our neighborhood, we'd play baseball in the summer, football in the fall, and basketball in the winter. We were so involved that one of the neighborhood kids, Peter Brothers, actually started typing a sports sheet of our weekly activities. He would distribute these mini-newspapers to each family in the neighborhood, listing scores as well as each individual's contributions to the game. In addition, each issue had an interview with a key player in the game, as well as a section on entertainment, which would give movie and record reviews. Needless to say, this was an ambitious project, and it inspired us to be the best athletes that a middle-class, white, suburban neighborhood could produce.

By the time I got into high school, I had decided to try out for the basketball team. Going onto the court for the first time—with all of the kids from other neighborhoods competing also for the coveted twelve spots—was intimidating, to say the least. My friend Jeff Radant, who was trying out for the team as well, said that we didn't stand a chance. But then, he was always a pessimist. He was my catcher when I pitched on our Babe Ruth League baseball team, and before every game, as he was warming me up in the bullpen, he'd come up to me in all seriousness and tell me, "Harris, today they are going to kill you." Nevertheless, somehow we'd won most of our games together, and our struggles through baseball cemented our friendship.

Well, in this situation, Radant was humblingly correct. Both he and I were humiliated before our peers as we attempted to keep up with those superior athletes. We were simply freshmen, and most of the guys who made the team were at least a year older than we were. Distraught, I felt like this was an end to my basketball career. Radant, however, came up to me and consoled me. "Don't worry, Harris." (Why do guys love calling each other by their last names?) "The church I go to has a basketball league. They'll let us on the team, and we'll have a lot more fun there than if we just sat on the bench with this bunch of bums."

Jeff explained that getting on the team was quite easy. "The only qualification is that you have to attend our church four times a month." That seemed a bit of a push—perfect attendance? "It's easy at a Baptist church," he assured me. "Look, we got high school Sunday school. That's one. Then 'regular' church right after. Two. Then you can spend the day here and go to the evening service, and there's always the high school Bible study on Wednesday nights. You can get your monthly requirements done in one week!"

This sounded great. I'd been on the school baseball team, and I knew that practicing all day and letting your grades slide just for the sake of riding the bench was not a pleasing way to spend a season. The thought of being on the starting team and playing the whole game seemed radiantly glorious. Where was the church? When were the tryouts? "Sign me up!" I thought. "I'm ready!" Still, I'd never heard of so many church activities before! Didn't anyone do anything else with his life? I soon realized that you could spend your whole life in a Baptist church, seemingly every day and night. At the Greek church, attendance was like renewing your library book; you just checked in once a week for an hour, made the rounds, ate a doughnut, and headed home. Minimal commitment. This church had something available every day. I loved it! My parents, however, hated it.

See, to my Greek mother, everything revolved around two major activities: sleeping and eating. If something detracted from one of these sacraments, it was considered anathema. There were few things more important to my mom than these two necessities, and if someone threatened to deprive her or her kids of them, well, *watch out*!

Going to play on a basketball team twenty miles away with a bunch of non-Greeks was bad enough, but she was slowly getting used to that. Suddenly, however, she realized that I would be gone anywhere from one to three other days a week and, therefore, would be *missing home-cooked meals*. That, of course, meant that I was going to do the unthinkable: I was going to lose weight and look thin, which is the ultimate insult to a Greek mother. The thought of it was too much for her. Suddenly, this church was filled with "damned Baptists" who were going to starve her son to death and deprive him of needed sleep so he won't grow up to be a big Greek boy and marry a lovely Greek girl. The family tree was definitely at stake!

After much cajoling, I was able to convince my parents that Jeff's mom would be able to take care of me when she took us to the practices on Wednesday nights or to the Sunday evening or morning services. (This was only after my mom had a very long talk with Mrs. Radant and made her promise my mom that I would get a very good meal somewhere and that I wouldn't get home tired.) To her credit, Mrs. Radant made good on her promise. She made sure we ate out for dinner or lunch, and she got me home in time to get enough rest to turn me into a Greek god.

TRIPLE THREAT

Growing up in middle-class Encino, California, I had never been exposed to anything but suburbia. Being told that the church team was in a town called Inglewood meant nothing to me except that I needed someone to drive me the sixteen miles to church for the games and practices. Jeff told me this was no problem; since he would be on the team, his mom would take us. Feeling all set and determined, I couldn't wait to get home and tell my parents of my latest sports adventure.

Here is where I learned another key lesson in life. Most of the time, you want to really grow or do something different, someone will try to dissuade and discourage you. It is one thing to stay at the same level as everyone else you know, but to attempt to do something above the bell curve is seen as a threat—as if the other people are being left behind somehow. Telling my Greek Orthodox parents that I wanted to go to a Baptist church in Inglewood was almost like telling them that I was no longer interested in being Greek—that I was abandoning my heritage. "Why can't you play basketball at the Greek church?" they challenged me. "Why do you have to leave our church?" Getting them to try to envision a basketball team loaded with short Greek teenagers did not endear them to my argument. But I also pointed out the fact that our church didn't even have a basketball team. Undaunted, my parents coaxed me into calling all of the local churches to see if *anyone* had a team of high schoolers that would accept a new kid on the block. No other church had a team; I was free to check out Inglewood.

CHAPTER 4

From Byzantine to Baptist

THE FIRST THING THAT STRUCK me about the Baptist church was how unassuming it was. My Greek Orthodox church had gigantic stained-glass windows, a dimly lit sanctuary, lots of smells from candles, and a hushed sense of foreboding. After being driven to the nondescript parking lot, Jeff and I entered a simple edifice. The main part of the church was a bright and plain building with a pulpit in the center and very tacky pennants draped along the wall with various sayings on them, like "Jesus is Lord." What was most astonishing to me was the casualness of behavior and conversation inside the building. People were walking up and down the aisle to the pulpit like it was just an ordinary passageway in a department store.

I flashed back to a time when I was about ten years old. I was all by myself in the sanctuary of the Greek church. Who knows what I was doing there, but as I was looking around, I slowly approached the area toward the back of the sanctuary, nearing the screen from where the priests came forward and did all of their secret ceremonial esoterica. I was overcome by curiosity, wondering what was on that table just beyond all of the carvings and mosaics, so I slowly started to ascend the steps to find out. As if I had set off an alarm, as soon as I touched the first step, I heard a loud and booming voice behind me that broke the stillness and warned, "Do not approach the sanctuary. Step back down." I felt like I was in a scene from *The Wizard of Oz*. Half expecting smoke to come out of the sacred doors, I hurriedly stepped down.

All of these images flashed through my mind as I gazed around at the simplicity of this unpretentious urban church. It was also peculiar to me to see people of all different ethnicities and colors gathering together to worship

God. At this church, people weren't there because they were Greek or *had* to be there but because they believed in God. This realization gave me much to think about.

Jeff introduced me to a bunch of his friends. They were all very warm and easygoing. He led us to the front row, right in front of the pulpit where the pastor was going to preach his sermon. I obviously wasn't going to miss anything from this seat. Some guy in a suit walked up to the podium.

"Is this the preacher?" I whispered to my buddy.

"No, he's the worship leader."

"What's that?"

We stood up, and Jeff handed me a little blue book, called a hymnal, that we were supposed to sing from. Jeff immediately turned to a page number with a song on it, as did everyone else, without the guy up front saying a word. I wondered how everyone knew what to do.

Jeff came to my rescue. "You see that sign right there?" he pointed to a billboard that had space for interchangeable numbers, almost like a scoreboard at a baseball game. There were three sets of numbers lined up vertically: 154, 299, and 78. If it were the Greek church, that board would have been up there to display how much money they had made from doughnut sales that week. "That shows us what hymns we're going to sing this week." This information was almost too much for me! In the Greek church, we had sung the same songs from the same liturgy every week since I could remember. They actually varied the songs in church?

After I had attended a few times, I fell into a routine. I would sit with members of the basketball team, and—just for the heck of it—one of the players on the basketball team, Ron, and I would go through the lyrics of the three hymns ahead of time. We'd look at the songs and try to figure out if each was a "cool" hymn or not. Our definition of a cool hymn was one that had two parts to the vocal refrains, such as…

(Part 1) "Greater than the mighty rolling sea!"

(Part 2, echo) "The rolling sea!"

Ron and I would always sing the bottom part. Sometimes, we'd be the only ones doing it. We thought it was great. After a while, we had about three or four other team members joining us. Not every song had two parts, but when they did, we'd get all excited in anticipation. There's something about singing with all of your heart that cleans out all your problems. I realized I'd never sung before with such gusto. I was becoming a Baptist!

Anyway, that first morning church service I attended there, the pastor walked up to the pulpit after the songs. He looked exactly like a pastor from an old movie: squarely built, graying temples, and a well-worn face from a lifetime of smiling at people he probably didn't really like. He confidently put both hands on the podium and gave a firm and impassioned sermon on something that I could barely understand. I had never heard a man preach for so long. At the Greek church, the priest would talk very calmly about some topic for maybe five minutes at most. As my dad would say, "He probably thought of the sermon while pulling into the parking lot." This guy here was going on and on for over half an hour. I looked around, and everyone was paying rapt attention to him. Some were even taking notes. Was there a test afterward that no one had told me about?

Once he started winding down, he hit upon a topic that I could finally understand, but that had never been brought to my attention before. Looking out over the congregation, he asked, "If you were to die tonight, do you know for sure whether or not you'd go to heaven?" I sat there completely dumbfounded. I'd been going to church my whole life, and I had never actually thought of that before! Oh, sure, I knew that I wanted to go there, and I flashed back to my days in Sunday school with that wonderful substitute teacher's lessons on heaven. But that just made me *want* to go there. Would I? How could I really know? I was sweating in my boots. I just wasn't sure. I knew about God. I liked Him, but suddenly, I realized I knew very little about Him! I felt doomed.

"If you want to go to heaven, you've got to ask Jesus to be your Savior!" the pastor declared.

"You've got to be kidding!" I thought to myself. "I've been going to church all these years and have been praying to God. I believe Jesus is my Savior, but I've never *asked* Him to save me. Does that somehow disqualify me?"

I sat in my pew a very confused person.

"If you want to go to heaven and want to ask Jesus to be your own personal savior, raise up your hand right now." Well, this seemed like a trap to me. I wanted to go to heaven, but I wasn't sure if I was going. I believed who Jesus was, so I couldn't raise my hand to go to heaven. Weren't there any other options?

During this time, a bunch of people raised their hands, and the teary-eyed pastor called these people to come forward to "accept Jesus" and become Christians. People in the congregation were cheering and clapping for those souls who went forward. They were treated like celebrities or like someone who had just won a sweepstakes! A few of those who were walking down to display their newfound faith were crying; others looked almost regretful. Why couldn't I be one of those who knew for sure they'd be in heaven forever? Well, the pastor must have been reading my mind because he glanced over the audience and said, "If there are some of you out there who have made Christ your Savior but want to rededicate your life to Him because you've slipped away from Him and want that assurance of heaven, with your head bowed and your eyes still shut, please just raise your hand. You don't need to come forward." Ah, I could feel comfortable belonging in this gang. Sign me up! So I raised my hand at this opportunity and didn't have to walk down the aisle and make a spectacle of myself. I felt like I was in!

Did anything powerful come over me? No. Did I feel a sudden sense of peace? Again, no major change. I simply felt like I was making something official that I had felt all along. When I went to the Greek church, I figured that I was a Christian by default; I wasn't Jewish, Muslim, Hindu, or Buddhist, so what else was there for me? After having raised my hand, I realized I had actually made a conscious choice, confirming to myself—and maybe to God as well—what "team" I belonged to.

I went home that Sunday feeling like I had done the right thing. What struck me as peculiar was that the following week at church, the pastor made the exact same plea, with the exact same emotions and tears. In fact, he did this every Sunday morning I went. I suddenly felt a bit manipulated, but the fact remained that I was glad I knew I was going to heaven. But was I tricked into eternal bliss?

After the first practice, we went to the high-school group to do what they called a Bible study. I had absolutely no idea what to expect. To my astonishment, they actually read from the Bible and talked about what they had just read. Growing up in the Greek church, the Bible was something that you owned but never actually read. The only Bibles I owned were a couple at home that I had received at the Greek Orthodox church for perfect attendance in fifth and sixth grade. I had never even thought of reading them. What for? No one had ever told me to. It was something only the priest was supposed to read and tell you what it meant. The only time I had ever opened one of my Bibles was to look at the pictures. Each of the Bibles I owned had the same basic pictures: Moses as a baby in a basket in some river, Jesus being born and being crucified, angels over a tomb, and Jesus in clouds, either going up or coming down. That was about it. I soon learned that this was not going to do for a guy going to a Baptist church.

After reading and talking about the Bible, all the kids sat in a circle and shared what they called "prayer requests." Each kid would mention something that was going on in his or her life. By the progression of the requests, I could tell that eventually it was going to be my turn, and I had absolutely no idea what I should pray for. I didn't even hear the last three or four requests before it became my turn because I spent all of that time trying to think of something that sounded good enough. To this day, I have no idea what I asked for, but at least I passed the baton quickly to the next person. Then, we closed our eyes and started praying for all of these things. This went on for about ten or fifteen minutes. I had never seen people praying like this before. They looked like they were actually talking to God—without incense and no "our Father, who art in heaven…" And they addressed Him as "Jesus," "God," and even "dear Lord." It was getting quite informal here. Was this something fantastically great or absolutely barbaric? I still wasn't sure, but I did like the freshness of it.

What really blew me away at first was the fact that I knew a lot of these stories already, as well as a number of the sayings. Also, I was really impressed with how Jesus always seemed to say just the right thing at the right time. He was always in control of any situation. Nothing seemed like an accident, and He never ceased to amaze me by His perfect response to every challenge and predicament. He wasn't like a TV crime hero, though—nothing terribly dramatic or brawny; He was just able to sidestep every assault, almost like a martial artist, but with words and gentle actions.

In order to qualify for the basketball team, I'd change my routine so I could attend the services that were the best to go to. For me, the highlight of each week was not only going to the Wednesday-night Bible study right after the practice for the weekly Saturday-night games (which we would inevitably lose, but at least we had fun), but then going out afterward to hang with everyone. It was really the first time I had gone out with people just to be with them and discuss things, and we did this every week. As soon as the Bible study was over, one of the two youth leaders—either Tony or Danny—who were all of around three years older than we were, but were in *college*, would cram us into their cars, and we would go to a local diner called Dinah's to get something to eat, usually the all-you-can-eat shrimp for $2.99.

We'd take up a long table, anywhere from six to fifteen of us, and discuss either current events or something related to the study we just had. This whole scenario opened me up to the world of debate and discussion. No one had been interested in my opinion about life matters since Mr. Floor. Sure, each of us would come up with some absolutely random thought, but that was the whole point: solidify your thoughts, and let other people hack away at them and see how well they stand up. I loved every minute of sitting and hammering out topics like that.

Tony once told us to bring a bunch of friends the next Wednesday night, as he had a special treat for everyone. It turned out he had bought an old clunker of an auto for about twenty-five dollars, drove it into the parking lot, and for twenty-five cents a swing, allowed us to smash the car with a sledgehammer! It was one of the most enjoyable nights we'd all had...until the cops pulled up and told us we couldn't do it anymore. To this day, I haven't been able to find a law that prohibits destroying your own car on church property.

Some of the Sunday-night meetings were quite fascinating as well, and others were amazingly intense. As I would walk into the church, some usher would hand me a sheet of paper. On it was the title "Prayer Requests," and the sheet was filled with typed, single-spaced lines of prayer requests people had written on little cards that were found in the pews during the week for the entire church to pray for. A lot of these requests were for things like "Aunt Harriet's warts to get better"; others were pretty intense, like serious illnesses. The ones that I could never understand were the ones that said, "Rick Jones has three unspoken prayer requests." I mean, since this guy wanted us to pray for him, the least he could do was to tell us what it was that was bothering him! What was I supposed to ask God? "Help Rick with his three things he won't tell anybody about?" Anyway, the pastor had no problem with it, and we'd sit there and pray for five to ten things that no one even knew about! The unspoken requests seemed to be from the same people all the time, and I ended up figuring they must just have had a lot of communication problems.

One Sunday night, there was a guest speaker at the service. He was a tall man, middle-aged, with a barrel chest and an ex-marine attitude about life. He stood up in front of the pulpit and—looking like George C. Scott giving his famous *Patton* speech—spoke with deep conviction that pierced me right between the eyes. What really hit me was when he gazed at the congregation in front of the pulpit and snarled, "If you don't have a quiet time with the Lord where you're reading the Bible and praying, and I mean *praying*, at least twice a day, you're worthless to God as a Christian."

He convinced me that very night, and while I understood very little in the Bible, I felt that I needed to start understanding at least something about this book, so I'd read a little every morning and again before I'd go to bed. I figured, "How can I really be what God wants me to be unless I put in the time with Him?" About this time, someone showed me the verse, "You will find me, if you seek me with all of your heart" (Jeremiah 29:13). I was determined, as much as a teenager can be determined, to seek Him, and—no matter what—I'd read the Bible, even if I didn't understand a word of it. I'd let it somehow, through osmosis, get into me. I couldn't make sense out of a lot of it, but I plugged away. The chase was on!

CHAPTER 5

Who? Me?

ONCE A MONTH ON SUNDAY nights, the high-school kids would get together at someone's home and just hang out. One of the cool college kids would give a Bible lesson, sing a few songs, and tell us what life was really all about from the grand and wise perspective of a freshman at college. One day, a lovely college girl named Norita came up to me and said, "George, why don't you give the lesson next week?"

I had absolutely no idea what to say, and trying to not look uncool (the goal of every teenager), I said, "Sure. What should I give it on?"

"Anything you like," she replied. "Just call me during the week with the part in the Bible you're going to teach from."

On one hand, I felt completely over my head and overwhelmed. I'd only been going to this church for a couple of months, and I was already giving a lesson? What did I know? I was sort of overwhelmed. I'd just gotten a new Bible; I hadn't read it in any detail. Nevertheless, I blithely assented, immediately sending my mind into a spin. What the heck was I going to teach about? I mean, there are certain topics you just can't fake your way through, and teaching the Bible at a Baptist youth group is definitely up there in the *un-fakeable* categories.

On the other hand, I felt like, hey, here was a great chance to get something out of the Bible and teach it to people. The idea attracted me. I couldn't wait to get started, but where? How many stories did I even know about in the Bible?

Suddenly, my prayers that week became a lot more intense! I felt like this was really the first time I had asked God for something semi-spiritual, something besides the Raiders winning a football game or having some girl notice I was alive. By Tuesday, I had the answer: go with the classics. I knew about the story of David and Goliath, so I figured I'd do that one. Somehow, I found out where it was in the Bible. "Why the heck is it in a book called 'Samuel'?" Made absolutely no sense at all. Anyway, I read the story, and—much to my surprise—while it had a little bit of what I'd heard in church, it had some very cool features that I'd never known before, like the fact that David was first offered Saul's protective vest, but he turned it down. Hmm, interesting lesson there about not accepting help from losers...

After working out my thoughts all week, I gave the lesson at the next Sunday-night meeting. I really liked teaching what I had learned, and Norita said it was a very good lesson. What impressed me most of all was that someone had trusted me with the Bible. I learned that anyone can use this great book, even a fifteen-year-old basketball player. I liked that feeling. How many people in world history had read and learned from this book? Lincoln. Washington. Newton. Suddenly, I was one of them. It was a great feeling of membership!

It wasn't too much longer after this episode that I faced my first black-and-white choice of my desires versus God's will. I was really into rock music at the time, and I had purchased tickets to see a band named Genesis in concert. It was their first time touring, and the show had sold out in a matter of days. One Wednesday after practice, Jeff asked me if I was going to the church's winter retreat. "What is a retreat?" I had never heard of one, much less been to one. I learned that it was a place you went in order to learn more about God. There would be a guest speaker, and he'd talk about what it meant to be a Christian. It sounded interesting, but then I found out it was the weekend I'd be going to the Genesis concert, so there was no way I could go. I'd already bought my concert ticket!

Well, Jeff said something to me that I'd never heard before: "Why don't you pray about it?"

"What do you mean by that?"

"Well, you know, ask God what He'd want you to go to."

That really seemed unfair. I mean, did I really think God was going to tell me, "Sure, George, go to the concert and skip learning more about Me." Well, I guess He could. Eventually, I realized that I should at least get God's OK on this, one way or the other.

Sure enough, after praying a couple of days, I realized that Genesis was just going to have to wait until next time to have me in the audience. I put an ad in the local record store's flyer, and by the time someone called me for the tickets, I was actually glad to get rid of them! I felt a freedom, knowing I could do something that was good for me and not just something I selfishly wanted to do. This was going to be an unforgettable trip, I thought. And so it was!

Our clunky van pulled up to the camp area, and as we twenty or so teenagers got out into the freezing weather, I realized that this retreat was not just for us but for about ten other churches as well. There were a ton of kids there, from all over the LA area. The place was packed! After getting us all together, having us sing some songs, and giving us a quick pep talk, the head counselor let us go outside to play in the snow. We were having a great time, throwing snowballs at each other, and I don't remember how it all got started, but somehow, the ball throwing got a little intense. Someone from our group nailed a guy from another church, and he got really ticked off. The rest of the afternoon was a fairly un-Christian exchange of snowballs being traded between cabins. I realized very quickly that this retreat was for people who needed God and that everyone there might have been a Christian, but there were different stations that people could be at.

The retreat went along pretty well until the second-to-last night. The head counselor called the kids from our church and another church together. We couldn't figure out what was going on. Having never been to a retreat before, I asked Jeff what this was all about, and even he didn't know. Finally, the counselor told us the news: he was calling the sheriff! "What for?" we all wondered. He then lifted his hand and showed us a collection of forks that had been bent to wrap around hands as weapons. Someone from the church we had hit with the snowballs was planning to have a rumble with us! The counselor had caught wind of it and was going to nip it in the bud. He assumed we were preparing to fight back as well. We were aghast and shocked! A gang war at a church retreat! What would my mom say when she picked us up at jail? That concern was replaced with another: the counselor said he was ready to have the sheriff call our parents to come take us home. There was no way I'd ever be allowed back at the Baptist church again. This would confirm every suspicion my Greek parents had of "those Baptists"!

Suddenly, one of our basketball players, BB, stood up and shouted, "I don't know about you, but I'm *scared*! I don't want to go to jail or have my parents know about this!"

We all agreed, and we somehow reconciled with the tough guys. It amazed me how Christians could be so tough and hard, but then, somehow, they could work it all out because they follow the same God and maybe avoid legal problems in the process!

What a crazy retreat! Somewhere along the way, I know we must have read the Bible once or twice, but believe me, I couldn't wait until the next retreat. What would we do for an encore?

By the time the summer retreat rolled around, I was ready for another spiritual shot in the arm. I had heard that the speaker was a guy named Ray Schmautz. What got my attention was that he had been a member of my favorite football team, the Oakland Raiders. Every Sunday I lived and died with that team. My happiness each weekend depended on a Raider victory. Luckily, they were a good team during this period; yet, they always seemed to lose the game that would make them champs. As any sports fan knows, victory brings joy, but defeat brings loyalty.

Anyway, I just couldn't contain my excitement as I was getting ready to go to the retreat. Sure, learning more about the Bible was great, but I was actually going to meet someone who had played with the Oakland Raiders! *Yippee!* I even had autographs of many of the players because I had sent fan letters to my favorite Raiders, asking for signed photographs. In those days, you didn't have to pay athletes for an autograph; you just had to like them.

By the time we got to the retreat area, I was looking all over the place for the Schmautz. There he was! Just as big and burly as I had hoped. All I wanted to do was ask him about all of my favorite Raiders and about certain games that I had watched, but he just didn't seem that interested. Oh, he answered all of my questions, but he would talk more about the players' spirits and souls than what he had done on the playing field. I had never thought that these guys I watched every week would have personal and private struggles. Weren't they all Christians? They all seemed like nice guys. Ray set me straight on that. Suddenly, I realized that these athletes had made football their god. That was one of the reasons Ray got out of the game. It was taking his soul down a path that was wrong for him. In a sense, I was a little disappointed in him; he seemed like a declawed lion, like all the fight had gone out of him.

Then all of us guys went out to play football one afternoon with Ray. While we were out there, I could see Ray was having a great time. What really struck me was when one of my friends, Roy, messed up on a play and let out a loud curse. Ray sort of sauntered over to him and gently explained how his cursing was making God unhappy. The sensitivity Ray exuded while he corrected Roy was quite profound. Here was a guy who, just a few years earlier, was pounding the living daylights out of opposing football players, and now he was about as menacing as a pillow. This guy had gone through a change. I'd never seen anyone actually transformed by faith before. Oh, sure, people had given up smoking or other stupid habits. But to have actually let go of something he had really loved...

I had to ask myself, "What do I hold on to that keeps me from being a stronger Christian?" Somewhere around the same time, I came across a verse in the Bible: "What does it profit a man if he gains the whole world, yet forfeits his soul?" (Matthew 16:26). I couldn't get that feeling, or that verse, out of my mind. What was I trading my life for? For something that would bring me closer to God or for something that just seemed alluring but would actually lead me away from my desired destiny?

CHAPTER 6

Just Gimme Some Truth

IT WAS ABOUT THIS TIME that someone brought up the question of whether the Bible was true or not. It was after a Wednesday-night meeting, and we were sitting around at Dinah's. The thought had never even crossed my mind. It's the Bible, for Pete's sake! What do you mean "Is it true?"? Suddenly, I started having doubts. I went to my faithful source, Norita, and she told me that there was a guy in his twenties, named Josh McDowell, who set out to become famous by disproving the Bible, and instead he ended up writing a book about how the Bible does actually stand up to scrutiny as to historical accuracy.

"Am I actually able to buy this book?" I asked.

"Yes, and in fact, there are Christian bookstores where you can probably buy it."

I'd never heard of such a thing! A store where they sold only Christian books? Who'd ever want to go there? It sounded very esoteric.

Well, Norita told me of a store not too far from where I lived. I drove up and parked out front. It seemed harmless enough. Inside, there were a ton of books scattered everywhere on the shelves. I was overwhelmed by the supply of books that I'd never heard of before. I felt like I was a member of some secret society. There was some intellectual-looking college student behind the register, his nose buried in a book, completely absorbed in the material—and completely ignoring my existence, even though I was the only customer. Didn't this guy want to make some money off me?

I was absolutely positive that if I mentioned the name of the author or book I was looking for, this nebbish guy would think I was a member of some subversive cult. When I asked, "Do you have *Evidence That Demands a Verdict* by Josh McDowell?" He actually looked up at me, as if I were a fellow member of the human race, and acknowledged my existence.

"Oh yes. Here it is. Good choice." That was it. I was not treated like a member of a fanatical cult; I was on an acknowledged path. This was getting good.

The problem was that once I got home and looked at the book, I was completely overwhelmed. The book consisted of hundreds of pages of outlines defending the veracity of the Christian faith. As I perused this tome, I recalled Mark Twain's famous quote of a classic being a "book you don't want to read but want to have read." I simply put that thick paperback on the bookshelf by my bed and kept it safely there as a reminder that, if I ever had any doubts about the Bible, I could always rest assured this unfathomable reference book had the answers for me.

CHAPTER 7

Nami Ho Ringe Kyo

SINCE I HAD STARTED READING the Bible for myself, I began to have some questions about things I read. I figured the best thing for me to do was to go to the pastor of the church and ask him some questions, so I made an appointment to see him.

Pastor L. was a short and stocky man in his early to mid-forties, it seemed to me. He always wore a dress jacket and slacks, and—since this was in the early '70s—he had that classic extra length of sideburns and hair over the back of the neck that showed he was at least trying to look hip to the younger generation. We met in his study, and there I was, with a list full of questions to ask him. But as soon as I started talking to the pastor, he pulled out a Bible that he claimed he had used during an exorcism with someone at the church. He even showed me the pages the person had ripped out of the Bible while under Satan's influence. He then went on for quite some time about all of the various demonic possessions he had been involved in and how there were lots more of these things happening because it was a sign that "the end is soon." Now, to be fair, this was during the time that the movie *The Exorcist* was really popular, so a lot of people were interested in demons and demon-possession kinds of things.

Gee, I had only gone there to ask a few questions about the Dead Sea Scrolls and about people who had never heard the gospel or to ask about how to pray, and I was getting Linda Blair spitting out green-pea soup! What the pastor was going on about had absolutely no interest for me and, in fact, seemed completely inapplicable to my life. Between the demonic forces and the imminent end of the world, I felt that this guy had no answers for me and would not assuage my doubts.

I left without answers, and then what confused me even more was when my church friends told me that I needed to go out with them and witness to people I'd never met. This *really* threw me for a loop! What the heck did "witnessing" mean? Jeff said that if I looked in the book of Acts, I would see Christians were witnessing to non-Christians and were giving their testimony. Therefore, if we were Christians, we needed to witness and "give our testimony" to as many people as possible.

The question for me was, "What have I witnessed?" This sounded like something very manipulative and confrontational. Why would I go up to complete strangers in a mall and tell them about my life as a Christian? It seemed very forced, and I sure wouldn't want to have someone come up to me while I was shopping and have them tell me why they were whatever religion they were. Once again, it seemed to have absolutely no relevance to the life I was living.

Around this time, I hitchhiked home from high school one afternoon, and the guy who picked me up asked me a simple question: "Do you pray?" Good question!

"Sure, every day," I told him.

"Do you chant when you pray?" That seemed a bit weird, but I was interested.

"No. Why? Should I?"

"Well, don't you want your prayers answered?" he asked as he was driving me home. "This is what you've got to do." And as I got out of the car, he handed me a little card that was blank except for a phrase in the dead center: "Nami Ho Ringe Kyo."

"What's this?"

"Just say this when you pray, and you'll get everything you want." And he drove off.

This seemed very interesting.

I took the card and put it next to my bed. Right before I went to sleep that night, I said my usual prayers, and after praying to God in Jesus's name, I added, "Nami Ho Ringe Kyo." I figured, why not hedge my bets with a Buddhist chant?

Just around this time, I read an article about a baseball player, Willie Davis. Previously a fair-to-middlin' hitter, he had a red-hot thirty-one-game hitting streak one year, and he gave credit for his improvement to the fact that he chanted "Nami Ho Ringe Kyo" every day. He said since he'd been chanting, good things had been happening to him.

Hmmm…what I thought might be a good idea for myself suddenly looked much more self-indulgent and selfish when seen in someone else. Looked at objectively, my faith seemed to be turning religion into a cosmic vending machine that was to supply my whims and desires. Was this the reason I became a Christian, or why Christ came on earth, to get me a "B" in geometry or some cute girl to like me? What about the verse about "gaining the whole world, but forfeiting one's soul?" I still had more questions.

CHAPTER 8

Never Goin' Back to My Old School

I SURVIVED AND GRADUATED FROM high school. I had stopped going to the Greek church for a while and was still going to the church in Inglewood, but I had gradually started to become disenchanted with the people there. I'd given up on the cosmic chanting; it just seemed like I was manipulating God…as if I were trying to use Him like some kind of genie by saying a secret code. Either God was going to hear me and answer my prayers, or He wasn't; some collection of sounds wasn't going to catch His ear. Besides, through reading the Bible, I'd never seen anyone using this phrase, and they did pretty darned well with their own prayers. So, I said "Sayonara" to the Buddhist chant.

But still, the people with whom I hung around at the church, for the most part, didn't seem to be that inspiringly dynamic or excited in their faith. Actually, their faith seemed to have absolutely no impact on their behavior. There were kids who were fooling around with each other and smoking pot, and a disarmingly high number of them just seemed to have negative and directionless lives. One guy in particular, Boris, had an incredibly disagreeable attitude, and he'd ridicule and put down people all day long. I finally confronted him about this, and he completely dismissed me, simply stating, "Oh, I can turn off or on this behavior anytime I want." When I challenged him to turn it off, he just laughed at me. These people didn't seem to take this whole thing of living like the Bible said very seriously, and that bothered me. The Bible seemed to be true; I'd finally read through the *Evidence…*book, and it seemed beyond reproof that the Bible was the Word of God, and Jesus was who He said He was: God in the flesh. So, why were these people living like it was a lie?

I started going to California State University, Northridge (CSUN), the local university, and because of the demands and intensity of these new classes, I was unable to go to the Baptist church I'd been attending for the past couple of years. It was just too far away, and my old friends there had no sense of making something of their lives. I felt like I'd outgrown these people, and while I felt like I was abandoning the place that had given me my spiritual impetus, I started looking elsewhere for guidance.

One day while at school, as I was walking to the lunch-court area, I saw a fairly good-sized circle of people milling around. It looked like some sort of commotion, so I wandered over to take a look. At the center was a female student, and not an unattractive one at that, but she was bespoiling her beauty with an angry and venomous diatribe against all of the listening students. She was telling them that they were all sinners going to hell and that they needed to believe in Jesus for their salvation. I watched this scenario unfold, and while I couldn't argue with the words she was uttering, her demeanor was quite embarrassing. She spewed anger and vitriol, which was just difficult to watch and, in fact, embarrassing to me, even though I didn't know this young lady. What was quite striking about the entire episode was that the students were taunting her in a way that made it clear they had no inclination of believing they were in need of any forgiveness or that their lives needed straightening out. Their arguments with her centered on justifying their own self-absorbed lives and comparing their live-and-let-live attitude with her self-righteous, judgmental, and condemning nature.

The preaching girl seemed oblivious to the mood of the audience and just kept her own tirade going—almost as if it were a monologue without a listening ear. It was amazing to see these two forces arguing at each other without any interchange. The darkness of the students was palpably apparent, as they had no sense of wrongdoing in their lives; ironically, their own self-righteousness conveyed their greatest sin—that of pride. These fellow students were blind to their need of cleaning up their souls, just as this girl was oblivious to the need to find a proper way to communicate their need of God to them. It once again seemed as if the truth of Christianity was presented as an irrelevant, impotent, and obsolete package. I walked away from the confrontation feeling that if I had first been confronted with Christianity the way these students were, I never would have bought into it.

During that first semester, I enrolled in an art class. I had a blast; not only was I doing something I had loved to do since childhood (painting and drawing), but the teacher was one of those young-and-hip types who allowed us to bring our own music to the classroom and play it on a tape machine in order to create an artistic mood. I felt like I was in collegiate heaven, being able to listen to my favorite tunes while drawing and painting for two hours. Besides, being a music snob, I felt that by sharing my exquisite taste in music with my classmates during this time, I was enlightening my scholastic peers with the high art of progressive rock music.

During the drawing sessions, one student in particular caught my attention. Ed always had something positive to say during the classes, but even more endearing to me was his appreciation of the music that I'd bring in each week. He really got into the groups I'd play and would always compliment me on my taste in music. It was one of those instances we've all experienced when you just feel a relationship click. I started looking forward to seeing him in class each day, just to see his reaction to the albums I'd bring in for him to listen to. We'd leave class together and sometimes talk about either music, the project, or who we thought the cutest girl in the class was. Good times!

Near the end of the semester, Ed and I were walking toward the food court, and he asked if he could talk seriously with me for a few minutes. I said sure, having absolutely no idea what he was going to bring up, but he definitely wanted my opinion on something. Well, we were sitting on one of the short walls that ran parallel to the path of the central outdoor plaza, and he asked me a poignant question: "Tell, me, George, what is your definition of a Christian?"

A myriad of thoughts immediately plunged into my brain: (1) "How confrontational is this session going to be, and what can I do to diffuse the potential confrontational heat of the dialogue?" (2) "Is this guy about to embark on the type of witnessing Jeff had told me about when I was in high school?" (3) "Hey, this guy really seems concerned about me; he deserves a direct answer, yet I really don't have a cut-and-dried answer to give him." (4) "What do I think he wants to hear from me so it won't turn into an intense discussion that I have no desire to get into at this point in my life?"

Was Ed going to get me involved in something that was going to be as trite, prepackaged, and trivial as every other Christian group I had run into the past year? Yet, there was no denying that Ed was sharp, sincere, witty, and not someone who seemed out of touch with reality.

After a pensive pause, I told him, "Well, the word *Christian* literally means 'little Christ,' so I've always thought that a Christian was someone who was trying to be like Jesus in everything that he does." I felt pretty darned good with that impromptu response; it answered the question without seeming rehearsed or contrived. We then talked about going to church, reading the Bible, and other points, and departed very comfortably. We still remained on good terms the rest of the semester, yet I have always deeply regretted not pursuing the subtle invitation of an honest friend to get more serious about following Jesus's path at a time when it actually would have done me a lot of good. I feel like I blithely dismissed him with a sleight of hand so that I could continue on with my own self-absorbed life of academia.

CHAPTER 9

Paper Chase

DURING MY UNDERGRAD YEARS, IT became obvious to me that I was sort of floundering spiritually, but I was at least treading some water by still intermittently attending various local churches, still reading the Bible, and still praying a couple of times a day. The major reason I did all of these things was that I had the underlying conviction that God still loved me and had some sort of a plan and destiny for me. If I were to really be useful in this life, I knew that I needed to be faithful to Him. I had so much of my life ahead of me—college, career, wife—and one thing I had learned from my limited knowledge of life was that if I was true to God, He would guide my path. So, even though I was weak in my faith, I was still hanging in with this God I'd grown up with.

Although I never found a church home during my years in college, I still prayed daily for God to guide me in school and in my relationships with my friends and family. There were lots of times I was tempted to do something that I knew was wrong, but my belief that God honored my obedience was a major motivation to follow Him. The amazing thing was that when I did go against His way—be it in what I said, who my friends were, or my motives for dating the girls I went out with—I could viscerally tell I was taking myself off my proper path. I could feel God saying, "Fine, go indulge your stupidity for a while. I will work through that. It's going to take you a bit longer now, and the correcting process will be a bit sticky, but I'll eventually get you back on the path."

The testing of faith for every college student has to be figuring out what he or she wants to do for a career. I had entered college with the intention of becoming either a lawyer or a cartoonist—sort of like the co-ed who can't decide between cheerleader and brain surgeon! Well, a couple classes of poli sci sucked the legal life out of me. I came to the conclusion that if I wanted to be of service to people, being an attorney was the absolute last field I should choose. At the same time, I soberly realized that being cooped up in a small room, drawing for hours, only to have some editor tell me that he didn't get— or like—my cartoons after hours of labor was too rough to endure. I drew cartoons for the college paper, and while I enjoyed the end product, the constant haggling with the editor just didn't seem worth the effort. I needed some other field. So, I decided to pray to God for guidance and to ask as many professors and professionals as I could what they thought about their own lines of work.

To my absolute shock and dismay, each and every teacher and professional I talked to couldn't stand his or her career and wanted out, if only he or she could find something else that could pay the bills. In a pair of revealing visits, I had one economist/accountant tell me that he would give anything to be able to chuck his career and become a psychiatrist; yet, when I visited the psych professor at my college, he said he dreamed of getting out of all of this "airy-fairy stuff" and becoming an accountant! No one, it seemed, was content with his or her vocation.

One morning, however, as I stumbled out of bed and went to the kitchen to make breakfast, my mom came up to me and said, "We've found your career." Well, that woke me up and got my attention! She said that she and Dad had gone out to a dinner at the Greek church (which none of us had attended for the past few years) and had run into some old friends, whom they hadn't seen in eons. Those friends had invited some new members of the church to the dinner, Bill and Michelle Scruggs, and introduced them to my folks. My mom said that Bill Scruggs was a chiropractor and was "just like you" (as only a mom can say). She said, "He would love to have you see him at his office, to see if you'd want to become a chiropractor."

I had absolutely no idea how to even spell "chiropractor," let alone what it entailed. But after one and a half years in college, I needed to try anything, as the careers that I *did* know about seemed to hold no future for me. Suddenly, I felt a nascent hope growing; this could work for me! For as long as I could remember, my dad would come home from his job as an electrical engineer and walk through the door, and before greeting us, he'd gruffly mutter, "Don't work for someone else." I had learned that lesson firsthand from drawing cartoons for a picky editor. Maybe I could meet my needs of helping people without having some boss lord it over me. I was intrigued!

On my parents' suggestion, I drove over to Dr. Scruggs's office to see just exactly what a chiropractor did. I had deep reservations about this whole adventure; what nineteen-year-old wants to have a parent-recommended career? Nevertheless, I pulled up to Scruggs's office, and the first person to greet me was a very cute and chipper receptionist. Hey! If all chiropractors had such attractive workers, count me in! How's that for using sober discernment for planning my life? Anyway, I was directed into his office, which had a wall of famous actors' pictures, all with notes thanking him for helping them get better. Was I in a doctor's office or an Italian deli? I thought it looked pretty cool.

Dr. Scruggs sat behind a desk. He was a warm, husky, sandy and gray-haired gent who gave me a firm and comforting handshake. He showed me around the office and demonstrated what he did. (Actually, all of the twisting and turning that he applied on each patient looked a bit like something from the Spanish Inquisition, but every patient seemed to love it.) Taking me back to his office, Scruggs explained that he made a good living, was his own boss, loved his work, and enjoyed helping people to feel better. Besides the cute receptionist (whom I never did get the courage to ask out) what more could a guy want? I was sold.

Scruggs told me that the best school to go to was Los Angeles College of Chiropractic (or LACC), simply because it had the highest percentage of students who passed the boards. "Remember that I tell you this," he wisely advised. "The only reason you go to school is to pass the boards. You'll learn to become a doctor and run an office later." Wiser advice was never given to a student.

I called LACC to set up an interview with the dean to help me decide if I was really interested in applying to the school—as well as if they were interested in having me. I met an avuncular James Stewart–type man. He told me that in order to be eligible for the college, I needed two years of undergrad classes, which had to include six units of biology and six of chemistry. After telling me this, he reached into his desk and pulled out a couple of postcards that showed an aerial view of a very fancy campus. "That's our new campus in Los Gatos. That's in Northern California, you know. It's going to be state of the art, and it will be completed and ready for enrollment in about nine months. If you wait a semester, we can get you into that campus instead."

That postcard sure looked nice; however, I didn't want to wait to get into chiropractic school unless I had no other choice. I looked around at the LACC campus; it definitely needed a bath, as well as some plaster to give it a facelift. It even still had some damage from the '73 earthquake. I remembered Scruggs's advice: get in, get out, and get the state-board certification. I told the dean this place was my first choice. He replied that as soon as I could prove I had the required six units each of biology and chemistry, we'd start the application process. I was on my way!

Or was I? At a year and a half into college, I had been preparing to be involved in political science. Therefore, I had only taken one three-unit biology class up to that point. What I suddenly realized was that in the next semester, I had to take not only one more biology class but somehow get six units (usually consisting of two classes) of chemistry. In one semester! Could this even be accomplished? This was the era before computers, so I had to go through the school catalog and scrutinize *every* science class to figure out whether it qualified for LACC. Finding and registering for the needed biology class was a piece of cake; there were scores of choices, and I grabbed one at random. The chemistry class, well, that looked a bit challenging.

There were a bunch of premed chemistry classes, but they were all five-unit classes—one short of my goal. There were lots of three-unit classes as well, but they all required the premed class first. I decided to take a shotgun strategy, and I simply enrolled in every chem class that was offered. I figured that, somehow, I would end up with six units out of two of these selections. Having enrolled in five chemistry classes, besides my other three choices, those first few days were quite harrowing for me, to say the least. I had to run from one class to another to meet with the professors to figure out if any of them qualified for my LACC enrollment. Each day, it seemed like I could hear the "William Tell Overture" racing through my head. Tada dum, tada dum, tada dum dum dum!

To my absolute dismay, each teacher told me that I needed to take the prerequisite five-unit premed chem class before qualifying for the other classes. I couldn't believe it. I was going to be one lousy unit short of enrolling to become a doctor, and I'd have to wait a whole semester to go to LACC because of this scholastic bureaucracy. Just what *was* this intangible thing called a "unit," anyway? Maybe I was supposed to go to Los Gatos after all. No, I wouldn't settle for delaying my destiny. I decided to go to the chemistry department at CSUN during enrollment week and figure out what configuration of classes I could take to get the elusive and precious six units.

I arrived about ten o'clock in the morning at the chemistry department office, and there were already about half a dozen lines of students. Each line was about fifteen to twenty people deep—all anxious to enroll in some type of chemistry class. Each student attentively waited his or her turn, with hands firmly grasping respective enrollment slips. (Again, this was precomputer.) All of us were filled with anticipation or dread as we sought a needed class to continue on our scholastic path to graduation. Patiently waiting and having heard every argument between the desperate students and the indifferent office workers that preceded me in line, I finally had my turn.

"May I help you?"

"Yes, I would like six units of chemistry, please." I felt like I was ordering lunch through a drive-in at Taco Bell.

"What do you mean by that?" replied the indifferent, yet harried, student who was behind the counter. This person seemed to have about as much interest in my future as a geophysicist has in yoga.

"Look, I need six units of biology and six units of chemistry to get my prerequisites to get accepted into a chiropractic college and out of here. I just got the bio classes lined up, and I would now like my six units of chemistry."

The nonplussed student thumbed through the card catalog with feigned interest as she peered through her finger-printed glasses. "Let's see…We have a five-unit class: Chemistry 101. Premed. You're almost there with that one! Oh, but it looks like every other class that we have for you requires that class. Here's a three-unit you can take; ah, but all the three-unit classes also require the five-unit class. Hmm," she concluded, as she feigned interest and compassion.

"So, what should we do?"

"Well, all I can say is that it looks like you should take the five-unit class and then come back next semester for the three-unit class. That will get you in, no problem," she concluded as she peered back at me.

"What do you mean, 'no problem'?'" I asked incredulously. This clerk was determining my future with the wave of a hand. I could see that this student was so enmeshed in university life that she had no concept of life outside of the ivory tower. I was losing my patience with this scholastic bureaucrat. "Are you telling me that I can't get out of this university this semester?"

"Well, you need to take the five-unit class first—"

"Can't you get me something for one, simple, itsy-bitsy unit? Isn't there something out there hiding in the chemistry department for me?"

"I'm sorry, sir," she indifferently explained with the pedantic patience that makes you feel like you're getting a lesson about life that you did not ask for, "but you have to take classes in the proper order, and there's nothing you can do about it."

"Isn't your job to get me an education and to get me out of here as quickly as possible?" I sternly asked. "I thought that a successful college is one that *has people advance into the world to be contributing members of society.* Why are you preventing me from doing that?" At this point, I was starting to lose whatever cool I had left. I had been trying to be as gentle and reasonable with her as a young Greek male can be, but I was obviously getting nowhere. As I had learned growing up, some people need to be rattled a bit in order to get with the program.

By this point, the conversation had gotten so loud that I was attracting some attention from the students who were in the crowded lines. Hot under the collar, I turned around to face them.

"Can you believe what this lady's telling me?" I loudly spoke to the interested gathered mass of students. "Here we are, trying to get classes so we can be productive citizens, and this lady is preventing me from doing that!"

The students were stirring and murmuring in agreement.

"What's the purpose of going to college if you can't get out and be a useful member of society? What school would want to prevent that? Yet this lady *is preventing me* from being successful!"

The crowd was getting excited and restless. By that time, the students were all watching me with encouragement in their eyes.

"This whole scholastic system is ridiculous!" I continued, as I could feel myself shifting gears like a sports car. "Here we are filling out these stupid slips of paper, trying as hard as we can to get the required classes that *they* tell us we need to take, and the school doesn't even want us to move on with our lives. Something is wrong with this system! Something's got to be done about this."

Looking around, my eye caught a tray on the counter beside my counselor that contained all of the enrollment slips for the chemistry department. Every student who wanted a class had his or her name on that tray. I saw my chance to gain some leverage for my argument...and with one fell swoop—like a pelican diving down toward its prey—I grabbed the box that was filled with the students' scheduled classes and their scholastic futures. Feeling and acting like a plane hijacker, I stood up on the counter with the coveted container and declared, "If I can't get out of this school, no one can! No one is getting their classes until I get my six units! I'm not giving up these papers until I get those classes!"

Every eye fixed incredulously like a beacon on me and my paper hostages. At first bewildered by the sudden change in events, the students suddenly became my allies, joining in with me and demanding my vindication. This was obviously during the era when people enjoyed protesting, even at the expense of their own scholastic advancement. (Try doing this now, and see what reaction you'll get from the students—let alone the armed school agents that are within shouting range!)

Here I had started simply trying to get six units of chemistry, and now I was leading a protest. "Gimme a class! Gimme a class!" I kept shouting over and over, and all the students were chanting with me. The sudden exchange of power was quite exhilarating and intoxicating!

After a few minutes of this, my exasperated clerk ran into an office, and a few seconds later, a gentlemanly Asian man emerged with her, looked at the scenario, and casually asked, "What's all this commotion about?"

From my perspective, standing on top of the enrollment counter, he looked quite calm and collected in the midst of this academic chaos. Hotheaded and filled with adrenalin, I shouted to him, "No one is enrolling in any more classes until I get my six units!"

"Just please put down the papers, come into my office, and I promise we'll work something out." I suddenly felt like the guy standing on the edge of a five-story building ready to jump. All that was missing was the guy holding a

megaphone and a spotlight on me. I figured I'd made my point, and I'd either get kicked out of school altogether or tricked into waiting another semester, but I didn't see any winning ways out at this point.

"All right…just get those six units," I pleaded as he calmly led me into his office.

Sitting across from me, he folded his hands and looked genuinely sincere as he asked what the problem was, which I explained. "I thought the intention of college is to get us *out* into the real world, not to keep us here forever," were my closing comments.

Dr. Lu looked truly sympathetic to my predicament. "I'm the dean of the chemistry department," he explained. "I understand your desire to get on with your life, and I even appreciate it." He looked at my current classes, gave me a quizzical look, and asked, "Are you the George Harris who draws the cartoons for the school paper?"

"Yes."

He gave a faint smile. "I like your work. Let's see, maybe there is some way we can get you out of here," he said as he turned away to get a folder overflowing with papers out of his filing cabinet. He laid it on the table in front of me.

"Here, look at this," he said. The papers were announcements of school meetings, events, and seminars. "I need someone to draw up and make brochures and posters for these things here. I know absolutely nothing about artwork and am trapped in a corner to get these projects done. If you can draw the brochures and posters for me during this semester, you've got your unit. Deal?"

I just couldn't believe this was coming so easily after all of the obstacles! Who would have guessed that my cartoon drawing would be the linchpin to my becoming a doctor? I felt an overwhelming, warm sense of God's hand being on this entire situation. I stretched out my right hand to shake his hand, while grabbing the folder with my left. "Deal!"

He signed me up for a one-unit special chemistry class, stamped my enrollment card, and handed it back to me. "You're on your way, Doctor." He smiled.

I felt nothing could stop me. When you feel God working in your life, it's thrilling.

CHAPTER 10

Next Stop: Chiropractic College

I WENT HOME AND CALLED the dean of enrollment at LACC to tell him the good news. "Great," he cheered back. "Come on in for the final interview, and we're all set. How about ten thirty tomorrow?"

That morning I got up, got dressed, and headed for the campus. I couldn't believe everything was suddenly going so smoothly now. Pulling up to the school in my '71 VW van, I pictured myself here for the next four years. It was a great feeling to know where you're going in life, I thought as I walked into the lobby. Then I saw an interesting group of people.

"Strange," I thought, "here it is in the morning, and a bunch of guys in their late twenties and thirties are here all dressed up in suits." I went over to a bunch of them to see who they were and what seminar or convention was going on.

"Hi! I'm enrolling here next semester. Are you all part of the faculty?"

"Oh, we're here for the interview," a well-dressed and coiffed guy about ten years older than I was said, looking at me like I was his valet. "We're enrolling next semester, after this last interview that we're waiting for."

"So, why are you all dressed up for some final interview, if you're going to the school anyway?"

"Well…" He sniffed, looking at my blue jeans and the Popeye insignia on my T-shirt. "You want to make a good impression. This school doesn't want just *anyone* here who doesn't look professional."

Hmm. Could there possibly be two completely different sets of interviews, or was I in a very uncomfortable situation? The fact was, at this point, there was very little I could do about my sartorial splendor, so I just sat among the

Brooks Brothers—looking like I just got out of a comic-book convention—and waited my turn to be called in.

At to this stage of the game, I felt that if God didn't want me to be a chiropractor, He wouldn't have gotten me this far, so it almost didn't matter what I said during the interview. The Popeye shirt would either close the deal or make for interesting conversation with the interviewer. I entered the room, and I saw the academic dean and two guys who looked like interns. They were dressed in short-sleeved medical smocks and had a confident air of knowing they were on their last lap before graduating—not unlike that of a parolee during his last moments behind bars. I felt like they were here to do the dirty work of the interview.

As I sat down, one of the interns looked at me. "Well, Popeye, we've got three questions for you: What makes you think you'll be a good chiropractor? How do you think you can afford this school? Do you like working with elderly people?"

I looked at them and said, "Can I answer them in reverse order?"

"Fine," they each said, as they simultaneously folded their arms and crossed their legs. Where was the lamp that was supposed to shine in my face?

"I love working with elderly people. I think everyone should be elderly at least once in life."

I think that eased the tension.

"Second, don't worry about the money. I've got that covered."

That got the dean smiling, while the interns looked at each other like they'd just caught an eight-pound rainbow trout.

"Why do I think I'll be a good chiropractor? Well, I truly think it's the perfect combination of using my hands and my mind. I know I want to help people in this world, and after watching another chiropractor do his job, I knew this is supposed to be my way of accomplishing my life's purpose."

The interns looked at each other with a smile, and the bearded one on my right leaned toward me and put out his hand.

"Welcome to LACC, Popeye."

CHAPTER 11

Dry Bones

MY YEARS SPENT AT LACC were filled with spiritual challenges: large chunks of time when I lacked a moral compass mixed with confirmations that God still had a hand in leading me in the right direction. Most comforting to me during all of the nebulous moments was the seemingly miraculous timing of my application. If I had applied to LACC any later or if I had decided to try for the new Los Gatos campus, I may not have become a chiropractor. As soon as I was accepted into the school, at the tender age of nineteen, the college changed the enrollment requirements by adding a third biology class and a physics class. I would have had to take an extra year of undergrad school to qualify! What's more, by the second year I attended LACC, we had students coming to our campus who had been waiting for over a year for the Los Gatos campus to open. They finally realized that campus was merely someone's pipe dream and decided to move south to the Los Angeles campus in Glendale. Somehow, God had prepared my path perfectly. I felt like I was in one of those adventure movies where as soon as you enter one room, the doors behind you automatically shut with a severe finality, leading you to the next room. It seemed that the vaults were slamming all right, coaxing me forward.

The first part of my time at LACC was horrendously challenging. I took challenging classes like anatomy, physiology, and histology, and the amount of information I had to assimilate in each class simply overwhelmed my gray matter. I added over five thousand words to my vocabulary the first year alone. As soon as I finished my day at school, I would lock myself in my room and try to study and memorize all I had learned that day, usually not coming up for air until I had finished at around nine or ten o'clock that night. I had to internalize all of the information from that day; there was no time for procrastination, as the next day of school delivered just as much information as the previous day had. I either had to get a grip on the information or drown in the tsunami of names, definitions, muscles, nerves, and bones. My program for success was to memorize everything given to me during the week and then to review it all over the weekend, studying twelve hours each of those two days. This was my life for the first two years at LACC.

Needless to say, my social life quickly turned into a petrified forest. There was simply no time to see anyone except for my classmates during the week. I made a valiant effort to find a church to replace the Baptist church, but with church requiring a commitment of time for transportation and attendance and with every minute for studying seeming like an ounce of gold, I simply could not afford the time away for anything short of a reunion of the original members of the Last Supper.

Besides, I started becoming disenchanted with the Christians my age whom I had associated with at that church. They all seemed directionless and uninterested in doing anything to make something productive of their lives. I would talk to them about the wonders of the human body or about nutrition, and they were just concerned about the fact that "Jesus was coming back soon" and that we needed to prepare. Yet, their idea of getting prepared for the imminent Second Coming seemed to consist only of telling other people "the end is near." They seemed to have no sense of living a quality life on earth, just of getting a ticket for the cosmic bus stop. They seemed completely out of touch with the world that I knew.

The only one who seemed to get it was Ron, my friend from attending the Baptist church and playing on the basketball team while we were in high school. He was interested in music, reading, and camping, but he was going to a seminary in Colorado, so he was out of geographic bounds at this point. The dearth of mental and spiritual stimulation at my old church made me realize that I had to get rejuvenated from some new, and henceforth unknown, source of people. I began my search.

My first stops were at the local Christian churches closer to my home and campus. I figured, "Hey, maybe I'll kill two birds with one stone—get some spiritual nourishment and maybe make a friend or two." Dating was essentially out of the question at this point, unless a young woman's idea of an exciting date was testing my knowledge of muscular origins and insertions, blood supplies, and nerve innervations, using the information on three-by-five cards. Somehow that didn't seem like much of a draw (not to mention that my bank account was dying of starvation), so I stuck to nonpredatory relationships.

A major turning point came when I had decided to join a church I had been attending fairly regularly. I started going to it because my mom had gone and said the pastor was a really good preacher. I went a few times by myself, and by Jove, the pastor not only held my attention, but he made the teachings of Jesus seem real and practical. He had a demeanor that was kind of a cross between the gentle warmth of Dick Van Dyke and the easygoing charm of James Stewart. I could get into this guy's sermons!

After one of the services, I went up to him and asked him about joining the church. He said they were starting a class on Sunday mornings before church for people who wanted to become members. In that class, he would go over the history of the church denomination (Dutch Reformed—good painters!) as well as the distinctions of this particular church. Every church has its own special shtick—something they emphasize more than other churches—be it the way they baptize, speaking in tongues, playing rock music, rolling in the aisles, or some quirky view on how the world is going to end. The pastor said if I agreed to everything, I could join the church. I would have to be baptized, however.

I had struggled with this whole baptism thing for a long time. Growing up in the Greek Orthodox church, I had been baptized as an infant, and I hadn't known there was any other way of doing it until I started going to these Protestant churches. Since attending the church in Inglewood, I had always liked the baptism services, usually held on a Sunday evening. They consisted of the pastor standing in or beside some giant water tank, with the converted soul standing in the water and giving a testimony as to how he or she had become a Christian. I found it fascinating that someone could tell his or her spiritual pilgrimage while standing in a bathtub wearing a white kimono. You could only be willing to do something that looked so surreal and ridiculous if you felt that God told you to do it; otherwise, it seemed completely bizarre.

While at the Baptist church, I was told, over and over again, if I wanted to get baptized, I could sign right up. And no matter how many times I told them I had already been baptized as a child, they told me this thing that I had gone through as an infant—which had been done to people for hundreds, if not thousands, of years—was not *really* a baptism; it didn't *count*. What it actually was, they couldn't say, but they knew what it wasn't! Needless to say, I hadn't been convinced. In fact, it seemed like an argument over some completely abstract point. This did not seem to be the essence of Jesus's teaching, so I never gave it major thought…at least, not until I realized any church I wanted to join seemed to have this fixation on me being baptized after some unknown magical age.

Anyway, I thought about it during the time I went to the Newcomer's Study with the pastor, and I gradually came around to concluding, fine, I could be baptized—if for no other reason than just to get everyone off my back and settle this thing once and for all. I told the pastor of my desire to get baptized and join the church, and he was delighted. "Next week, come to the service about fifteen minutes early, and we'll get you ready for everything." He beamed. I caught his infectious enthusiasm; warm up the water!

"You don't have to do it, George," Pastor Clark reassured me. "We are one of the few non-Catholic churches around here that consider an infant baptism a *real* baptism, just as your Greek Orthodox church does. You only have to be baptized by submersion if you want to. It's your choice."

What a contrast there was between this gentlemanly fellow and the fire-and-brimstone guy at my old church, who felt everything had to be done a certain way. The fact that he was so easygoing about the whole thing actually made me want to do it—just to cover my bases and so the Baptists wouldn't bother me about it anymore. "I'd like to do it, Pastor Clark," I said.

"Fine. The week after the last lesson, you'll walk up to the front with me, answer a few really basic questions, and get baptized."

The four weekly lessons were done an hour before each service. There were about a dozen of us, all sitting in a small circle, with Pastor Clark patiently going over the essential beliefs of Christianity and the distinctions of the Dutch Reformed faith. I was fascinated by the history and how intellectually it was all presented. Gone were the emotional manipulations. This guy made Christianity seem quite logical and actually reasonable. By the last session, I was sorry to see the classes end, but I was greatly anticipating the following week when I would finally become a member of a church by choice. (The Greek church didn't count, as I had been born into it. Besides, you only had to give twelve dollars a month as a donation to be a member. "Ten dollars if you're a senior citizen," the church secretary once told me.)

Mixed about fifty-fifty with anticipation and resignation, I got dressed that Sunday for church, not even bothering to tell my parents of my ecclesiastical exploits. I decided to just head for church, get everything over with, and move on with my spiritual journey.

Pulling into the church parking lot, I look around for the pastor. He was nowhere to be found. Not only that, but the church congregation had a buzz of activity. I went up to a matronly adult and asked, "What's going on here?"

"Oh, didn't you hear? The pastor is no longer with us."

"What happened? I just saw him here a week ago?"

"We had a congregational meeting last Sunday night and voted to remove him," she sniffed. "No one liked his wife. She was a real troublemaker."

And she cheerfully walked away.

I stood there dumbfounded. I couldn't believe that a church could just dump a pastor like that. And over his wife! At the Greek church, people openly hated the pastor's guts, but they still went every blessed week simply because that was what Greeks were supposed to do.

I looked around at all of the members at the church. I assumed that all of these people milling about were the mutineers. I went over to a sweet-looking middle-aged lady who was standing nearby to see if what I had heard was true. "Oh, yes," she replied, "we had to get rid of her. She was nasty!"

Glancing around at all of these people, I realized that I knew absolutely nothing about any of them. The only people I had gotten to know were the pastor, who was just charming, and the three or four other people in the weekly small group who had met every week to get prepared to join this church. So...no pastor. I realized I sure wasn't going to get baptized *this* week. Small cliques were huddled in discussions, some with laughter, some with a vicious intensity. Did I want to get to know a group of people who had just exiled the guy who convinced me to join this organization? This just didn't make sense, so I left the premises of the HMS Bounty Reformed Church and went back home—unbaptized, unaffiliated, and unimpressed with the local Christian community as I had come to know it.

It was at that time that I started becoming disenchanted with just about *all* of the Christian congregations that I had visited. I tried to get involved with some of the small groups of Christian people at my age and station in life, but I seemed to always run into peers who just didn't seem to be as excited about their faith and life as I thought they should be. In contrast, while in chiropractic school, I was surrounded by people who were beaming with direction and a laser-like focus. They were excited about what the future had in store for them. What's more, because of the nature of the chiropractic field, most of the students were into things like a holistic lifestyles, nutrition, exercise, and generally improving the mind, body, and soul. I was fascinated by how so many of these people really cared about what they ate and put into their bodies. This was completely foreign to me. At the functions I attended at the Baptist church, the only thought of nutritional value was asking God to bless the meatloaf and potluck. That was the best chance the food had to do us any good! As a friend of mine used to say, "Gluttony is one of the few acceptable sins left!"

CHAPTER 12

New Sights and Sounds

SELF-EVALUATION IS ALMOST AN INHERENT part of going to a school that teaches about health care. You can't learn all these wonderful lessons about how amazingly complex the body is and how to take care of it, without wondering about your own mind, body, and soul. Many of the students at LACC were highly religious—be they Christians, Jews, Mormons, Buddhists or Sikhs. This led to a plethora of interesting discussions about how to best take care of our complex and multidimensional selves.

Because of the inherent fact that the school specialized in helping people become healthy without ingesting medicine, instead relying on natural remedies such as the body's own healing power (as well as healthy nutrition and lifestyle choices), I heard lectures, went to seminars, and participated in discussions on just about every type of self-help technique out there. A lot of these sessions were pretty esoteric and loony, but each person teaching or selling some type of product or healing technique emphasized the importance of doing something constructive for your own well-being.

One of the guilty pleasures of my life has been listening to music—either in concerts or via records, tapes, CDs, or, nowadays, downloads. When I was in high school, I had almost one thousand record albums of various rock 'n' roll styles and genres. By the time I got into chiropractic college, I had come to the conclusion that almost all of the lyrics, attitudes, and lifestyles of rock were based on nihilism and usually focused on problems rather than solutions. Sitting in an arena waiting for a concert to begin one time, I blithely glanced over to my friend Steve, who was right next to me with his head in his lap. He didn't look up when I called him, so I lifted him up; he had been holding his face over a Frisbee that had been thrown and had hit him just above his lip while he was sitting in his seat. The Frisbee contained a pool of his blood. The final straw was when rock singer Patti Smith declared in the opening of her initial album, "Jesus died for someone's sins but not mine." I came to the conclusion, like that of rock singer Ian Hunter, that "rock 'n' roll is a loser's game." After having enough anger, vitriol, and cynicism literally thrown my way—at a concert or via a record album—I decided to stop going to these dens of decadence, get rid of my rock collection, and look for something a bit more life affirming.

But where to start?

The problem was I didn't know what to turn to musically. I had taken a classical music course in college, and it wasn't bad, but going into a classical record store with only a beginner's knowledge was intimidating and overwhelming. I mean, which of the twenty versions of Beethoven's Fifth Symphony do I buy? Secondly, since I was in chiropractic school, I had absolutely no money to buy any of these records. Still, I felt I had to honor God with this meager act of sonically going in the right direction, so I gave away some of my rock records and simply dumped others, like the Rolling Stones' *Their Satanic Majesties Request* into the trash can. It actually felt pretty relieving, like I had lightened my load a little bit.

Because of all the school hours, combined with studying all of my waking hours and a financially Spartan lifestyle, I hadn't been into Moby Disc Records in over a year. I took a few of the albums I thought were sellable to this local used record shop, thinking I could get a little money to help my poor collegiate wallet. Bob, the manager, looked up to reunite with his long-lost customer.

"Hey, George! Good to see you! Where've you been?" Thin, with long straight hair and a bicyclist's physique, Bob leaned over the counter, sincerely glad to see me. When I was in high school, he was one of those cool college guys who had what seemed to be the dream job—the manager of a record store. Soft-spoken, he had that intangible quality of mellow that was so prevalent back in the '70s. Nothing seemed to faze him. Was it his disposition or a lifetime of pot smoking?

"In the Twilight Zone," I answered. "I've been going to chiropractic school, and it takes all of my time to get through the classes. Besides, I have *no money* for albums, which is why I'm bringing these in for some cash."

"Sure. I'll give you ten bucks for these. Chiropractic school? That sounds cool!" he said in his classic relaxed, yet affirming way. "I love chiropractic! I've even seen one myself for my stiff neck and shoulder." Bob was about four years older than I was, but when you're nineteen, that is like the equivalent of an Old Testament prophet. "Can you do the chiropractic adjustments yet?"

"Sure. Why do you think I'm going to school? I'm not the best at it, but I'm getting there." I started seeing some light shining behind the clouds, like a glorious sunrise. Something good was coming...

"I've got an idea. Why don't you come by here once a week or so to give me and the owners a treatment. Do you have a massage table of some sort that we could use?"

I had just bought a portable adjusting table for ninety dollars. It was about to become the best investment of my young life.

"Yeah. I could do the treatments in your storage room in the back. I can't take money for this, however...That would be illegal since I don't have my license."

"Look...how about every time you give me a treatment, I'll give you a few albums. Deal?"

My head was spinning over the possibility! Unlimited access to music! Could anything be better for a poor and musically starved student? How close to heaven could I get?

"I'd love to do this, but I want something besides just rock 'n' roll, but I don't know what to get."

Bob looked at me incredulously, with that kind of look that only an older and wiser sage could give. "George, don't you know that my real love is jazz? I'll turn you on to some of the best music you'll ever hear! Ah! Virgin ears!" he exclaimed as he took me over to the jazz bins, an area of the record store I had not even known existed, let alone approached. I felt like I was entering some dark inner sanctum of a medieval castle. Bob fingered through the different sections...

"Here, even people who *hate* jazz like this one." He handed me an album by Herbie Hancock titled *Maiden Voyage*. "Let's see, you need to start on some Ellington, Coltrane...Here's a Miles Davis album. OK, you're set for this week. Listen to them, let me know what you think, and we'll go from there."

Could this really be happening to me? Suddenly, after giving up something I liked—even though it was bad for me—I felt like God was dropping a giant Reward for Obedience card in my lap, with this new and positive music.

Determined to expand my music repertoire further, I found out that a student in the class behind me at college used to be a classical cellist. Armed with pencil and paper, I walked up to him and handed him my writing utensils.

"What's this for?" asked the bespectacled colleague.

"You play classical music, right? Well, I know *nothing* about it. Would you do me a big favor and write down fifty pieces of classical music that any self-respecting music fan should know?

Sitting at the lunch table, he peered over his glasses, smiling the perfect condescending smile of a musical snob. "I'd be glad to!"

I was musically set for the rest of my life!

The reason that I bring up this simple story is that while I was on my spiritual trek, I was on a musical one as well. I figured that if I was going to get myself on the right track spiritually, a proper musical intake was going to be just as vital to my attitude and demeanor. How could one part of your life be in conflict with some other facet? Slowly and methodically, I saw the importance of everything that I was imbibing—be it food, literature, music, media, or even friends. Everything seemed to be calling me to fit together into a cohesive unit, where one part of my life seemed like a complement to the rest of my life.

My second venture into alternative musical forms was to go to a series of free concerts at UCLA. Surely this center of education could offer me something in the form of the fine arts. The first was a baroque concert (not bad!) and then an acoustic blues/folk duet. The third had a sign at the entrance that said "Indian Music." I had no idea what that entailed; back in the seventie'70s, Ravi Shankar was not a big name yet, but I figured, "Hey, it's worth checking out for free." I noticed a couple of cute girls about my age, and I decided to sit by them to try to remember what it was like to be a human.

Valerie and Virginia were a pair of sweet, good-humored, and very bright ladies, and they had a demeanor I found very attractive. They also had a sensibility that the Christian girls I'd known did not have, but they had an innocence and lack of guile that seemed to indicate a sense of morality and higher purpose. I was intrigued…

"Have you two been friends for a long time?"

"Well, we've known each other about two or three months. We met at an Emissary Center."

"What's an Emissary Center, and what's an emissary?" I had never heard of such a thing.

Virginia looked disarmingly confident. "An emissary is just someone who follows the teachings of its leader, Martin Cecil. It's not an actual religion or anything like that. It's more of a philosophy about life. We have people in it who are Catholics, Protestants, and all other belief systems. It's just a way of looking at life."

This sounded both intriguing and confusing. Was this some sort of a cult? Were these the kind of people who went around collecting money at airports or offered free personality tests in order to sucker you into some program that was going to cost you thousands of dollars? When did the mind control actually start? Was it actually already happening? This piqued my curiosity. These girls seemed very grounded in reality and practically minded. They didn't have that otherworldly look in their eyes that some of the people who hung around airports or DMVs handing out flowers for a donation had. No, these ladies talked a lot about nutrition, exercise, and the importance of being productive and useful. They knew a lot about the chiropractic field, which impressed me. How could they be so culturally aware, so seemingly in touch with the cusp of health, but evoke an image of innocence that reflected the prepsychedelic '60s?

"Oh, we have a lot of people in our group who are into healing, health, and nutrition," Virginia commented, as she glistened a disarming look at me. "You should come to one of the lectures; I think you'd like it."

The demeanor and aura of these two young ladies was strangely alluring, but not for any romantic reason. I was drawn to their complete peace with themselves and their lack of self-absorption. They truly seemed to be enjoying the simple things of life.

"Well, are there sermons or reading from the Bible?"

"Sort of. You'll have to come to see."

After some thought, I decided to go. It turned out the meeting room was in someone's home in Westwood, a town better known for WASPish materialism than self-denying spirituality. Nevertheless, I pulled up to the ritzy Spanish-style home in my '71 VW van, not knowing what to expect.

I walked into the open, spacious, and windowed living room that had about ten rows of chairs facing a podium, which was in front of a fireplace. On the mantle and also on one of the lampstands was a black-and-white picture of a man who looked to be in his sixties. Each of the frames contained the same picture, sort of a generic bust shot of a semiserious gray-haired gentleman. Why two pictures? Was it a relative? The ringleader of some cult? It looked a bit funny yet also slightly ominous.

I scanned the room and saw almost every chair was filled and the people were all sitting in quiet anticipation. No one was really conversing; they were all just facing forward in blissful repose. I looked around and saw someone I actually recognized: Dave Rice, a very friendly mid-to-late-twenties guy who sold and distributed vitamins to various chiropractors. He'd come to the office I was interning at, and I always found him very engaging, friendly, and in possession of an infectious laugh. "He's pretty normal," I thought. I had heard him speak once at a health seminar, however, and had found that he spoke in generalities and platitudes that sounded good but lacked substance.

I waved to him, but I had also noticed Virginia, so I sat next to her and a friend of hers. The oppressive silence was not conducive to small talk, so I just sat and soaked in the quiet atmosphere. Someone went up to the front, offered a few greetings, and then read for about twenty minutes from a sermon by Cecil, who I later discovered was the guy in the pictures. The reading was encouraging and practical; it mentioned taking care of your body, mind, and soul. Parts of it sounded really deep and thought provoking. Hmm. Maybe this was what I was looking for. I liked that it didn't just come off as a series of dos and don'ts; the speaker talked about the importance of thought life and being aware of what's going on around you, the importance of making yourself useful, and how everything you do and think is interconnected—not just with yourself, but with other people as well. I really was attracted to that last part, as most of the Christians I had met and had known seemed to spout off verses from the Bible about what was right but never seemed to be able to back it up by their actions.

I was intrigued by the lecture; it sure was a different format than I had been used to—no singing, incense, or references to a Bible verse, just people taking in this guy in the picture's thoughts. What was even more interesting was that after the reading, the man at the podium invited the audience to speak about their reflections on what we'd just heard. Some of the comments were quite insightful. I was impressed by that; I just couldn't imagine Father Kezios or the Baptist pastor finishing a liturgy or sermon and then asking, "Are there any questions?" After the Q & A, I got up, spotted a counter with a handful of booklets that contained Cecil's other lectures, and put some of them in my pocket. I figured I would see what this guy had to say over a period of time.

After the talk, I caught myself thoroughly enjoying Virginia's positive and slightly silly attitude about everything, and I mentioned that we should get together, hang out, and just do something. "I give great foot massages," she boasted. "Why don't you come over sometime? We'll go out and come back for a foot rub!"

Now, that was something to look forward to!

About a week later, I actually had a free afternoon, so I decided to go on something that might resemble date and gave her a call. I went over to her place in Venice Beach. It was a cute and funky little apartment, just a short leap from the Santa Monica Pier. She wanted to take a walk along the beach and was wearing one of those old-fashioned, roaring-twenties-type bathing suits that is part bathing suit and part skirt. This girl was something different! I had a ton of questions for her. I asked her about the meeting. Was it a denomination? A religion? What?

We went back to her place, and on closer inspection, I noticed that the same picture of Cecil was in her living room. What was it about this photo? Weren't there other shots of him?

"It's not a cult or anything like that," she replied. "We don't worship it or anything. It's sort of like a picture of a member of your family."

We settled down on the couch, and I kept asking her questions. The answers always seemed interesting and well considered but were never completely revealing. She went over to her bookshelf, grabbed a couple of little booklets, and gave them to me. They looked like various lectures by Cecil, as well as other people. "Here, read these, and see what you think about them. Ready for a foot rub? What music do you want to listen to?"

She went over to her record player while I took my shoes off and pulled out *Lady in Satin* by Billie Holiday, which is one of the most desultory recordings in history. Holiday's scratchy voice, from years of drug abuse among other things, is barely tolerable in its self-destructive agony. She's backed by the lush strings of Ray Ellis's orchestra, and the commingling of the two is like dipping an egg roll in both hot mustard and sweet sauce.

We continued these platonic, podiatric, musical, and spiritual meetings for quite some time, and it always ended with me on her couch with my feet getting rubbed to Billie Holiday's crackling "I'm a Fool to Want You." I'd lie there thinking about this whole situation, both while it was occurring and afterward. What was actually going on here? Was I being attracted to her mix of innocence and quirkiness? Her foot rubs? Her pursuit of spiritual truth? Or was I just trying to figure out if what she believed was the real thing? Was she on the threshold of some really deep truth that I was searching for as well? I analyzed and cross-analyzed my motives for a series of weeks, even as Virginia's heat-seeking fingers were atom bombing me on the foot reflexes.

I figured there was only one way to figure it out; I'd have to make a move on her. One night after our ritual of discussion, *Lady in Satin*, and foot reflexology, as I was getting ready to leave, I went to the door and planted one on her. It was one of those moments when—something like 90 percent of the way bending forward to kiss her—I realized I was going to get a completely nonplussed response from her, and I did. It was like the proverbial "kissing your sister." For some strange reason, this confirmation of our platonic relationship made the spiritual quest a lot easier; I didn't need to get all of my information from her. She had a network of acquaintances that I was being introduced to, and all of them were particularly enjoyable in their own quirky way.

What fascinated me about these people was that they were all deeply and enthusiastically interested in something. No matter what it was, they had a passion for their direction. I found myself drawn to one guy, Paul, who was a guitarist. He was spending a lot of time practicing to become a master jazz guitarist. He was also the first vegan I had ever met. He was just trying to figure out if eating such a strict regimen of food was going to be beneficial or not.

Still, even Paul was either unclear or noncommittal about the essential teachings of this group. He felt that the teachings of Martin Cecil helped him get more clarification about his direction. He said he used to be involved with drugs, but he had changed, so he wanted to really take care of his body, mind, and spirit. These people certainly appeared to have their lives together. No one I met at the meetings seemed to lose his or her temper. They were always so cheerful, or at least friendly in a matter-of-fact sort of way, and held themselves up to a high level of personal integrity. I was trying to figure out this group, and while the readings they gave me were interesting, they weren't conclusive.

Somehow, I was going to have to get this thing resolved. I decided that once I got out of chiropractic school, I was going to travel around the United States, visit some more of these emissaries, and figure it out once and for all. In the meanwhile, I'd just hang with them and read their material, with or without massaged feet.

CHAPTER 13

Dates, Travels, and Signs

I HAVEN'T WRITTEN MUCH ON my dating life at this time for a few simple reasons: I was taking premed classes in undergraduate school and then going to a chiropractic college that sometimes had me taking *thirty-one* units a semester, so I pretty much had the social life of the local mortician.

Oh, not that I didn't try. There were a few girls I dated in undergrad and even a few fellow students at chiropractic school, but there was just no time to be able to commit to making a relationship work. It seemed that I also had a simple case of terrible judgment in women. Like most guys in their twenties, looks were the initial draw, and it wasn't until too late that I'd realize that I was pursuing a superficial relationship for shallow reasons. I knew that the Bible said to be committed only to fellow Christians, but the Christian girls I had known seemed even less interested in spiritual growth than the agnostics!

Essentially, none of the young women I was meeting were on the same quest that I was. I was slowly learning that when it comes to choosing between security and adventure, most ladies will take the safe and cautious route. Most women were intimidated by a guy like me, who was searching for something intangible in life and therefore unsure of the destination. I felt that most of them preferred (and understandably so) someone who was grounded in his ways and focused on his plans. While he may be good or religious, nothing is less attractive to women than a guy who takes things too seriously. Most people liked the comfort and ease of social religiosity, but my fervor to find the inner core of God's truth didn't fit into the plans of most of the ladies I met; they wanted a guy, a home, two cars, and a golden retriever. If I was going to commit to this sojourn, it seemed that I was going to go it alone.

Maybe when I found the answers I was seeking, I'd be ready to share my life with someone else.

I sat down by myself and tried to think through my future plans. I had no girlfriend, I was becoming a doctor at twenty-three, and there was *no* way I was going to get pinned down into a job commitment for the rest of my life. One thing I had learned about being a doctor was that if you set up a practice, that was *it*; you were going to be there for a long time. There were no transfers, so you'd better choose wisely and carefully where you put down your stake. With my survival of chiropractic school pretty well secured, I figured maybe it was time to travel around and see the world outside the framework of classrooms and labs.

Besides, I decided that the only way for me to figure out this emissary thing, once and for all, was to visit a number of their centers throughout the United States. I'd wanted to do a bit of traveling anyway, so here was a means of killing two birds with one stone. I decided I would take a trip around the United States in my '71 van for a number of months, and Ron's book would definitely accompany me.

First semester would end in December, and then I would have an eight-week break; I could take some of that time to drive around and see part of America. Being wintertime, the best place to go would be the southern United States, as it would have the best weather for driving.

As far as meeting people and determining where I would spend each night on my trip, my strategy was fairly simple. I was still involved with the Emissaries, so I contacted Dave, who was the leader of the group I frequented, and asked him if he knew other people from the Emissaries who lived in the areas I'd be visiting. I figured this would be a great way to see their belief system in action, and sometimes, when you're a stranger, you can ask questions and get answers that you normally couldn't get because of the barrier of familiarity. Dave got me an Emissary directory. (There *was* such a thing? Interesting!) It included the names, addresses, and phone numbers of Emissary Centers throughout Texas, Louisiana, Alabama, and Mississippi. I called a bunch of them up before I set off on my trip and told them the general date I'd be visiting. Everyone I talked to seemed sincere and friendly, though a few in the Deep South were pretty hard for me to understand because of thick Cajun accents. This was going to be fun! I'd stay at these centers when I could; that way, I could save a bit on the traveling expenses and I could also spend some time with these people in order to really figure this whole thing out.

Things were getting exciting!

My beautiful 1971 VW van had an ice-chest type mini-fridge and a sink, as well a roll-out bed. I'd always had the travel bug, and I figured, with my camper, I could go just about anywhere as long as there was a street where I could pull over and park for the night. I had very little money, so this trip had to be done as cheaply as possible. My two-pronged approach was very simple: (a) Fill the van up with breakfast cereals, sleep in the van as often as possible on private streets (to avoid state-park fees), shower in college gyms, and (b) mooch off of as many strangers as possible. I got a Coleman stove, which fit right on a little table. The van had a ton of storage space, and I jammed the crevices with cans of baked beans, corn, vegetables, boxes of granola cereal, and dried milk, along with cans of chili, soup, and stew. I figured if I could eat my own cooking as much as possible for six weeks, I'd save a bundle of money. I had a bunch of Emissary books and *Mere Christianity*, as well as some Mark Twain stuff—figuring that would get me in the mood for going through the South—as well as my journal and a Bible. Bob had given me a ton of records by then, both classical and jazz, and I made twenty cassette tapes—two albums per tape, divided evenly between jazz and classical. By the time this trip was over, I would know those albums *cold.* I filled my sink's tank with water, checked my tires and oil, and tucked my *Idiot's Guide to Volkswagen Repair* in the storage spot behind my seat. I was on my way!

I had never traveled by myself for such a long time before. I'd taken a weekend trip or two down to San Diego and had gone camping by myself in the backwoods of Yosemite for a week to see if I had the stomach for prolonged periods of solitude. Each of these short treks was a test of my ability to travel without any company—no one to talk to or share responsibilities with—and I actually seemed to enjoy this style of travel. I soaked in the quiet and intro-spection of going it alone, and I was sociable enough to initiate a conversation with some stranger (which I once heard defined as "a friend you haven't yet met") if I craved company. I felt refreshed from being alone for a while. Maybe the fact that my great uncle was a monk in a monastery in Greece inspired me—something in the gene pool! I was mentally ready for life on the road.

Traveling by myself through the open spaces of Arizona, New Mexico, and Texas was just exhilarating. The great thing about driving around in a van is that you can pull over any time you want, find a residential street that looks fairly safe, and park for the evening for a good night's sleep. I always picked upper-middle-class neighborhoods, as they were not only fairly safe, but I figured that—if it were a typical suburban neighborhood—each home was so uninvolved with neighbors no one would notice an extra van on the street for one night. I'd usually wake up and get going before anyone would suspect anything from seeing a van with California license plates. For basic washing and facilities, I'd either use a local gas station or I'd find a local college and just wander into the men's gym locker room. One thing I learned by traveling in this way was that you can get away with just about anything if you simply act like you know what you're doing. This system worked pretty well, except for the gas stations that used some funky, hard blue powder for soap. That stuff could really burn!

The first family I stayed with had nothing to do with the Emissaries; the Niels were Jamie's parents. Jamie was a really nice Houston flight attendant I'd met when driving around and hanging out in San Diego. I had a crush on Jamie's friend Glynda and, as so often happens, ended up becoming friends with the one who hadn't broken my heart. Mrs. Niel was a lovely, down-to-earth lady who let me stay at her San Antonio house for a few days to get the feel of Texas. Mrs. Niel, her husband, and their ten-year-old son and I played a number of board games, which were a ton of fun, and went out to the shows along the famed River Walk. We had a few spiritual discussions; I was bemused by the classic hardworking and drinking behavior of the white-collar Mr. Niel. He never appeared to actually enjoy the board games we played; each move and act during these games seemed like a personal war maneuver, and he was demonstratively—as well as vindictively—happy when he won. Seeing his behavior, I knew I did not want to end up like this kind of guy, just another horse on the merry-go-round of the business world.

Ever the generous hostess, Mrs. Niel opened my world to various indigenous ethnic foods by taking me to cute little divey Mexican restaurants for local Tex-Mex fare. "Try this!" she said, pushing a bowl of soup in front of me. "It's called 'menudo.' Very popular here." It contained a bunch of vegetables and other assorted articles.

I took a bite; it was delicious! It was love at first sip! I completely polished off the bowl in record time and asked for seconds. From then on, whenever we went out, I asked for a heaping serving of it.

On my last day in San Antonio, Mrs. Niel took me to an antique market, where I was overwhelmed by rows and rows of classic American artifacts. Mostly catching my eye were the gorgeous, old-fashioned metallic signs that advertised things from Coca-Cola to bread to root beer. I connected with the small, round Coke signs; they seemed to reflect a nostalgic part of Americana. I was drawn to the simple beauty of these reflections of a bygone era, and I knew that I somehow had to get one on this trip. I had no money to buy one. (They were going for as much as five hundred bucks!) I had to figure out some other way to get my hands on one—or two!

After the market, we went to my final Tex-Mex restaurant, just me and the missus. She ordered my soup and glowed with a mother's protective pride over my appetite as I devoured my gastronomic discovery.

"My, you sure do love that menudo!" She beamed.

"It's just fantastic. Thank you so much for introducing it to me."

"My pleasure. You are really an adventurous young man, traveling around like this," she declared as she leaned forward with her arms folded in confidence. "Even in the fact that you try different foods."

"What do you mean?"

"Well, most white people I know would never even try menudo."

"You've got to be kidding! It's delicious!" I responded as I slurped my opening sips.

"Well, some people are just turned off by the fact that they're eating intestines."

At the exact moment the word *intestines* hit my ears, I can honestly say that the taste and configuration of the soup that was in my spoon completely transformed before my very eyes and taste buds. No longer was this material going into my mouth a wonderful, exotic delicacy, but it magically changed into a putrid and stomach-churning piece of *pig's gut*. If Mrs. Niel weren't there, I would have immediately spit it out with a full spray of enthusiasm, but instead, I bravely swallowed it with a hard and final gulp, holding back the nausea and vomit that was trying to work its way up my throat. For the rest of the meal, I simply stirred the soup around; I swear I saw the spoon dissolving in the questionable mixture in the bowl. I never tried another sip that evening, and I have not ever considered sampling it since, simply because I now know what was in that witches' brew. First lesson on the trip: attitude is *everything*! Nothing had changed except my opinion of what I had eaten. It was a big lesson with implications galore.

My purpose for this trip, however, was not to feast on menudo, but to see the South and get some spiritual direction. Traveling on through Texas, driving along long, lonesome highways, I became obsessed with the ubiquitous metallic soft-drink signs that appeared on every drugstore and market.

I had never seen them before that antique store in San Antonio, and I was more convinced than ever that I had to have one to put on my wall back home! While driving through Leggett, Texas, I came across a strip of stores, and—lo and behold—I saw a vacant store that had two beautiful Coke signs up on the front-entrance overhang. The store looked like it hadn't been open in years, and I was tempted to just get up on a ladder and take them. Who would know?

My sense of decency and honesty temporarily overcame my acquisitive materialism, though. All of the stores on that side of the two lane were closed for the day—or for the duration—so, I ran across the highway to find the only store that seemed open, a hardware store run by a taciturn, old buzzard of a guy. I asked him who owned the shop with the Coke signs. "I'd like to have them."

"That'd be Mrs. Davenport. She retired a long time ago."

"Could you please get me a phone book so I could call her? I'd like to ask her permission to have them."

Sighing with the silent resignation that comes with having a peacefully boring routine broken, Mr. Buzzard reached under the counter and plopped a thin and worn phone book on the table. I scanned through the book, looking for her name...Curtis, Darling...The phone numbers had only five digits! I was definitely in small-town USA! I finally found her name and number and gave her a ring.

"Mrs. Davenport?"

A fragile voice responded on the other end, "Yes. Who is this?"

"You don't know me, ma'am, but I was passing through your town, and I saw a couple of Coca-Cola signs on the front of your old store, which is closed down. I'm from California, and we have nothing like those signs there. I was wondering, since your store is closed down, if I could have your permission to take them off your hands, so I could keep them as a souvenir of your state?"

She seemed a bit bewildered and hesitantly replied, "I'm not sure what you're talking about."

"Your old store!" I answered louder, as if that would help her understand. "I would like the signs from your store!" She seemed to be fairly senile, but as long as I got the signs, honestly, who cared?

"I'm not sure what signs you're talking about, but you can have them, sonny."

That was all I needed to hear. With that, I triumphantly thanked her, hung up, and told Mr. Buzzard, "She said I could have them! Do you have a ladder that I could please borrow to get them with?"

"Right there, young man," he drawled with the indifference and feigned politeness that only a store manager can exude while waiting for the store to close.

I looked both ways up and down the long highway and carefully crossed with the ladder. I couldn't have been happier. I thanked God for helping me do this project the right way as I carefully unscrewed the signs from the over-hang. The screws were so old that I ended up bending and twisting some of the support brackets, but I figured that since Mrs. Davenport wasn't going to use the sign or store anymore, it didn't make too much of a difference. After tucking the lovely red cylinders under the seat of the VW, I folded up the lad-der and victoriously took it back to the hardware store.

"Here's your ladder, sir. Thanks for everything," I said as I headed for the door.

Mr. Buzzard slowly turned to me from behind the counter and said suspi-ciously, "Just where did you take those signs from, son?"

"Why, Mrs. Davenport's. I asked you whose store that was, and you saw me call her," I cautiously answered as I put my hand on the exit, smelling a rat.

Buzzard's eyes seemed to get larger. "That wasn't Mrs. Davenport's store you went to," he said as his stentorian voice slowly increased in intensity. "Her place is next door. You just took the signs from Old Man Farner, the meanest man in this here county!"

All the blood drained out of my face. "What should I do?" I asked as every instinct within me told me to run out of the store as fast as I could and drive my van as quickly out of town as my four cylinders would allow.

"I don't know what you should do, but you're sure in a heck of a lot of trouble, boy!"

Trying as hard as possible to avoid panicking, I assessed my predicament: I figured that honesty had gotten me into this situation, so I might as well try honesty to get me out of it. Besides, how far could I get, trying to escape a county filled with Ford and Chevy trucks that had stickers that said, "This vehicle protected by Smith and Wesson"? I grabbed the phone book again and found Farner's number…

A voice that sounded like something from *In the Heat of the Night* answered the phone. I could almost hear him lazily rocking back and forth in his chair, a shotgun on his lap, and a couple of hound dogs at his feet. "Ye-ah?"

"Mr. Farner?"

"Ye-ah?"

"You don't know me, but my name is George Harris."

A couple of agonizing seconds of silence passed as I could sense the wheels churning in his head. "Ye-ah?"

"By mistake, I took the Coke signs off of your store roof, thinking the store—"

"You did *whaaaaaaaaaaaaaaaaaaat?*"

"I took the Coke signs off of the display of your store by mistake. I thought it was Mrs. Davenport's store. I am willing to buy them from you, or I can—"

"Yew betta put them signs back up raght nayow!" And the phone clicked off with a tremendous and resounding thud.

I looked at Mr. Buzzard, who was leaning forward with both hands pressed firmly on the counter. "I need to borrow your ladder again."

Having heard Farner's voice blaring from the phone, Buz suddenly came to life with the excitement of holy fear. "You ain't gonna involve me in this hea' problem of yours!" he declared as his head shook and then scuttled into the back of his store like a cockroach exposed to light.

Abandoned to my own devices, I grabbed the ladder, crossed the highway again, and got the signs out the van. Just as I was ascending the ladder and beginning to put the antiques back on the roof, an olive-green truck came careening up, jarring to a dusty halt right in front of the store. Two Dobermans jumped out of the bed of the truck, and a sunglasses-wearing, stocky, grizzly guy in army fatigues sprang out of the truck, a pistol in each hand. I felt like a sitting duck, so I moved *very* slowly.

He didn't say a word…just chewed his tobacco.

"Hold on! Don't shoot! I'm putting them back."

Sizing up the situation like a parole officer, he spoke more calmly than he had on the phone. "Don't bother, boy. Just come on down."

I slowly and methodically got down from the ladder and explained the mishap to him, with the Dobermans sniffing me up and down the whole time, as if I were tonight's meal.

"Well, boy, you did the right thing. I'm letting ya go 'cause you might be dumb, but you're honest. If you'd have driven off, I woulda then had to cut you down."

I didn't want to ask the details about that expression; I was just glad to escape in one piece, albeit without the signs. I learned a valuable lesson, though, about being strictly honest. One variance from absolute integrity would have put a .357 in some part of my van or body. God's ways do give life, or as W. C. Fields paraphrased the Proverb, "You can't cheat an honest man!"

CHAPTER 14

Louisiana Hayride

AFTER SURVIVING TEXAS, I HEADED to Louisiana, where I had the addresses of a few Emissary Centers that could provide me free room and board. The Centers actually ranged from communes that had ten to twenty residents of various ages and social statuses to a bachelor pad or small family home that followed the teachings of the leader/founder, Martin Cecil. I found it bemusing that every residence had the exact same picture of the guy on a desk or on the wall, almost giving the appearance of an icon.

Arriving in Natchidoches, I pulled up to a lovely ranch house and was greeted by some friendly people my own age. Each person here seemed warm and genuine. The same was true of my time in Lafayette, where I stayed a few days with a bachelor who had a career as an advertising editor. The thing that really impressed me was how even-keeled everyone seemed. If I broke something or was abrupt in my speech, the people around me were very patient. I never saw one of these people lose their cool. Nothing got them irritated, and they were very generous in how they let me stay with them as long as I liked and fed my hungry, traveling body with aplomb and grace. I wondered if I could ever be that insouciant about life, while still being productive.

I was intrigued by the teachings that were read each evening. The message usually consisted of something about making something out of your life and not getting wrapped up in the things in the world that people strive for, like power and fame. It was pretty level-headed stuff, and I couldn't really find anything that Jesus himself would have objected to if He had heard these readings.

Arriving at New Orleans, I knew that I was now entering a completely different world. The energy of the French Quarter was intoxicating, with sights, smells, and sounds that overwhelmed the senses as I'd walk down streets like Bourbon and Burgundy. I had very little money to live on, so I just parked my van on some side street and slept in it during the night, leaving it there while I'd check out the local colors and flavors.

I didn't know what to expect from the Crescent City, but it certainly wasn't being propositioned by a couple of guys whom I had simply asked for directions. It was done so matter-of-factly; they said I was "cute." Suddenly, I empathized with the countless number of women who have been treated like a piece of meat. Being a man, I'd never been on the receiving end of such a situation. I felt violated; the education definitely continued!

Sometimes, you take in a lot of information all at one time, but it takes days, weeks, or even longer to digest it. That's what happened to me while I was traveling along the Mississippi River to the historic town of Natchez in order to check out the antebellum homes. I was having a great time of solitude, listening to some bebop music by Charlie Parker and Dizzy Gillespie, and really starting to appreciate this intricate yet visceral music for the first time. It was becoming mid-afternoon, and I'd have to start looking for a place to park my van. Plus, I needed to go to a store to get some groceries to tide me over through breakfast.

I pulled into a market and entered the store. There was a really tall, pasty-skinned, lanky guy setting up a display of soup cans. He was whistling; it sounded like a song I knew from the Baptist church: "Father, I Adore You." I gently stated, "Nice tune you're whistling there."

"D'ya know it?" he drawled at me as he turned suddenly with a smile.

"Sure do, buddy."

Well, he looked at me like I was a long-lost friend. "I'm Duane, and I'm sure excited to meet a Christian brother!" He beamed. "I'm getting off work in a few minutes. Why don't you come home with me and have dinner?"

Following Harris's number-one rule of travel ("never turn down a free meal"), I gladly accepted. He seemed sincere and quite enthusiastic about his faith. I hadn't seen anyone like this since those speakers at CSUN.

He started peppering me with questions. "How long have you been born again? How long have you been saved? How did you come to know Jesus?"

This guy was really into it. I felt a bit overwhelmed by his enthusiasm and even intimidated. I was *never* this excited about being a Christian. While we were driving to his house, I asked myself, "Is the problem, therefore, with him or with me?"

We went to his little apartment, a funky and modest place with just the bare minimum of furniture. Dinner consisted of spaghetti with store-bought tomato sauce, iceberg lettuce, and bottled Italian dressing—simple, basic. There was something about this guy: he almost looked like he'd just gotten out of prison or something. He was still going on and on about how important Jesus was to him. I noticed a saxophone in the corner of his Spartan living room. Hmm…maybe a different topic.

"Duane, do you play that?"

"Used to," he said, munching down the salad, "but I gave it up for Jesus."

"What do you mean by that?"

"Well, when I was in high school, I really got into jazz. At one point, I could play everything Charlie Parker ever did. And I mean *play* it."

My ears perked up. "You could play 'Moose the Mooche,' 'Ornithology,' and 'Yardbird Suite'?" I asked enthusiastically (and a bit enviously).

"Knew them all," I could hear him say through the crunching salad. "But I had to give it up."

I started to feel an uncomfortable tingle in the back of my neck. I was anticipating some pious, self-righteous speech, but I got something else.

"I thought music was the greatest thing ever. I wanted to play just like Parker. I'd practice eight to twelve hours a day, until I mastered it. Then, just like Bird, I got into drugs. Took all of that bad stuff, and it just ruined my life. I spent all my money on that junk. Lost my job, friends, direction, and almost my life. Someone told me about Jesus, and I'm now slowly getting back on track. My life has meaning again. Praise God." He just kept eating his dinner, matter-of-factly.

"Wow," I thought to myself. "I can't argue that this guy (who seems like he's *now* on the next-to-bottom rung of life) is trying to better his situation. He must've really been down and out when he turned to faith in Christ. Is that what Christianity's really for? The real losers in life who just can't seem to get it together any other way?" Was the music I was being drawn into the real loser's game, and was Christianity the true hip thing, when it was all said and done? Which one of us was buying low and selling high? Which was going in the right direction?"

I spent the night on the shag-carpet-covered floor of this guy's humble abode, had cornflakes for breakfast with him, and drove off the next day with my head spinning with questions about who the real fools and wise ones are in life. I realized that my spiritual horizons needed more fine-tuning.

I felt even more confused after I arrived in Mobile, Alabama, and met an Emissary who was a chiropractor. While he was old enough to be my father, we hit it off like longtime buddies; even better, I felt an attraction to his receptionist. This just might be a nice stay! Gladys was about my age, and we talked quite a bit about the general teachings of the Emissaries. She seemed to be just starting her journey with them and was enthusiastic about finding some truth and integrity to life.

The night before I was to leave and head back to California, Gladys invited me to a friend's house, just to hang out. I was introduced to three Persian guys who seemed nice enough, but somehow, after a few minutes and drinks, they made it clear to me that I was the only straight person in this home. It turned out that Gladys and her friends were all homosexual and very assertive about it. They put on some disco music (which was just starting to get popular at the time) and began delving into some fairly lascivious dances that made me feel very uncomfortable. Was there someplace I could hide from all of this? I started asking myself, "If the world ended right now, and I was caught here at this evening of debauchery, how bad would that look on Judgment Day?" I figured I would not get a pass on this one and that my ability to discern people's character had been once again proven quite poor in my travels. I was developing a healthy skepticism of my own judgment concerning people— and women in particular. Somehow, I got out of that place with some semblance of decorum and went directly to bed, pulling the covers over my head.

When you travel by yourself, you have *a lot* of time for reflection and self-examination. During my long hours behind the wheel, I'd think about my relationships with women and wonder why they seemed to fail so profoundly. Was it my initial judgment? Was I expecting too much? Could I really be so wrong in my first impressions? Well, the girl in Mobile put some fuel to that theory! I was amazed at how I liked the wrong girls for all the wrong reasons—and it wasn't until it was too late that I would retrospectively appreciate the more subtle qualities of a female companion who was long gone from my life. What was Groucho Marx's old joke? Oh, yeah. "Why would I want to join a club that would have me as a member?"

Right before this trip, I had been dumped by a girl I'd been dating for a short while and had developed a crush on. I started questioning my ability to find the right mate. And besides, what would I do if I did find her? Could I be mature enough not to ruin the relationship? Here I was, in the middle of trying to figure out what I believed about God, life, my purpose, and eternity. What good would it do me if I found someone who was just perfect for me at the present time but at odds with me if I changed my belief system? What if I became an Emissary...or ended up rejecting it? Or if I converted to Judaism? I realized that if I were to find someone to share my life with, I had to get my own spiritual act together so as not to frustrate either one of us.

I came to this quick realization while I was in good old Austin, Texas, slowly working my way back home. I was taking an afternoon off in an art museum to detox from the long drive from Louisiana, and my eye caught a tall, lithe, blue-jeaned girl about my age. Somehow we started talking, and we were bewildered at how much fun we were having by simply being together. Susan took me around town and showed me a bunch of sites. We went out for dinner and took in a good old-fashioned country-and-western concert at the famous Armadillo. The whole time I was with her, I was wondering to myself, "How could I feel so comfortable with someone so fast?" It was scary when things worked out so well.

We went over to her place, and she played some records by Bob Wills and his Texas Playboys. I'd never heard western swing before, and I just fell in love with it. We had some great philosophical and religious discussions. She was a big fan of Nietzsche, about whom I knew nothing. We had some stimulating debates back and forth about reality and why we are on earth. I was excited to have a really intelligent discussion with someone who cared! Well, here we were, all cozy together, and I had to be back in California within four days to resume school again. Why did I meet her at the end of my trip like this and not at the beginning when I could've just spent the whole time with her?

Well, we've all been in those situations when the night is late and the resistance is down. It's difficult to say what would have happened if I *had* met her at the start of my trip, but I sure wasn't going to have some physical fling just before leaving for home. This was really the first time I had felt that the flesh was willing, but the spirit was more willing. I told her that if it was right for us to be together, it would work out. She agreed and said she was actually relieved there was no sexual pressure, which was refreshing for her. I gave her a good-night kiss, told her I'd keep in contact with her, and headed back to San Antonio for my last leg home.

After leaving Susan behind like that, I was wondering even more about my timing and judgment. As I lay down in the bed of my van that night in some suburban neighborhood, I felt that I wasn't as smart as I thought I was when I initially set out on this trip.

When I arrived in San Antonio, I stayed at the Niels' house again for a couple of days to get ready for the long twelve-hour drive to El Paso. By this time, I had accumulated so many signs that advertised things from Coca-Cola to bread to root beer to laxatives (loved that one!) that I could barely even fit into my van to sit and drive. I had to move my signs all around in order for me to pull out the bed and get a good night's sleep.

Well, the radio said there was going to be a cold rain in the late morning in San Antonio, so Mrs. Niel and I figured I'd better leave really early to beat the storm. Bless her beautiful hide, she got up early and made me a nice, warm breakfast and sent me on my way, about four o'clock in the morning. I could feel the cold nip in the air, and I detected some ominous clouds overhead, with the half-moon peeking out between them. But I figured I could outrun the torrent and make the drive without too much difficulty.

I was driving in the early morning darkness, feeling like a real trucker after those six weeks of being on the road. Semis were passing me, but you get used to that when you're driving a '71 van. The great thing about traveling is that you get a real feel for your own vehicle; you can sense a problem by the slightest sound, smell, or feel. I loved that intangible ability.

Cruising along steadily at sixty miles per hour, I started seeing drops of water on my windshield. Rats, it was still dark. I had put about one and a half hours into the drive and was in the middle of absolutely nowhere. I wasn't too concerned until after about another forty-five minutes or so, I started to hear a funny noise coming from the back of the van—sort of a tumbling sound I'd never heard before. Now, what could that be? Maybe a piece of mud? A belt that was breaking? The rain on the windshield seemed to be turning to sleet. I drove a bit longer, and the sound went away. Then it came back. I knew I had to pull over and check it out, so I slowed down to get over to the side of the highway.

Whoa! The car glided quite a bit, and it felt a little shaky as I brought it to sort of a sliding halt. Not sure of how bad the problem could be, I figured that I'd better not turn the car off. I needed to see if the sound was coming from the engine anyway. I opened my door—or at least, I tried to. Man! Why was this thing so stuck? Finally, I threw my whole shoulder into the door and opened it so I could step out. Whoosh! Immediately, I slipped on the ground. *Ice*! The van was covered with about two inches of ice all around, and the highway was as slick as a hockey rink! I had been driving through a storm of snow and sleet and hadn't even known it!

I started inspecting the van. First, I checked the tires for a flat; maybe that was the sound. But the tires looked pretty good. The area around the tires was pretty well caked with ice, so I chipped off some of it and poked around to see if there was enough air in them. They seemed fine. Next, I opened the back hood. I loved the look of those spinning belts. It wasn't making the weird sound right then, so it couldn't be the engine. It had to be some clump of dirt that had gotten caught between the ice and the tire. That was the only thing that made sense. I chipped off a bit more ice around the back and hoped that would solve the problem. I had just passed a sign that said there was a gas station in forty-five miles, so I decided I'd check out the situation better once I got there. My van would be lighter by then as well, and with gas stations about ninety to one hundred miles apart in this desert, I'd sure better get a fill-up as well.

Driving toward the gas station, I again heard the clunkety-clunk rolling around. Dang it, I didn't chip off enough ice, I reckoned. Finally, just before getting to the off-ramp to the station, the sound suddenly stopped. Hmm, maybe it just corrected itself. I felt relieved to finally get rid of that problem; all I needed now was some gas and a bite to eat. I pulled into the station and lined up at the gas pump. The attendant came up to my window (this was before self-service), and I rolled down my window to address the frozen and craggy-looking attendant. "Fill'er up!" I braved through the freezing and howling wind.

The guy gave me a quizzical look and slowly drawled, "Ya know, yer back wheel is missin'?"

All of the blood drained out of my face. So *that* was the problem! Somehow, the wheel had loosened and had finally fallen off. I had been literally driving on ice!

Not wanting to look like a complete buffoon, without missing a beat, I replied, "Sorry, I didn't mention that first. Get me the gas, and then let me buy a wheel from ya."

Shaking his head in bewilderment, he walked back to the pump and then to his station to find a matching wheel. I don't think the guy bought my confidence, but he did scrounge up something that fit my van.

I was astonished by my inability to figure out the situation, but I was similarly awed at how God had gotten me through a potentially disastrous situation. It was obvious to me it was not my time to die.

Driving through the snow along Highway 10 toward El Paso in my '71 van with one gimpy wheel was a real lesson in dealing with objective truth. Not having anticipated any snow this journey, I had not brought any chains for my tires, so I was completely on my own in my battle with the elements on this long, lonesome, and snow-covered road. Through trial and error, I figured out that if I kept her in second gear, going twenty to twenty-five miles per hour, I could chug along without any problem controlling the drive. If I started to get a bit impatient and wanted to go even a tiny bit faster and I popped it into third, I would immediately spin out of control. I was able to live by my disciplined standards for an hour or two, but the sheer frustration of crawling along that desolate highway made me pine for just a little more speed at times. But within a minute of changing gears, I'd spin right into a snowbank. I must have done this test a half dozen times. I sure got experience practicing my high-school driver's education lesson to turn into a spin!

Fortunately, I had stocked the van with some food—if you call two loaves of multigrain bread enough food for over eight hours of driving. Besides food, what else did I need but music? It was on this drive through the Southern states that I grew to love the music of Clifford Brown and Max Roach's mid-1950s quintet; Miles Davis's band with John Coltrane, Dizzy Gillespie, and Charlie Parker from the '40s; Art Tatum's masterful piano playing from 1955; Duke Ellington's orchestra from 1941; Count Basie's band with Lester Young from '36; Benny Goodman at Carnegie Hall; Fletcher Henderson from the early '30s; Billie Holiday with Teddy Wilson; and Joe Williams belting out "Every Day I Have the Blues" with Basie's '50s band. These bands, these artists, became part of my blood system and were my friends and loyal travel companions.

Arriving in El Paso late at night, I pulled into a church parking lot that seemed safe enough to set up for an evening of well-deserved and much-needed sleep. I had seen a lot of America and Americana, met some fascinating people, and just as important, learned a lot about life and myself. I realized that I could stomach traveling in solitude. As the Tom Waits song said, "I get along with myself so well, I can hardly believe it!" I enjoyed meeting and learning about different people: why they believed or didn't believe and what motivated their lives. I met a devoted mom, some sincere adults, some people around my age who were searching, and others who seemed to have already given up their quest. I'd heard a good sermon in New Orleans by a sincere pastor and had listened to some practical teachings from the Emissaries. I had eaten red beans and rice with some down-and-outers in dives in Louisiana and had spent time with live-for-the-moment hedonists in Alabama.

I was pleased that I was flexible enough to sleep in my van, on couches, on floors, or in a nice home. Outside of gasoline costs, my expenses had been under two dollars a day; I had learned how to be frugal. While in Mississippi, I had traveled to Natchez to visit some of the most beautiful plantations on earth. It struck me that these men of the nineteenth century had given their lives to build their small empires. Yet, none of the properties were still in the original family; after only four generations, the results of their labors were under someone else's ownership. What seemed so important to one man, that he was even willing to go to war in order to protect it, was completely obsolete in barely over a hundred years…a blip of time when compared to world history or eternity.

All of these thoughts raced through my mind as I lay in the stillness of my van that night, just a couple of days short of being home. I had left Encino to get some of my questions answered about the validity of the Emissaries and about life in general. I was returning with more questions than before.

CHAPTER 15

Dancing in the Dark

BACK AT CHIROPRACTIC COLLEGE, I returned to my regime of classes. After the first year, the strain and burden of studying started to ease up, and I actually found time to occasionally come up for air and socialize a bit. I had befriended a classmate named Evan Loundy. He was just a couple years older than I, with a similar middle-brow temperament and peculiar sense of humor. Growing up in a Jewish community in Encino, I had an appreciation for Evan's Semitic mix of dry comments and his warm zest for life. Somehow, we realized that we both liked international folk dancing; I had done it countless times at Greek church festivals, and he had cut his teeth at various Hillel houses.

The thing that really impressed me about Evan was his lust for life. He had been afflicted a few years prior with Hodgkin's lymphoma, and the combination of the disease itself and the radiation treatments he had undergone had consequently made his body quite weak. I noticed slight clues of deterioration over the course of our first two years of school together. The folk dancing that we did required us to hold hands in a circle, and I could see Evan struggle to lift his arms up. Eventually, it started to take him longer to dress, as well as get out of the car when we'd go out to dance or to a concert. It never affected his joy of life, however.

For some reason, we talked deeply about a lot of things, but we never talked too seriously about religion. Maybe I wasn't *that* convinced Jesus was the cure for his searching heart, or maybe I just didn't want to jeopardize our friendship with an inevitable argument. Who was I to tell one Jew that another Jew, whose name was used for unspeakable atrocities against the Chosen People, could actually save his soul? I looked for opportunities, but I never saw one.

Evan and I figured that since we were going to a school that had about seventy-five guys for every girl, one of the best ways to meet women was through folk dancing. So, we strategized—on Thursdays we headed to USC to meet the Jewish girls at Hillel, on Fridays we hit UCLA to meet the WASPs who were learning international dancing in the girls' gym, and on Saturdays the destination was a funky place in Silver Lake called The Intersection, which focused on Greek dancing and gorgeous Mediterranean women. Girl-wise, we probably struck out more times than a .167 hitter, but we had great fun nonetheless, laughing off our flirtatious failures and celebrating life and the hunt.

After a few rounds of these dancing places, we began realizing there was a regular crowd of attendees, almost like a secret society of folk dancers, and we got to know them quite well. One guy who got our attention was Paul, a college student about our age who seemed to have an attractively good attitude on life. We had similar quests in that we were all trying to figure out just what were our responsibilities on this planet. Like us, he enjoyed reading—particularly biographies and autobiographies. Sitting at a table after a strenuous hour of dancing, I asked him what he'd learned from all the books he'd read.

"There are always a few things in common with each person I read about," he observed. "First, once you start following the person's path, you can see the logical projection and sequence of his life. One thing leads to another, and then eventually there's a crossroad—kind of a crisis of sorts—that gives the person a major choice, whether to make a decision based on integrity or not to complete his vision.

"The other thing is that most people who are really famous have to sacrifice their personal and family lives. The most interesting thing is almost everyone I've read about seems to come to a point where he or she either makes a big public impact and then ends up having a disastrous private life or makes a big impact personally—with a small group of people—and doesn't have much of an impact on the great mass of people. Most of the people who are well known are disastrous on the home front. To me, therefore, the trick of life is to follow your quest but not at the expense of leaving a wake of broken relationships behind you. You can either affect a lot of people a tiny amount and have no effect on those closest to you, or you can have a great impact on a smaller number of people you come into contact with, but not have popular renown."

Both Evan and I agreed that Paul made a lot of sense. The question we all agreed on was simple: what should our quest be? What was worthy enough to spend our lives on, so that we could look back someday without regret? My mind flashed back to the verse written at the back of the Greek Orthodox church I attended as a child: "What does it profit a man to gain the whole world, yet forfeit his soul?" (Mark 8:36). Then and there, I determined to figure out which, if any, of the religious groups I had come in contact with to embrace.

I realized I had more traveling and discovering to do.

Meanwhile, I kept working on getting through chiropractic school and trying to retain some vestige of sanity in the process. The college required classes and labs from 8:00 a.m. until 3:00 p.m. every day, which required an inordinate amount of studying and prep work. Students were flipping out over the amount of stress that came with the demands of such a heavy curriculum. A number of them relieved their anxiety with drugs and alcohol; many of them came to class quite plastered and incoherent. These were the brightest guys in our class, but they just couldn't handle the pressure.

Contrarily, my non-Mensa friends and I went the more subversive route in terms of scholastic survival. Instead of becoming overwhelmed by the Sisyphean burden, we'd keep ourselves distracted from the unrealistic deadlines and perpetual exams by running football pools, publishing our own gossip paper, forming our own social club called Sorenity (a combination of "sorority" and "fraternity"), and making the class time pass more easily by doing things like practicing jumping jacks or throwing paper airplanes when the teacher's back was to us while he wrote on the chalkboard.

I observed that people handled being in a highly demanding and stressful environment in various ways. It was sort of like all of those old World War II POW movies I had seen; each prisoner coped with the situation by surviving in a myriad of ways. Some worked on escaping through a tunnel, others were collaborators, and others simply went mad.

During my years at LACC, I befriended Sikhs, Mormons, and tons of what we'd now term New Agers, and I was actually quite impressed with all of them, for the most part, in regard to their integrity and healthy lifestyle and diet. I was struck by how informed the Sikhs were on nutrition and various forms of mental and physical discipline. One of my friends was a Sikh convert named Parthap. He told me of his journey to Sikhism; he was not some otherworldly type of guy. We'd listen to the blues together during lunch and discuss his religion's teachings a bit. He even could take a joke pretty well, as when we told him he must have been from the "Hyden-go" sect, making him a "Hyden-go Sikh." Besides, it was pretty cool back in the '70s to go anywhere in public—like to a movie—with an Anglo guy wearing a turban.

My Mormons friends impressed me for other reasons than the Sikhs. I was quite amazed at how many people in chiropractic school with me were Mormon (about 10 percent of my class). They explained that Mormons are generally interested in health and improving one's life. They were by far the most studious and most intently serious of my classmates—as well as the most wholesome people in the school. They never made waves and were what you'd consider model American citizens—clean cut, almost embarrassingly so.

They never laughed (or at least not too obviously) at the crude jokes that were said during class time. One of our class clowns, Clarke, had a cheesy slide of a naked woman in a tacky and provocative pose that he'd sneak into the teacher's slide projector during our X-ray analysis labs. The first time she flashed on the screen between slides of femurs and hip sockets, the class howled in surprise. After that, like a scholastic version of Russian roulette, as the teacher would display various slides of cells and tissues for the class, we future doctors would wait in anticipation for Clark's Playmate to project onto the screen. When Alice (as we affectionately started calling her) finally came on the screen, the guys in the class would erupt in victorious laughter—all except the Mormons, who stoically either looked down or sympathetically smirked at our infantile reaction. They always seemed to have a bemused and benevolent detachment to everything like this that went on in the classroom.

Most of the Mormons were amazingly even-tempered. But a number of them had a suppressed fiery emotion or underlying anxiety that they seemed to be afraid of admitting. Alan was one of those guys who always seemed to be holding back more than he wanted you to know. Another was Bill, a big, heavy bull in a china shop whom we affectionately called Orca after the famed whale. Displaying a sense of hidden insecurity and hostility, Bill always seemed to be bragging about some scientific or chiropractic book he had read, and whenever he'd ask the teacher a question, it always seemed like he was actually showing off how much he knew. He would preface his questions with some statement like, "While I was studying through *Gray's Anatomy*, I read that the sartorius muscle allows abduction of the femur, so I wanted to ask you in relation to that…"

The Mormon classmate that I respected the most was Alan. He was unobtrusive and pensive, but he'd always be the one we'd go to if we wanted a problem solved or a question answered. A deep thinker, he was also an incredibly great blues guitar player. He had a reflective stoicism that made me wonder just what he was thinking about all the time; what were those cogs in his brain conjuring up? We regular guys would kill time in the X-ray or chemistry labs by having various discussions about politics, the injustice of the administration, or the latest movie, and Alan would stand by silently until one of us called him to join in. Invariably, he'd give a comment or answer that immediately resolved the discussion, making us wonder why we had never thought of it.

One time during a biochem lab, my friend Dave and I were trying to pass the time by asking ourselves various important metaphysical questions, like "What are the names of the Seven Dwarfs?" or "What were the names of the hired hands in *The Wizard of Oz* who turned into the Scarecrow, Cowardly Lion, and Tin Woodsman?" Our all-time favorite was "What was Hoss's real character name on the TV show *Bonanza*?"

After working out these incisive topics, I once asked, "Name the one person you'd like to have dinner with." Someone said, "Hitler, so I could poison him." Another guy said, "Einstein," and the answers went around. There stood Alan by himself, concentrating on the Erlenmeyer flask. He looked up, turned to us as he took off his protective goggles, and said, "The Man."

"What do you mean?"

"I'd like to meet The Man: Jesus."

Once again, he brought the discussion to a halt. What can you say to that impressive reply? But, during the silence, as we returned to our projects,

I couldn't help but wonder why he referred to Jesus Christ as "The Man." It seemed a strange moniker. I'd gotten into some discussions with Mormons while in school and had found them fairly astute about the Bible. I didn't seem to agree with them on Christ and what it took to make it to heaven, though. I would keep telling one guy, Mark, that Jesus said it took faith in Christ's sacrifice to make it to heaven, but he kept coming back with the verse "Faith without works is dead" (James 2:26), meaning that your faith has to be accompanied with actions to truly show that you are qualified for eternity in heaven. He brought up good points, and I couldn't disagree with the fact that most of the Mormons I met were pretty clean-cut and upright people. Maybe if I could meet a nice Mormon girl…

One of the Mormons told me that his temple had monthly dances that were really good, and we could meet some girls there. I thought that sounded like a pretty good idea to get myself out of my study cave, as well to get to know a bit more about the Mormon culture. I'd only read a few books on Mormonism, and I would like to see more, I decided. Plus, I was intrigued by the fact that there still might be some wholesome ladies out there in the Babylon of Southern California.

I found out where the auditorium was that was hosting the dance, and I decided to give it a try. As I walked up to the building, I could hear the dance music blasting out of the doors. I peered in and saw a room filled with well-dressed and coiffed guys and attractively and conservatively attired ladies. Most wore dresses, but some had slacks on. This could easily have been a snapshot from *Back to the Future*. On the stage was a snapping funk band of Filipinos who were high-stepping through dance tunes like "Boogie Nights." This was, after all, in the late '70s, and disco was the absolute rage. (I didn't expect anyone to be playing the big-band swing and bebop that I loved.)

Working my way into the room, I noticed the place was packed. Even though these people were college age, the place had a high-school sock hop feel to it. All the girls were against one wall, standing all so cutely and looking around the dance floor, and opposite were all of the guys, with their arms folded, just talking to one another or with cups in their hands, drinking something. In front of the band were maybe a handful of couples actually dancing with each other. I walked over to the refreshment counter and looked over the selection—classic *Leave It to Beaver*–era snacks: doughnuts, Rice Krispie treats, brownies, chips, and punch.

I began mingling, and after a while, I was having a nice time getting to know a very attractive and quite accomplished co-ed. She was not only bright and well-read but a cellist as well. We hit it off quite nicely and had fun dancing together. After one of the numbers, I went to get something for us to drink. While over at the refreshment stand, I started talking to one of the guys; I assumed he was a Mormon, as I was probably the only one in the whole gym who wasn't.

We started chitchatting, and I casually mentioned the number of attractive ladies there.

"You're wasting your time, bud," he deadpanned.

"What are you talking about?"

"The girls here, they might dance with you and talk to you, but it will never get past that."

"Why not?"

"It's been drilled into them since they were kids that they can only seriously date and marry a Mormon. Oh, they'll be polite with you and all, but unless you convert, you're not even in the running. And let me tell you, the guys here all know it. They treat the girls terribly because they know that—even though they behave like jerks—when push comes to shove, these girls *have* to marry them."

"Whatta ya mean by that?"

"Well, the word is already out that you're not a Mormon. These guys here all know that. The girls *have* to marry a Mormon—like I said—and since you're not one, you're not a threat. You're not even in the equation!"

"You're kidding me!"

But he was right. My relationship with each Mormon girl I dated came to a dead end as soon as she realized I wasn't going to become a Mormon. Just like that, the switch would flip off. It was quite amazing.

These experiences did lead me to getting a Book of Mormon to check out what it had to say. I also read some material in the *World Book Encyclopedia* about Joseph Smith, the founder of the church. He claimed that he prayed to

God, asking which church he should attend, and that an angel told him he should go to none of them, as they were all an abomination to God. Upon further reading, I learned that the Mormons believed that the Christian church had become an abomination around the year AD 300. Hmm. Could Luther, Calvin, Tertullian, Augustine, Wesley, and Billy Graham all be part of an abomination?

One night at a dance, I looked around and saw all of those lovely girls—all dolled up in beautiful dresses—on one side of the gym and the crew of guys—completely ignoring the girls and indifferent to their charms—hanging out with each other. Each group seemed to know its lot. If I was somehow going to penetrate generations of expectations and traditions by going out with some Mormon girl, I had to either dedicate my whole life to it or realize its futility. I chose the latter, left, and drove home, realizing that my mother lode had just caved in.

I'd have to find smart and down-to-earth ladies some other way.
Back to the Emissaries!

CHAPTER 16

What to Digest?

ACTUALLY, I DIDN'T RETURN TO the Emissary meetings simply for female companionship. After attending a few lackluster Christian church services with disinterested peers, I figured that I just wanted this group to answer some questions about life and faith. As I mentioned, there were people from all spiritual viewpoints at chiropractic college, including lots of people who followed the Eastern philosophy that you are your own god—the inner light (or divine nature) is within you—Mormons, Hindus, Sikhs, Buddhists, and Muslims. It really made me start wondering if there really could be a definitive thing called "truth." I was struck by the fact that most people I met who weren't Christians seemed sincere in their beliefs; it was the Christians who didn't seem sold on their product.

After one Emissary meeting, Paul the vegan guitarist gave me a handful of booklets that had Cecil's teachings. I knew I'd have time to read them fairly soon, as my graduation from chiropractic school was on the horizon. I had decided to take another journey in the van and drive around the Western states—taking my Oregon and Washington state boards as I went. My feet were itching to hit the road again after getting my degree.

For my graduation, my parents threw a small party with some of my closest friends. I opened the presents, and one of them was a book from my friend Ron: *Mere Christianity* by C. S. Lewis. I'd never heard of the author or the book before. I thought to myself, "What a peculiar name for a book. Is Christianity a 'mere' religion? Why would a guy use that title?"

The relief of graduating was tempered somewhat by having to study for the required chiropractic state boards that were about six months away. I knew I had to start preparing for them, but I also didn't want to burn out or peak too early for the exam, which can happen when you study for a big test. I decided to pace myself by studying about six hours and then spend the rest of the day taking care of other aspects of my life by exercising, playing pool, listening to music, and getting into the C. S. Lewis book. Balance, baby, balance, seemed like the best way to get ready for the upcoming trial.

Six hours of daily studying made my brain feel like chow mein, but exploring Lewis's book remedied my brain fog. Having gone to church for years, I had read books by Christians before, but never books that were this in-depth and intellectual. I had read books by the Emissaries and a bunch of Eastern books like *Siddhartha* and *Zen and the Art of Motorcycle Maintenance*. I had always found them interesting, but this one was different. Most religious books simply conveyed the benefits of their religion, while subtly attacking the other belief systems as being faulty for various reasons. Lewis, however, went the opposite way; he would paint certain essential (or "mere") beliefs of Christianity into a corner, giving a myriad of objections to believing their veracity, and then he would come up with a logical answer that would vindicate the claims of the Bible and, therefore, Jesus.

The one that really hit me was Lewis's argument that if Jesus was *not* God, He was not a good man, as so many people claim. Throughout His time on earth, He declared Himself to be the source of life, the creator of all things, and the forgiver of the world's sins. Therefore, if He wasn't God, He surely knew it and therefore was a very evil person intent on deceiving people—or He was an absolute nut case, on the level, as Lewis said, of "claiming to be a poached egg." I realized Jesus's claims *had* to be taken seriously. As Lewis said, I needed to either dismiss Jesus as a loon, fight against Him as an evil deceiver, or fall down and worship Him as Lord. This got me thinking and made me want to talk to other people about Jesus and see what their thoughts were on this perspective.

One person I had good discussions with was a Bulgarian woman from LACC named Lana. (I liked her because she enjoyed folk dancing as much as Evan and I did, and she would occasionally join us.) It turned out that Lana went to a Buddhist temple. I'd never been to one and wanted to know what it was like, so one evening, we went together to her temple, which was like a dimly lit auditorium. There were many rows of seats with a small platform in the front. On top of the stage sat a man with a harmonium—sort of like a traditional organ. He played a few meandering chords on the keyboard, but he didn't say anything except a few vague phrases. I looked around and saw there were maybe fifteen to twenty other people seated around me. Lana sat next to me, and as soon as the leader finished speaking, she closed her eyes and bowed her head in silence.

I guessed that was my cue to do the same thing, so I also sat in monastic solitude. I couldn't help but think, "What am I supposed to be thinking about? Am I just supposed to empty my mind? Where is there any guidance or leadership in this thing?" I decided to pray for all of my friends, family members, acquaintances, civic and government leaders, teachers, and the like. I found the collective silence with a group of complete strangers and the forced introspection peculiar.

Years later, I met a guy who had converted to Christianity from Buddhism. I asked him if he felt that he had lost something by giving up the Eastern mysticism of Buddhism by replacing it with the more Western and materialistic Christianity. He looked at me in surprise. "Are you crazy? The people who go to the Buddhist monasteries don't go there because they're searching for some type of truth but simply to escape the reality of the cruel and harsh world they live in. They replace the noise and evil in the world with a spiritual bondage that insulates them from reality. Christianity is reality, man." His response made me think about my Buddhist temple experience.

As I mentioned, I had decided to also take the state board exams in Oregon and Washington—as well as the one for California. I figured I might want to live in one of those states someday, and since I was preparing for California, the information would be fresh in my mind, so I might as well drive up the coast and get those licenses before my memory began failing me.

I also realized that since I was only twenty-three years old, this was as good a time as any to broaden my horizons a bit. I'd spent my whole life studying for tests and preparing to get some sort of profession under my belt. Now that I'd done that, did I really want to start the lifetime grind of working a nine-to-five job? I didn't know what kind of lady I wanted to marry, and I was on the fence as far as belief systems went. I at least realized I wanted to spend my life with someone who was on the same spiritual wavelength as I was, though. I'd dated enough times to know that, eventually, the strength of the relationship depended on the firmness of the spiritual foundation.

One thing I remembered from the old Inglewood church was that a relationship was like an egg: if the hardest part is the shell, with nothing solid inside, then the whole thing will eventually burst under pressure, but if the deepest part inside is firm—as in the case of a hard-boiled egg—it can withstand outside pressure. And, to be perfectly honest, I'd had enough "egg on my face" from broken relationships by this time to know that an outer shell of a girlfriend did not last very long.

I had to figure out my faith and the resulting spiritual lifestyle for my own survival—not only for myself, but also for the sake of my future marriage. At a wedding I'd recently been to, one of the speakers wisely said that "love is not staring into each other's eyes, but facing the same direction together." Why should I take some woman down my lost path? I needed to figure out what I believed, so I would know what kind of spiritual partner to share my life with. And I didn't feel I could do that in the confines of suburban LA.

After some thought, I decided to expand my sights even further and to travel for a while in Europe, the Middle East, and Africa to see how Christianity fared outside the confines of the American church. I also wanted to see what competing religions like Hinduism, Judaism, and Islam looked like in their own countries and turf, instead of the American brands. I wanted to meet more Emissaries and find answers to finally satisfy my curiosity regarding their perspective on how to live. Lastly, and most important, I wanted to visit and work with Christian missionaries to see what the frontline followers of Jesus actually looked like in the trenches. I wanted to meet the people who believed so strongly in their religion and followed Jesus so deeply that they were willing to go to a foreign country and live among people they didn't know. They were so convinced of their beliefs that the only reason they were in foreign lands was to tell total strangers about this religion. Did they have the answers I was looking for?

CHAPTER 17

Planning Trips, Writing Letters...Is This How Livingstone Did It?

WHILE GETTING READY FOR MY trek to Oregon and Washington for their respective state board exams, I realized that this other journey after I got my licenses was not going to be some quick and superficial two-to-three-week vacation. If I was going to do it right, I'd have to stay in some of these places for quite some time, getting to know the people and culture. Once my traveling came to an end, I'd be obliged to settle down back home and start a practice. So, this trip needed to last months, if not years, in order to take in all the places I thought were important in my educational journey. Really experiencing these three continents and deeply learning anything worthwhile while on the road was going to require a big time commitment. After reading a few travel books about Europe, the Middle East, and Africa, I realized I needed to be willing to invest two years of my life in this quest.

There were two areas I needed to particularly concentrate on in my planning. First, I had to figure out if I could travel for that long a time by myself and not go crazy. But I was not too worried about that. I had learned from my short camping trips and drives around the States that I could indeed survive in solitude without losing my sanity. Also, I could travel a lot more easily and with more flexibly when I had no one else to consider. I would be able to stop and go whenever I wanted, and I could take as much time in a given area as needed. I could still link up with someone if I so desired; besides, who did I know who was able to travel for two years?

The more pressing issue was I needed money—money to travel abroad and money to keep traveling. I figured the best way to finance my travels was to work as a chiropractor (or even in some other field such as X-ray technology or physical therapy) in a clinic or hospital in various places abroad. Before the days of Internet—when finding this kind of information is simple—the only way to find what I needed was to go through books, magazines, and catalogs that listed the chiropractors throughout the world, along with hospitals that might want a chiropractor on hand. All in all, I wrote somewhere around three hundred letters to chiropractors, chiropractic organizations, hospitals, missionaries, and various Emissaries from England to Israel to Egypt to South Africa, telling them I wanted to work for them on their schedule and at their convenience. I figured some of the places would pay me, and others would simply provide room and board until I was ready to go to the next place on my pilgrimage.

While waiting for return letters, I continued studying for the California boards; once I took that test, I set out for about five months to take the trip to Oregon and Washington to take those state boards, with a side trip to Canada to visit my grandmother. I figured the more traveling in solitude I got under my belt, the better prepared I'd be. So, off I went again in my trusty van, a dress suit for the oral state boards, a box of notes, a few hundred bucks, *Mere Christianity*, my Bible, some John Steinbeck books, and a new collection of jazz and classical tapes to keep me company as I explored the people, faith, and sites of the Pacific Northwest.

During those months of travel, I came across some amazing people. When I arrived in Portland, Oregon—in order to take the board exam—the volcano Mount St. Helens had erupted only a short time before. The entire city was covered in ash; people were walking around in a gray haze with masks covering their mouths in order to breathe! I was going to stay here for three weeks in order to study for the boards? It looked like I was going to have a very cozy time in my van, I reckoned, as I pulled up to the parking lot of Western States Chiropractic College, the site of the test.

In order to pass the Oregon exam, a chiropractor had to be proficient in a wide array of talents. One had to be able to cast an arm, perform minor surgeries like stitches, deliver babies, and even do circumcisions! (The reason for this variety was that sometimes in the small towns, a chiropractor could be the only local doctor.) Because of this, I figured I would probably have to learn how to do all of these tasks on the run. As I registered for the exam, I asked the secretary if it was true that I would need to be proficient in these things I had not learned in California.

"Well, yes," she replied. "You will be tested in all fields that are under the umbrella of chiropractic."

"How do I learn all of this in three weeks?"

"My suggestion is that you go to the library and start studying."

The breadth of material sounded overwhelming, and I was scrounging for any specific hints on what to study.

"Can you give me any ideas on what to spend most of my time studying?"

"Well…" She sighed. "You'll probably be required to draw an anus."

I didn't know whether to laugh or cry. I wanted to say, "Isn't it just a small circle?" but I knew she was referring to all of the muscles, nerves, and vessels, and I didn't want to get on this lady's bad side, so I thanked her, left the building, and walked back toward my van.

At moments like that, when I felt overwhelmed and discouraged, I could tell God was still on my side and that He was coaxing me along. Just like the lost wheel or me making it into chiropractic school, He seemed to do little acts that would let me know I was on the right trail. As I headed back to the parking lot, I heard a voice, "Hey!"

I turned around, trying to figure out who was being called, and I saw a guy a few years older than I was walking toward me.

"What are you doing here?"

"I'm going to take the boards in a few weeks, so I'm registering here at the administration office."

He sized me up and brought his hand to his chin. "Where are you staying?"

"Probably in my van. I've used it as my home in the past."

"Look. I just finished taking my last final. I'm about to go on a four-week vacation to get out of here, with all of this ash. Why don't you stay at my house and feed my cat while I'm gone? You'd be doing me a big favor."

I had met this guy for five seconds, and my residence was taken care of! We went to his place—a cozy one-bedroom shack on a quiet street. It was perfect for studying, and I was set to learn about the anus!

My entire time in Oregon I spent either going to the college to learn procedures or studying all the new terms like a madman. The gray sky was a perfect backdrop for my hermitage, until one day—for just a brief period—the sun actually poked its eye through the soot and clouds. I looked out my window and couldn't believe the contrast of the speck of light against the darkness. I peered up and down the neighborhood as I walked through the front door; other people were noticing it as well. People were coming out on the sidewalk just to see the sun. I couldn't figure out why so many of them dashed back into their houses until they all sprang back out, wearing shorts and T-shirts and carrying towels and lawn chairs. They threw the blankets on the lawn and sat basking in the radiance. It was one of the most amazing sights I've ever seen, sort of like people experiencing the joy of forgiveness. It seemed like a religious experience.

I went over to the sunbathers and introduced myself. They were a very pleasant group of people in their mid-thirties. "Being from California, you must think we're all mad to be out here with this puny amount of sun," stated a cheerful lovely, pasty-white lady. "But you must understand, we haven't seen sunshine in over a month, and we're just so thankful for this moment."

It was one of the few instances in my life when I've witnessed true gratitude. They had absolutely no control over the forces of the environment. Here they were, at the mercy of the weather, being truly appreciative as they literally soaked in the sunlight like one would a cup of water to satisfy a parched throat. I had a lot to learn about thankfulness.

While studying in my little home for those three weeks, I had gotten a call from my parents. They told me they received a letter from the California state board. I'd passed my exam! I was officially a doctor! Just as exciting were a couple of letters from chiropractors in Italy who wanted me to work in their offices. One was from a health organization called STATIC, and the other was a guy in a private practice in Rome. *Roma*! I couldn't wait to get home to read the letters and figure out my trip. I was on top of the world! I saw my path opening up for me.

I finished studying for the Oregon board and took the test. Next, I said good-bye to the cat as I returned it to its owners, drove up to Washington, and took the State Board there. I could check off the West Coast, as far as exams went. Now it was time to travel up to Vancouver, hang out at my grandmother's home, and see a bit of western Canada.

When I wasn't visiting my grandmother, I spent a lot of time driving and camping throughout British Columbia and Alberta, seeing and hiking through the gorgeous Canadian Rockies. My mom, a native Canadian, had told me about the Calgary Stampede, which is basically a Canadian version of a good old-fashioned rodeo. I decided to catch the opening-day parade and see a few of the events. By this time, I had become pretty adept at finding a place to park my van for the night—usually on a quiet street close to a college, so I could sneak a shower…or at least near a gas station where I could freshen up a bit.

During one of my long periods of contemplative solitude, I started thinking about my singleness again. Here I was, just turning twenty-four years old, and I was absolutely no closer to a long-term relationship with someone than I had been when I was in high school, getting dumped by girls who were attracted to jocks or stoners. Still unsure of myself spiritually, I wondered if I'd *ever* get settled in that sense. I think everyone who is without a mate wonders if there is something that makes him or her unattractive. I loved the scene in Woody Allen's classic film *Annie Hall* when Allen asks a beautiful couple why they have a relationship that seems to work so well. "Well," the young stud replies, "I'm shallow and empty, and so is she."

"So there's nothing deep or meaningful about the two of you?" Allen queries.

"That's right; it's totally superficial," beams the yuppie, with babe in arms.

That was how I felt about myself. Was there anything about myself to prevent a shallow and meaningless relationship?

It's funny how God gives little affirmations about life at just the right time. After taking in the whole day at the Stampede, I headed for the bus that would take me to my van. While sitting quietly in the back, I noticed a group of about six or seven guys and girls stumble onto the bus, drunk as skunks. One of the girls, quite attractive except for being sloshed, was ranting and raving about all the problems with the world. "All men are %$#& jerks!" she bellowed. "They're all no-good @*&^%!" I sat about two to three feet away from her, bemusedly observing this pie-eyed commentator. Just as she was about to get off the bus, she gave one more assault on mankind: "Men are all ugly and nasty &#^%. I wouldn't give a nickel for any one of them." Descending to the exit, she gave a quick look at me, stopped, and said, "Except you—you're not bad at all!" and she stumbled off into the night.

Why a sauced lady's uninhibited alcoholic rantings would make my day or why I'd still remember it is beyond me. The fact is that she gave me an emotional pick-me-up when I felt no one noticed me anymore. I had faith in my destiny once again! (It doesn't take much!)

I decided that on this trip, besides my C. S. Lewis books (I had graduated to an excellent one called *The Screwtape Letters*, a cleverly written correspondence between a head demon and one of his young pupils), I'd get into some John Steinbeck. I had loaded up with classics like *Tortilla Flat*, *The Grapes of Wrath*, *Of Mice and Men*, and *Cannery Row*. After downing a few Steinbeck books, you just start waiting for the tragedy to come. You know it's coming right around the corner; it's just a matter of time...

For this reason, I was pleasantly surprised by the joyful tenor of his last release, *Travels with Charley*, which is basically Steinbeck writing about his journey through America with his faithful four-legged companion. It captured the excitement of being on the road—independent and adventurous—better than any other similarly themed book I'd read. (Kerouac's *On the Road* was a self-important letdown.) I don't know if it was the fact that I'd passed my boards, gotten the letters from Italy from doctors wanting me, read about the enthusiastic travel excursions of Steinbeck that paralleled mine, or just the thrill of the road, but one morning, I simply woke up and felt an indescribable, deep love and appreciation for God. Suddenly, everything seemed tied together for me. I felt His love and His guiding hand, and I felt an assurance that no matter what happened, I was going to be all right. For a guy who at the time had no job, no money, no girlfriend, a few books and tapes, and just two changes of clothes, it was a comforting balm that kept me encouraged. Some instances of life suddenly feel so focused and clear for no objective reason; this was one of those times for me. I fell in love with this thing called "life" at that moment, and no matter what else, I was determined to see what this life that God had given me was all about. I knew I *had* to travel to see the world and these other faiths if I wanted to live, really live, and not just exist to make enough money to pay for my funeral.

Arriving back home in Encino a number of months later, I was glad to see my parents, but I was also ready to get on with my travel plans. My mom said there was a letter in my room for me from "a real nice girl who stopped by two days ago." Wondering who on earth it could be, I opened the envelope, and to my surprise, I found a note from Susan from Texas! She said she was in town visiting some friend and wanted to surprise me. *Rats*! We had written once in a while, and I always enjoyed hearing from her. I wondered would happen if things were different—if we lived closer…if we hadn't just missed each other—but there seemed no way to pursue our relationship at the moment. I felt like I had let something valuable slip through my hands, yet there seemed nothing I could do about it.

After sitting down to think about it, I realized if I did pursue something with Susan, it wouldn't resolve the quest I was on. It was simply ludicrous to invest in a potential relationship that would have to be put on hold while I traveled for two years. Take her with me? That would defeat the purpose of the trip. As Tom Waits wrote in the song "Foreign Affair,"

Most vagabonds I know don't ever want to catch the subject
That remains the object of their long relentless quest
The obsession's in the chasing, and not the apprehending
The pursuit you see, but never the arrest.

I realized I'd just have to chalk up this inconclusive relationship as a casualty of my desire to see the world and find where I fit in it—Susan or no Susan.

CHAPTER 18

Sha Na Na...Get a Job!

I GOT A JOB WORKING in a local chiropractor's office back home to get some quick cash to use for my trip. I figured I'd work in the United States until I got some concrete confirmation as to where I could work overseas. Once I had that information, I could set up a two-year itinerary through my foreign jobs. It only took about a week or two back from my excursion of taking the West Coast boards before I got some of the letters back. The most encouraging were two from Italy, one from Israel, and one from Lesotho, a tiny country in South Africa.

My parents had told me about the letter that was from a big Italian corporation of health clinics called STATIC. In Italy, a doctor of chiropractic (DC) had to work under a medical doctor's license, so STATIC hired chiropractors to work in their clinics. They usually wanted a two-year commitment, which had its good and bad points. The good was that I'd have a steady job for quite a while, and at the end of that time, I'd practically be an Italian, totally submerged in a foreign culture. That sounded very cool. I could just picture myself sitting in my office, wearing chic Italian shoes and gesturing with my hands as I spoke.

The drawback was that living two years in one place was not in my plans; it would possibly mean I'd be away for three years instead of two, or maybe I'd just end up living there indefinitely. The letter said they would find a town for me to practice in once I got there. They would pay for my airplane flight to Italy, get me a car, and find me a place to stay until I got settled in the assigned area. Hmm. Reading between the lines, I thought it sounded like they wanted me to owe them a bunch of money for these perks, so I would be starting off in debt to them. Sounded very Cosa Nostra–ish (Italian Mafia). I was already learning the Italian way! I felt like there was a lot to consider on this one.

More innocuous and inviting was the other Italian letter from an expatriate doctor, Tom Rigel, who apparently had his own private practice in Rome. He was planning on taking a two-week vacation and wanted me to fill in for him during that time. He'd pay me in US dollars or equivalent (a very good sign) and would put me up someplace, which would be in addition to my salary (another nice sign!).

The chiropractic doctor in Israel was a guy named Robert Small, not only the first American chiropractor in Israel, but the first chiropractor from any nation in that country! He said he was planning on taking a leave of absence from his practice and wanted me to take over for him for a few months. He hadn't had an extended time off since he initially left his home in New York and went to Israel during the 1973 war. He said the time for my arrival was open for discussion and to contact him when I thought I was within six months of coming to Israel. This guy sounded very flexible—my kind of job!

Ditto for the Seventh-Day Adventist hospital in Lesotho. They simply said they were very interested in the chiropractic field and wanted me to work with them for three months in their orthopedic department. As far as I was concerned, my trip already seemed fairly planned and financially supplied.

Things got even better when I got a letter from a missionary in Nairobi, Kenya, who was a friend of my old friend Ron. The missionary, Les, said I could stay at his house any time for as long as I liked. Ah, the allure of free room and board in an exotic land felt enticing. The draw of the wild was beginning!

Other letters drifted in from all over; relatives from Greece said that they were ready for me. Emissaries who were "friends of friends" would welcome me with open arms whenever I'd arrive in South Africa and Zimbabwe. Things were starting to fall into place.

Most peculiar of all was a meeting by sheer happenstance. Out of absolutely nowhere, I got a call at home in the middle of the night. The guy had a peculiar accent. "Who is this?" he queried.

"George Harris."

"Where do you live?"

"What do you mean? What is my address?"

"No! What country do you live?"

"America. Where are you calling from?"

"South Africa."

This just seemed weird and a bit scary. However, I liked mysteries...

"What's your name?"

"Tubby. Where in America do you live? Oops, gotta hang up now...I'll call you again another time." And he hung up. Click.

Periodically, I'd get calls from Tubby, and we'd talk about life in the United States and in South Africa, and then he'd suddenly have to hang up. This went on for a number of weeks, but I ended up getting his address and phone number; I figured I'd be able to visit him and stay with him in South Africa.

"Oh, no. We'll be able to get together, but you can't stay at my house."

"Why not? Is it too dangerous where you live?"

"For me it is."

Something didn't make sense. "Why for you?"

"I'm part black and part white, what they call 'colored.' By law, I can't have a white person stay overnight in my house. We'll figure something out by the time you get here, however. Gotta go!"

I couldn't wait to meet this mysterious guy.

CHAPTER 19

Well, My Bags Are Packed...

I USED THE LETTERS THAT offered me employment as references in my remaining letters to doctors in Europe for other jobs. Thinking this was a great enhancement, I was dumbfounded when I got a letter from a doctor in Denmark who told me that, while he had no job opening for me, "employment by STATIC is nothing to be proud of." That sort of jolted my confidence. What kind of deal was I getting into and even worse, what was I getting set up for? After that letter, I called STATIC and told them I was interested in working for them, but I'd pay for my own expenses. Somehow, having someone loan a car to me in an accident-prone haven like Italy seemed like a sure way to get hopelessly indebted to this company. If I were to work with them, I did not want to start from a point of weakness.

Meanwhile, I called Rigel and told him the situation with STATIC. He sounded very sober, calm, and collected and simply said, "I'll take care of them and work it out so you can work with me first. Don't worry; I'll handle them." He seemed to end this assurance with a chuckle. Did this guy have ice in his veins? I definitely wanted to work with him for a while.

We got the dates set for me to work in Rome. The cheapest way for me to arrive in Italy was to fly to London, take a boat and then a train to Paris, and from there take a train to Rome. While in Paris, I would stay with a married couple, Gille and Katel LeGalle, chiropractors I'd met through my letter writing to European doctors. They said they had no chiropractic work for me but could find some work in a vineyard picking grapes for some good food and spare change. Why not?

I was ready to go!

Getting packed was easy. One thing I'd learned while driving around in the van was the golden rule of the road number 3: *Travel light*. The basic rule of thumb is to figure out the exact minimum you need and then cut it in half.

Since I'd be doing some working along with traveling, I settled on two dress shirts; two pairs of nice pants; a pair of jeans; a pair of shorts; two pairs of socks, underwear, and T-shirts; one pair of dress shoes (which I'd discard once done with office work); one pair of tennis shoes; and one pair of hiking boots. The total weight in my backpack was about twenty pounds. Nice! For extra security, I sewed flaps over the front pockets of my shorts, and I had two pockets sewn into the inside legs of my jeans, where I could safely store my passport, tickets, and cash. Kicking my ankles together to check to be sure all of my papers were where they belonged would soon become one of my habits of travel. It must have looked quite silly, like some ex-Nazi soldier!

The only extra weight I would carry was my newly acquired thirty-five-millimeter fully manual Nikon camera, with two lenses and a very cool ninety-degree attachment, so I could take pictures of people without them knowing it. I read in some *National Geographic* that this feature could come in very handy in third-world countries, where people are very suspicious and superstitious of photographers.

The person I bought the camera from had given me one quick lesson on how to use it. I was new to the world of photography and was told that fully manual was the way to go, as the camera would be able to take a beating during travels in buses and trains, as well as survive inclement weather. I packed all my film ahead of time (I'd mail it home to be developed) in a special X-ray-proof, lead-lined bag. That was an extra weight but a necessity, as I had heard that film was very expensive and sometimes hard to come by in Africa.

Waiting at the airport with my parents, I was just chomping at the bit to be on my way. There are only so many different ways your parents can tell you to be careful and to write. We developed a system where I'd number all of my letters to them, so they would know if they were out of order or missing. I'd write once a week and try to call once a month, if possible. The goal was to earn as much money as I could in Italy and have it sent back home, so my dad could wire it to me in whatever country I might be in when I needed it.

That way, I would never be traveling around with too much money, in case of getting rolled by someone in a dark corner.

As they announced the boarding for the flight to London, I realized that I wouldn't be seeing my parents for two years. Would they still be alive? How would they do without me? I always felt I was the one who kept my mom happy and sane. Would she cope all right? Dad seemed very quiet and stoic about the whole thing, until I was just about to board the plane. Then, he abruptly came up to me, gave me a Greek kiss (one on each cheek), and for the first time I could ever remember, told me he was proud of me. As he was backing away from me, tears welled up in his eyes. It was a part of my dad I'd never seen before. The last time I had seen him cry was when his dad died, about twenty years before. Why wait until now to tell me his feelings about me? It was one of the mysteries of parents who had grown up in the Depression.

I spent a night in London and then caught the boat and train to Paris. While on the train, I got to know some of the other travelers. "How long are you traveling?" was the main question I asked. Everyone seemed to be on one- to two-week trips; no one was on the road indefinitely besides me.

Arriving in Paris, I met the lovely and genteel chiropractic husband-and-wife team of Gille and Katel LeGalle. They had a room for me to crash in for a few days while I saw the sights, and then Gille said he had a job for me, if I wanted, picking grapes in the Champagne area of France. That sounded nice! First, though, I wanted to see some Parisian sights and try out my camera, so I walked along the Avenues de Champs-Élysées to get a feel of September in Paris.

I hadn't kept up with the news while I was traveling, so, to my surprise, I walked into a hornet's nest. A synagogue had been bombed a week before, and people were taking to the streets in protest of the anti-Semitism. The Champs-Élysées was packed with demonstrators; people were arm in arm, shouting slogans of unity. There were Orthodox Jews dancing in a circle. It was quite exhilarating, and I thought this would be a great thing to photograph, so I took some pictures. Suddenly, I felt surrounded.

"Give me your camera," a bearded man said in broken English.

"What's the problem?"

"Don't take pictures. Give me your film. Now." This was the only English these guys knew. They were Orthodox Jews and probably thought I was taking photos for some secret organization, since there were Orthodox Jews spray-painting slogans on the walls. I tried to explain in my nonexistent French that, being Christian, I was sympathetic to them, but they didn't care.

"Please. Give me your film. No problems."

Being surrounded and not exactly in control of the situation, I gave them the first two rolls of film from my trip. All because of fear and hatred. Welcome to Europe.

CHAPTER 20

A Case of Sour Grapes

GILLE HAD BEEN ABLE TO somehow find a job for me picking grapes near Lyon. He drove me to a side street in Paris where there were a bunch of other guys about my age preparing to get onto a bus. Gille talked to the guy who looked like he was in charge, came back over to me, and said, "You're all set, *mon ami*! When you're done working there, come back to our place and stay with us again." With that, he was gone; here I was...an official undocumented day laborer, with a doctor's degree! While we rode, I found out there were workers from several parts of the world, including Gabon and Senegal; there was one other American, an Aussie, and a bunch of locals.

The farm we were taken to was true bucolic beauty. The rolling hills were filled with vines heavy-laden with luscious, juicy grapes, just waiting to be picked. The twenty or so of us looked around at the serene beauty of the farm, with the green hills and dark clouds overhead. The gentleman who owned the farm looked like he was about in his late forties, about five foot six, stocky, with gray hair and a weather-worn face. He sported a gray-and-white-striped hat and wore overalls. Embedded in his left hand was a pair of pruning shears, his tools of the trade. Wearing the serious, concerned look that men who work on the land seem to have, he walked over to size us up. I understood absolutely no French, so I relied on a Moroccan guy named Magi who spoke French, Spanish, and English to translate for me.

"He says that we get three warm meals a day, work from eight until five, with a one-hour lunch. Breakfast is at six thirty, dinner at six. We'll get our checks when we're done with the work, in about two weeks."

We slept in a dorm, and after a good night's sleep, we were taken to the top of the hill, given our clippers, and shown how to clip the grapes off the vines before putting them into a collective pail.

The work was monotonous, difficult, and repetitive. All the while, I thanked God that I did not have to do this all of my life. Some of the guys I worked with had done this for a couple of years and were quite good at it. I lost my enthusiasm for it after about the third day, especially after working a whole day during a relentless rainstorm.

The day after the storm, with my hands covered with blisters, I decided this work was not going to enhance my ability to treat patients. If anything, it was going to strain my wrists for my job in Rome. I figured I'd take my chance of incurring the boss's wrath by telling him I didn't think I was cut out for the work. If I could just get my payment for the few days I'd worked and he would show me the way to the train station, I'd be all set.

I went with Magi into the little office, and Magi explained the situation. The boss didn't even flinch; he'd obviously dealt with workers like me his whole life. Wearily and perfunctorily, he pulled out a giant ledger, wrote me a check, and gave it to me. "Cash this when you get to the train station," explained Magi. "He doesn't have any money for you here."

One of the permanent hands had to run an errand in town anyway, so he took me to the station and bid me adieu. I checked the schedule; the next train to Paris was leaving in one hour. That was plenty of time for me to cash my check at the bank and buy a ticket.

I went to the bank next door and presented my check, along with my passport. The clerk coldly and silently looked at the check, went back for a moment, and returned. "I'm sorry," he said to me in broken English, "but there is no money in this account for you."

"What do you mean? This is a brand-new check."

"I'm sorry, sir."

Ripped off by a shrewd farmer! I wanted so badly to go back and at least warn all the other workers, but I had absolutely no idea where the farm was, the guy's name, or how to get there with no money. I was truly trapped.

My only choice was to get a train ride back to Paris and go back to my only familiar turf. But how was I going to do that without any money? I'd left all my cash back with the LeGalles. Only one way out seemed possible; I'd have to beg.

I spent the next hour going from person to person at the train station, with absolutely no knowledge of French, begging people for enough money to get a ride out of town. Here I was, a doctor, having to ask the most arrogant people in the world for a bit of financial mercy. The well-suited citizens haughtily looked down at me with disdain as I pleaded my case to them, sniffing at me like I was some addict begging for enough loose change to buy my next bottle or fix. I felt trapped in my own language; I couldn't explain myself or my situation. "I'm not what I appear to be! Please believe me!" It was one of the most humbling experiences of my life, and it made me look at all beggars differently ever since.

I finally cajoled enough francs out of the people who created the motto "Liberty, Equality, and Fraternity" to buy a third-class ticket. While the train clickity-clacked to Paris, I couldn't stop thinking about all the people I'd met at the farm, who were unknowingly working for a bounced check. People can be so cruel. I suddenly flashed back to the innumerable days my dad would come home from work, open the door, and mutter to me, "Never work for anyone else; be your own boss," before going into his bedroom to change for dinner. It's disarmingly humbling and humiliating to be totally dependent on someone else—be it the cheating boss or the snobby people who judged me by my begging and outward appearance.

Was it going to be a struggle like this for the entire two-year trip?

Back in Paris, I stayed with the lovely LeGalles just long enough to get a train to Rome and finally handle some actual cash! The train was supposed to arrive in Rome about five o'clock in the evening; therefore, I would still have plenty of daylight left to get around safely. One thing that had been ingrained in me from my various excursions is basic traveling rule number 2: *never arrive at your destination at night.* (Rule number 1 was "never turn down a free meal.") The problem with arriving in a city or town at night is the darkness makes getting the feel of the new environs astronomically more difficult than negotiating the traffic and layout of the area in the daylight. You feel more vulnerable walking around with a pack around your back, the banks are closed—so you can't exchange for the local currency—and hotels are harder to negotiate with when you're reeking of desperation for some sleep.

Since this was my introduction to the Italian railway system, I had no idea that a train that was scheduled to arrive at five meant it would arrive sometime after five—like, let's say, ten at night. When the train finally wheezed into Roma Termini, I stepped out and checked out my surroundings. I saw a nearly empty and dimly lit station that looked like it was in a hurry to close down for the night—janitors mopping the floors and shops and kiosks that looked like they'd been closed long before my arrival. Searching my mind for inspiration, I tried to figure out where I should go for the night to get a bit of sleep or at least where to find someone to tell me which direction to head to once I stepped out of the station. I looked around for someone to talk to, but at this point, my ability to speak Italian consisted of my knowledge of four years of Spanish. I was tired, hungry, and lost—a bad combination for arriving in the Eternal City.

I pulled out a little white book I had put together of contact people in each country and city: missionaries in Kenya, potential jobs in Israel and Egypt, business acquaintances of my dad's in the Middle East, distant relatives in Greece, Emissaries, and friends of friends scattered throughout Europe and Southern Africa. I was basically looking for anyone who wouldn't throw me out into the streets if I mentioned the proper connections.

In my Italian chapter, I had a couple of names in Rome: (1) Tom Rigel, the guy I'd be working for the first few weeks before moving on to STATIC; (2) Mario, Rigel's father-in-law from Argentina (just anticipating the Cosa Nostra factor in this connection intrigued me); (3) Mr. Cucinello, who was a business associate of my dad's; and (4) Liza Radziwell, a lady who was a member of the Emissaries. Someone in the LA gang had given me her name; I had contacted her before leaving home, and she had said she'd love for me to visit her and her daughter. Someone said she was a princess and lived in a palace. Hmm…

Of all these contacts, who would be best to call late at night? Just couldn't picture calling a princess or my dad's business associate, so Rigel was my first try, since he knew I'd be in town for the job around this time. No answer. Just some Italian operator. This was going to be tough! Next call…Mario! I got an answer, and the voice was deep, from an Anthony Quinn–sounding guy speaking Spanish. This had to be him! At least I knew enough Spanish to let him know I had arrived and that Tom was not home. He asked where I was, and I told him. "Take a bus to Tom's place" was all I could understand.

I had about 2,000 lire (three dollars) that I'd scrounged up from begging at the station. (I was getting good at this! I had now begged in two different countries!) I somehow found the bus stop, and as each bus pulled up, I showed each driver the address I wanted. I finally found the right one, and he took me within a mile of Rigel's place. The driver graciously pointed me in the general direction. Walking that last twenty minutes, at about midnight by then, I regretted every single piece of luggage I was carrying with me. I determined that by the time I went to Africa, my pack was going to be a lot lighter!

I found Rigel's place, but no one was home. There are not too many options when you have no money, so I just put my pack down, scrunched up my jacket, and lay down on his porch, trying to get a semblance of a night's sleep...

After a bit, I was startled by a barking Pomeranian. Where was I? Who were these people? Was I being arrested for vagrancy? I looked up and saw a tall, very sophisticated-looking American with a dark trench coat wrapped around his shoulders. ("People still do that?" I wondered.) There was also a very exotic and luxuriously dressed woman, with stole in tow. "You must be George Harris," he stated formally as he literally looked down at me while I sat on his sidewalk. "I'm Tom. This is my wife, Maria. My father-in-law has been looking all over town for you. We just got back from a party; you should stay with us for the night." It was about half past three in the morning. These Italian doctors kept peculiar hours!

Sleeping was easy that night; the sheets felt so comfortable. When I awoke, I was ready to check out the town and where I would be staying for the next four weeks.

CHAPTER 21

The Eternal City...Since When?

FOR THE FIRST TWO WEEKS, I was to observe Dr. Rigel, see how he treated his patients, and then slowly work my way into the rhythm his patients were used to. The offices themselves were like luxury apartments, with beautiful chandeliers, artistic wallpaper, and arched doorways. The office secretary, Anna, would present each patient to me, one at a time, in my office.

Anna was just unbelievable. Olive-skinned; dressed in an airtight pencil skirts, white blouse, black brassiere, and stiletto shoes; and smoking a cigarette from a four-inch filter, this lady was my connection to learning the ins and outs of handling the patients. The toughest part was I didn't know a word of Italian, and Anna's English was as good as my Italian. I wondered how much my Spanish was going to help me once a patient walked in the door and started telling me his or her problem in Italian. Every time I would need to open the Italian-English dictionary to understand what the patient had just said, I wondered if they wouldn't feel like quietly escaping out the door. I mean, how would *you* feel if you went to a brand-new doctor in your hometown, and he only understood Italian?

"Don't worry," Rigel comforted, "these people are very appreciative of the fact that you're even here. The entire country is designed to make people outlaws, so if you play by any semblance of propriety, honesty, and sincerity, the patients are on your side."

I learned what he meant firsthand the very first week. Anna brought in a couple of extremely well-dressed patients. Serious and staring right through us, these men spoke to me and Rigel about their condition. I nodded along with Rigel in acknowledgment, pretending to understand what they were saying. Rigel wrote some notes down on their charts…

"These guys are Cosa Nostra," he whispered to me in English.

"What do you mean?"

"You say in America, 'the Mafia,' right? Don't get jumpy."

I tried to get my pulse down to under 120 as I nonchalantly peered at them. "How can you tell?"

"Their dialect is from the south; the way they speak gives them away. Also, their clothes and the way they're presenting themselves to me," he continued as he casually wrote in his chart.

Nervously, I examined and treated my hit man, while Rigel did likewise. They came in a couple more times that week for treatments. By their last visit, I just couldn't understand something…

"Tom, you've got to ask them why they're coming all the way up from southern Italy just to see us—and to *pay* to see us—when they could get free medical care probably anywhere else."

Rigel raised his eyebrows. After we treated them, he quietly and professionally conversed with the men. Then they formally nodded at me, shook our hands, and departed.

"They said, in their circles of people, this office is known as the only honest health-care facility in all of Italy." Reputation matters, whether saint or sinner!

CHAPTER 22

O Sole Mio...

RIGEL WAS GONE, AND I was on my own. I had learned my lesson about the Cosa Nostra well; as long as I was direct, honest, and sincere, these wonderful, patient, and gracious Romans would put up with any stupid mistake I made. They were just glad to know someone was at least trying to help. I loved them.

Figuring I'd only be in Rome for two more weeks before taking my one-to-two-year job with STATIC somewhere else, I decided to see as many sights as I could. I was staying in a really nice, furnished suite right next to the Spanish Steps. Rigel's Argentine father-in-law, Mario, had found it for me. "How'd you get this?" I asked him in Spanish.

Looking as much like Anthony Quinn as he had initially sounded on the phone, he just broke eye contact, laughed, and said, "Don't ask." I had a feeling I was going to like this guy.

High on my list of things to see was the new pope, John Paul II. Though he'd already been there for a couple of years, Rome was still excited about him. He was relatively young at sixty, energetic, had a great big booming voice, and—like the previous pope—didn't look like Peter Sellers. Being Polish, he seemed a bit exotic to the Italians, especially since there were a lot of political happenings in Poland at the time.

During this period, the fledging communist-resistance group Solidarity—led by Lech Walesa—was just starting to make headlines. The Russians had put a puppet leader, Wojciech Jaruzelski, in as prime minister of Poland, and the Christian-led Solidarity Union was demanding freedom from the clutches of the communist reign. At the same time, in the United States, President

Ronald Reagan was on TV and radio encouraging Walesa—as was the pope, who spoke out against atheistic communism every chance he got.

Due to his political convictions and support for his fellow patriot Walesa, Pope John Paul II was at the center of the world's attention. He was going to speak at a cemetery for the celebration of the Day of the Dead. I thought this would be a great time to actually see and hear him out of his normal environment of St. Peters. I was warned that he attracted a good-sized crowd, so I got to the cemetery early to get a ringside view.

I've been to a lot of rock concerts, as well as baseball and football games. Let me tell you, the enthusiasm and excitement at those events is nothing in comparison to the cheering, waving, and hollering the crowds of nuns emitted in anticipation of the pope. These ladies were lined up four deep, and they weren't going to give an inch to some young American. They wanted to see their guy!

By the time the pope arrived, the place was raucously cheering him, as he was slowly driven by in his little "Popemobile," which gave him access to his flock. Even this was iconoclastic; no pope had ever mingled with the people like this one did. Most previous popes had seemed remote and aloof. Having grown up working class and blue collar, this guy wanted to identify with the salt of the earth. When he spoke, the crowd hushed, and he delivered a sermon with sober authority. I understood very little of it, but I sure could feel its weight. This guy was no buttercup.

The Italian papers (and there were a *lot* of them: communist, capitalist, pro-union, fascist, and sports, sports, and more sports) were always mentioning something the pope was doing. He would sneak into a confession booth for a while and listen to his sheep; he'd be at some place in the slums, taking care of the homeless; he shamelessly spoke out against communism in Latin America; and he scolded priests in public for their liberation-theology teachings. This guy was *tough*! I liked him; he was comfortable with what he believed. How many people I knew could really say that? Quite impressive.

This was a stark contrast to the American church I happened to find and visit for Sunday worship. Completely unenthusiastic and listless, the service seemed as if it had been done a thousand times the same way. The pastor, a nice enough guy, just didn't seem to want to be there. He gave the impression he'd lost his will to fight and that the Roman Empire had conquered him. Shouldn't it actually be the other way around, with him declaring victory? There had to be something else to inspire me here, or wherever I'd next work. Hopefully…

The two weeks had smoothly passed. Rigel came back and saw that I had run the place quite well in his absence. He laughed when I told him how amazing it was that the price for the same number of tomatoes got cheaper each time I went back to buy some in the market. "They realize you're part of the community, so you're not a target any longer," he quipped.

In walked Mario with his black-market look. Something was up. Rigel sat down, leaned back, crossed his legs, lit his cigarette (I was amazed that doctors in Italy smoked in their offices), and looked me right in the eyes.

"How'd you like to stay two more years?"

"What do you mean?"

"You've done great here, and I'd like someone to work with me. Stay."

My head suddenly became filled with thoughts and questions. Two years? What about my trip to Greece? Israel? Africa? What about working with STATIC? Was I destined to marry an Italian? Was that good or bad? Was Rome going to conquer me like it did that American pastor? How would I look in linen suits and Italian shoes?

Now it was my turn to ask Rigel some questions:

"What about my working with STATIC?"

"You don't want to work there."

(Why did I hear the strains of *The Godfather* theme running through my mind at that moment?)

"How do you know that?" I hesitatingly asked, looking around for Al Pacino.

"I used to own a quarter of it." He sighed as he blew out a puff of smoke. "I got out. You don't want to work there. You're like I am; you want to be a doctor, not a technician."

"I made a promise to STATIC."

"I'll call them."

"But I'd probably make more money there."

Rigel's calm expression didn't change, Mario became hot and agitated. He only spoke Spanish and Italian, but—like every streetwise guy—he had understood much more than he let on. He started peppering me in Spanish…

"You don't understand what it's like over there. Here, you're a doctor in a professional office, with respectable clientele. There, you'll be treated like an animal, and you'll treat your patients like animals. Look around at this office," he said, as he waved his arms around. "This is a nice place, and you're a nice guy. They will own you over there, and you'll have a heart attack. You'll hate it there!"

"Let me call my dad and get his advice."

They handed me the phone.

My dad was surprised to hear my voice and even more surprised that I had called him without there being a problem. I explained the situation and asked what he'd do in my place. "Well, George," he said as he measured his words like the engineer he was, "I'm not there, so I can't really assess the situation. You're really on your own, and it's up to you to make the right decision. You'll figure it out."

Stunned at the passing of the decision-making baton, I said good-bye to him.

We all have those moments when we realize we are finally people responsible for ourselves. As soon as I hung up, I realized my life was my own, and I was no longer under the shelter of my father's guidance and protection. I had to live my own life. Independence Day.

"OK," I said to Rigel and Mario, after working out how much I'd be paid. I told Rigel I only wanted to stay a year, but then I'd find someone else to take my place. I called a friend of mine back home to see if he was interested. He said he'd be there in exactly a year, so I let Rigel know.

"How well do you know this guy?" he asked.

"Really well. He's Italian American and really wants to come live here for a while, so he's going to fit in great."

"What's his name?"

"Dana Cancaro. He graduated a semester after me."

Rigel looked at me in askance. "Dana Cancaro? Do you know what *cancaro* means in Italian?"

"What?"

"Cancer! You're sending me Dr. Death!" He chuckled. "Fine. He'll work it out."

So far, so good. "Now, I've got three conditions: one—I get paid in dollars or dollar equivalent. None of this funny-money lira stuff."

"No problem. I'll pay you in lire—but at the dollar's current rate."

"Two—you get me a place to stay."

"You've already got the place, and it's nice."

It was *very nice*, and I was only paying $300 a month!

"Third—you've got to find a way for me to get the money out of the country when the time comes for me to leave, as I'll be saving it for the remaining year of my trip."

THE SELL...

Rigel took a deep puff and thought for a few seconds as he stared at the fancy molding on the ceiling. "It will be tricky, but it will get done."

"You call STATIC. I'm going to take a few weeks off first and see Italy before I start earning my next year's salary."

We shook hands. My year was set.

CHAPTER 23

A Non-Roman Holiday

RIGEL SAID THAT IF I was going to take a few weeks off before working full-time for him, I should go see a few of the popular tourist sites like the Leaning Tower of Pisa, Siena, and Florence, but that I would also appreciate less visited places like Ravenna, which he said had mosaics that were beautiful beyond description. Armed with my pack of clothes and a bit of money, I set out for the great north.

You may not remember, but back in the early '80s, there was a lot of internal terrorist activity going on in Italy. A group called the Red Brigades was kidnapping people, as well as bombing places like bars and restaurants that were frequented by various social/political groups. On my train on the way up to Ravenna, the ticket taker told me that a bomb had gone off in the Bologna train station and, therefore, our train would have to be rerouted and delayed. My primary rule of arriving in a town before sunset would once again apparently be broken by the daily struggles of the Italian railway; I probably wouldn't arrive until way past dark. Also, due to the fact that we were stuck on the train, I had no chance to get off to find some food to eat. By the time I arrived at the Stazione Termini in Ravenna, it was about eight o'clock at night—a five-hour delay of my trip that had started at nine o'clock that morning.

After getting to a nearby public phone, I called the three youth hostels that I had listed in my *Let's Go Italy* tour book. The first one was disconnected, the second one gave me some undecipherable recorded message in Italian, and the phone rang off the hook at the third one. Which one should I take a chance on? I decided odds were the third one was run by some lazy manager and that I could find him and convince him to let me stay in a room or at least sleep on his porch.

I got on a bus and showed the driver the address. He waved me in. We started to leave the center of town and headed for the outskirts. As we proceeded, the streetlights got sparser as the sky got darker and darker. I was really getting hungry by then, and I started scouring the streets for anything that could be open and sell me a bite of something. The prospects looked very discouraging. I hoped there'd be food at the hostel.

The driver stopped at a street that was completely unlit. In fact, there were no lights anywhere except at the top of a hill about a mile away. The driver motioned to the building up the long driveway. "That's the place." As I stepped off, the bus doors slammed in finality, and the orange bus whisked away, abandoning me. It was sink or swim at this place. I headed up the hill, getting hungrier and more tired with each step. Boy, was that bed or floor going to feel good.

Completely spent physically, emotionally, and gastronomically, I reached the front gate. It was locked! There was a message on the gate. To the best of my ability, I could make out the words "Closed," "October," and "April." I had the sinking feeling this place was not going to be my haven.

Then—just as I was reading the note—like the famous train-station scene in *Casablanca*, I saw raindrops hitting the ink, causing it to run. I felt the splat of water on my head—light at first and then steadier and heavier. Rain! What else? I was tired, hungry, frustrated, and now wet. I had nowhere to go and had no idea of where to stay.

There come various times in each of our lives when we're faced with a series of bad choices. This was one of those times. Fed up with this situation, I figured my only hope was to find something open by walking all the way back to town, which I estimated to be a full two-hour jaunt. In the rain. Hungry. Tired.

Disgustedly heading toward town, I reflected back on a dinner I had eaten at a cafeteria in Rome near my apartment. I had sat down next to a guy who looked American and had struck up a conversation with him. He looked like he needed some cheering up. I asked him how his trip had been going.

"Great until I arrived in Italy," he replied. "I arrived in Rome two days ago, and last night, I decided to go to one of those hip-looking dance clubs.

I sat down in a booth, and a very attractive lady came by and started talking to me. We headed to the bar, and I ordered a couple of drinks and so did she. After a couple of hours, I felt like I was really connecting with this girl, and I asked her if she wanted to go out for a walk. She said no, as she had to go somewhere else right away, so she left.

"So, I'm sitting there, and the bartender hands me the bill for the two of us! I told him she wasn't with me, but he claimed to not understand English. The bill was three hundred fifty dollars! I couldn't believe it! I told him that it was a setup—which it obviously was. I was about to leave in disgust, when suddenly three big guys who work in the bar surrounded me and told me to pay or else! Fortunately, I had some traveler's checks, so I wrote out my last remaining three hundred fifty dollars and gave it to the bartender. The whole thing was an organized roll; the girl was obviously a plant to trick me into buying expensive drinks and then sticking me with the bill. My trip is now over."

I felt so sorry for the guy. "I didn't know that travelers were such targets."

"That's not all. If you're hitchhiking here or if someone offers you a ride, forget it. What they do is, just before you get in the car, they put your back-pack in the backseat or trunk, and then, just before you get in the car, they drive off without you, with all your possessions. Happened to a friend of mine."

This whole episode flashed before me as I treaded along in the rain. I'd have to take this walk alone. Who could help me? My Italian after just three weeks was only good if you had a back problem; finding a place to stay was not in my linguistic powers. I kept walking, soaking on the outside, and sweating up a stench inside from the mix of fatigue and frustration.

Thirty minutes into this lonely march, a solitary car slowly passed by me. A few moments later, it crept by again, slowly tailing me. I didn't like this; I was feeling like I was getting sized up for something. There was no way to shake this guy; besides, whom could I call? What could I say?

He shouted something in Italian that I didn't understand. I ignored him, feeling all the more agitated by this situation. I figured that I was going to get rolled, and there was very little I could do about it. I had taken a year's worth of martial arts and self-defense in preparation for this trip; this just might be my opportunity to try it out. The general rule I learned from my sensei was that you usually get one good shot, so you should use it *very* well.

The fact was, though, I was too tired, hungry, wet, and frustrated to put up a prolonged fight with this guy. Besides, I was loaded down with a backpack. It had to be around midnight by now. I trudged on.

He circled around again, following me. This time, he spoke in English. "Where are you from?" he asked with a thick Italian accent. I still walked on.

"Are you an American? Where are you walking to?"

This was going to be some fight. Maybe one good punch. But then what? He probably had some friend in the back of the car.

"I'll take you anywhere you want!"

Wetter, hungrier, and more tired than I had felt before, I was fed up. Sometimes, you just hit a wall and don't care anymore. If I was going to get mugged and ripped off, so be it. It was better than slogging along in the rain being tailed. "OK," I thought, "let's play out this setup."

"I'm an American," I sternly grunted. "The hostel's closed. I need to get to town to find a place to stay."

"I love Americans! I'll take you!"

My options seemed limited. I turned around to check out my ride. This did not look good; he looked too eager. I looked inside the car. The guy looked about my age. No one was in the backseat, at least.

"Get in. Put your backpack in the trunk."

Ah! The old hitchhiker trick!

"No," I said in a sober monotone, "I'll hold on to it." Maybe I could somehow use it in the fight if I got cornered and outnumbered. Focused and steadfast, I sat down and just muttered, "Let's go."

Off he sped, trying to butter me up with small talk—just like the girl who reeled in the American at the bar. "Keep talkin', bud; I almost believe ya."

"I'm Marco," he said. "What's your name?"

"George…just get on with it, *amico.*"

He sped off like some sort of race-car demon. We made it to the center of Ravenna in nothing flat, and he went veering in and around the narrow streets. He was obviously trying to get me lost and confused, and it was working. I had absolutely *no* idea where we were, as each road got narrower and windier. He was going to pull up to some dead end, and a bunch of his buddies were going to be there to work me over. I had my first punch all planned out.

We pulled up to a little building, and he stopped the engine. "Wait right here," he advised. He got out and talked to a couple of guys, and then he jumped back in the car. "This isn't the right place," he quipped as we drove off. I looked around. Definitely not—it was too well lit…too easy for me to escape.

We traveled more winding roads, and my head was spinning from all the twists and turns. This guy was good at what he did!

Finally, we came to a street with about three of the giant, faceless, and dull-looking multistoried apartment buildings that are peppered throughout all of suburban Italy. "We'll go here," he stated, as we pulled up to the curb.

So, when was it going to come? Maybe as soon as we got inside the apartment lobby. With my pack on my back, I had my hands positioned for a good punch. No one was inside the entrance. Marco took me to the elevator. They must be inside; that was what he was telling his friends at the other place.

The doors opened…and nothing. We stepped into the elevator and went up a dozen or so floors. As soon as we stopped, I was ready to throw the punch at whoever was there waiting for me when the doors slid open. Empty. He took me down a nondescript hallway to a room, and he knocked on the door. My fists were in position for the first blow.

A pretty young girl answered the door. She and Marco entered into a subdued and—even without translation—personally intimate conversation. My guard started to drop.

"You can come in here."

I entered, and the young lady took me to the kitchen. There were some scrambled eggs cooking in a frying pan.

"This is my girlfriend, Luiza. She's making dinner for you."

What was going on here? Who were these people? I was not going to argue, so I wolfed down the scrumptious meal. Boy, did *that* hit the spot! The eggs were enhanced with some Parmesan cheese! Good call, Luiza! Suddenly, I realized that the guy I had thought was my enemy was an angel sent by God to save me! I felt an overwhelming sense of protection in this place. "What now?" I cheerfully asked.

"I take you to my house. My mom has a room for you." And off we went.

We arrived at a humble apartment about five minutes away. The house was filled with crosses, pictures of Christ, and photos of Marco and his brother, who was in the service. Simple and unpretentious, it was the most inviting place I'd seen. Marco's mother came up to me and gave me a hug, and then she showed me to my room. It was cozy and simple, and the bed was like a heavenly cloud.

"You stay here as many days as you like. You are our guest," Marco sweetly explained.

Lying on the bed and staring into the light-blue ceiling, I had an overwhelming sense of God's protection. At my most miserable state, God delivered me from the valley of the shadow of death. He had more faith in me than I had in myself and was looking out for me better than I ever could. Through this whole crazy day, He had showed me the depth of his commitment to me.

What a great night of sleep this was going to be! Nothing like the warmth of safety in a comfy bed.

Deep in my sleep that first night, I was suddenly jolted out of my bed by what felt like the world turning and twisting all around me. What was going on? Was the earth spinning out of orbit? What happened that November day in 1980 in southern Italy was a 6.8 Richter-scale quake that was so powerful I felt its venom hundreds of miles away. I rushed out of bed to see if Marco knew what was happening. He was listening to the radio, fascinated but unalarmed.

"They say Naples is filled with destroyed buildings, dust, broken pipes, and panicked people," he soberly said as he turned to me. Then, with a smile, he added, "Just like normal."

My days in that area were the beginning of my love affair with Italy and its people. Orson Welles said it best when in *The Third Man* he stated, "They had warfare, terror, murder, and bloodshed, but they produced Michelangelo, Leonardo da Vinci, and the Renaissance. In Switzerland, they had brotherly love; they had five hundred years of democracy and peace, and what did that produce? The cuckoo clock." The intensity and ferocity of their lives made everything they touched, from the most devotedly religious to the most hedonistic secular, radiate with passion.

I visited a series of Medieval and Renaissance-era churches in Ravenna that were noted for their mosaics. Since seeing the sights in Rome and now in Pisa and Florence on this short trip, I was, in fact, already getting churched out. How Catholic could the Roman Catholics go? The art at the Vatican was a testimony to the power and inspiration of the Catholic church. The churches at Ravenna were built before the veneration of Mary and had a much simpler beauty, which made the glorious mosaics in these churches all the more sublime; yet, I still found them overwhelming.

Pure devotion to God and Jesus were presented here in works of art that made me gasp at my initial sight. I couldn't stop gazing at them. One of them had a little light that required fifty lire (about seventy-five cents) to illuminate for about three minutes. I must have put ten coins in there; I just didn't want to leave. I could not believe anything could be so beautiful. True worship of God inspired this. It made me want to be that devoted to something. What would my year of work in the Eternal city inspire me to accomplish? *Could* I become that inspired?

CHAPTER 24

Meanwhile, Settling into La Dolce Vita...

ARRIVING BACK IN ROME, I figured my first necessities were to get settled into my apartment, get a phone, open a bank account for stashing my earnings, and find some transportation. Returning to my chiropractic office, I went to Rigel to figure out whom to contact to get these things.

"First," he admonished, "you don't need a car. Bad idea. It will get beat up, and fixing it will eat up your savings. Be an Italian; walk and take the bus or subway.

"As far as everything else, you have two options. One is to do things aboveground. What that means is that you go through the proper bureaucracies to get what you want, which usually takes around two years for something like getting a phone installed. What I recommend is to have my father-in-law, Mario, get you in touch with some people who work in the black market."

This again sounded like something from *The Godfather* or *Goodfellas*. Was I going to get involved with a bunch of cloak-and-dagger "paisans"?

"It's nothing like that," Rigel soberly reassured me. "Italy's system is such that there are so many government regulations in order to get anything accomplished, the people just get around the bureaucracy by doing their business without reporting it to any authorities. You're forced to be an outlaw. Your apartment, for example, do you like it?"

"*It's fantastic!*"

"You're not living in it."

"What do you mean by that?"

"The government put in rent controls in order to keep the prices down. The prices were so low that none of the apartment owners would have made any money by officially renting out the rooms. So, they just keep putting out an ad that the rooms are for rent, but they actually rent them out under the table to people who are willing to pay cash, but they don't report it to the government officials. People like you."

"You've got to be kidding."

"Not at all. In fact, we've got a patient coming in today who works for the phone company. Watch this."

In came a conservatively dressed, serious, plainspoken lady in her early thirties. Rigel asked her a question, and she looked straight at him as she delivered an answer. Rigel turned to me. "She just said that because she's a patient here and knows Mario, she can have someone from the phone company have your phone plugged in within nine months. Just in time for you to leave!"

"Now, I'll ask her about having her brother come in and install the phone after he gets off work."

Even I, with my beginner's Italian, was able to make out her unemotional phrase: "Tomorrow night at nine."

I was seeing before my eyes the entire motivation of Western Civilization unfold—regular people trying to figure out how to get around the oppressive bureaucracy of ruling empires. Italy had conquered the known world, as had Roman Catholicism, and anyone who didn't have power or access to it via connections had to figure some way to beat the system. I was seeing this concept right before my eyes.

I also saw it in the office where I was working. The Italian law dictates that in order to legally practice his or her profession, a chiropractor has to work under the auspices of a medical doctor. He or she can only treat a patient if an MD gives him or her a referral. These draconian rules can seem quite overwhelming and stifling, but Rigel figured a way around the system—the Italian way.

"Because the medical system is socialized," he explained, "the average doctor makes about as much as a bus driver, about six hundred dollars a month. So, I found a doctor and told him I'd pay him five hundred dollars a month to hire me. All he has to do is come in each day for the hour we see our new patients, examine the patient, and then write a letter of referral to us, and we're all set. We get our patients, and he gets his regular wage almost doubled!"

Sure enough, at two o'clock, just as we each had a new patient to treat, the door flew open, and bursting into the office—with his arms halfway through his lab coat—was Dr. Santoro, greeting us all with a very gruff *buon giorno*. We made our formal introductions, and he proceeded to give the most cursory patient exams in medical history. "I see this patient has scoliosis and arthritis," he soberly declared to the patient. "You need three to four weeks of spinal manipulation performed by Dr. Rigel and Dr. Harris." He would then go sit behind our desk, read the newspaper, and blurt out his commentary on the daily news as we proceeded to actually treat the patients. He repeated this routine with every patient who walked in that day—with the exact same diagnoses on each patient. He did this the first hour of every single day for the entire time I worked there. It was the most fascinating way of working a system I had ever seen. I realized that first day that I was working with a true genius.

"Oh, you do have to be smart here," he once told me. "But that's not what makes the difference. The key is to be up front, honest, and aboveboard at all times. I hire Dr. Santoro, as well as a couple other doctors to do my X-ray and lab work, and they know I never cheat anyone. Every other chiropractor here has been told to leave the country at some time because of some illegal activity. The black market is standard procedure; cheating and the like is a whole different thing, and you must always be aboveboard as well as crafty."

CHAPTER 25

Royalty and Great Expectations

SO, RIGEL AND MARIO WERE meeting all of my worldly needs. Rigel, while very moral and having grown up with a Christian background, was not a churchgoing man, so I was on my own as far as fulfilling my own spiritual needs. The American church I had visited a few times was not going to cut the mustard, so I needed something else. I went back to my little white book of connections and remembered Princess Liza Darziwell was an Emissary. I'd written to her a couple of times from the United States, and she was anxious to meet me. I knew nothing about this family and was very intrigued when she gave me the address of her supposed palace. What kind of royal blood ran through these Emissaries?

Her residence was about a half-hour walk through the streets of Rome from my Spanish Steps apartment. What a wonderful way to get through town, sliding and gliding through all the narrow and winding streets. I arrived at the given address, and it was a palace all right, but the kind of old-money type in the center of a city. Its courtyard had high walls and a very quaint fountain that led to a very tall and foreboding door. Answering the bell was a lovely, fair-skinned, slim lady about my age, with a light-brown bob of shoulder-length hair. She had an air of genteel and restrained aristocracy. Obviously. I was meeting Liza face to face.

"So pleased to meet you. Let me introduce you to my mother."

I was taken to the study where Ann was sitting in a chair quite regally. Looking a bit like Mrs. Havisham from *Great Expectations*, she exuded restraint and old-world charm. I later learned that her family had been quite rich in Europe but had to escape their home (it was either in Germany or

Poland) during World War II for some reason, and they had lost most of their money. Her demeanor conveyed dignity and self-respect, things that can never lose their value over time.

"We have weekly meetings with a group of people. We sometimes go over Martin's lectures or simply talk about the spiritual aspects of some issue. The discussions are always lively and quite stimulating. Please come to our next one."

Having few other social options at this stage of my stay in Rome, I decided to make the meetings part of my Tuesday routine for a while. After work, I'd make my dinner, hit the streets to frequent my favorite *gelateria*, and enjoy my latest flavor while sauntering over to the palace for some spiritual sparring.

The usual attendees consisted of Mrs. D. and Liza, a couple of middle-aged men, and a priest. It almost sounds like the introduction to some sort of a joke, but these were actually those who frequented the weekly gathering. Some of the discussions got quite interesting. I did a lot of listening to feel my way into the group. The priest was surprisingly witty and erudite in his explanation of Catholicism. In fact, he quoted C. S. Lewis a few times, which got my attention.

After one meeting, I went up to the priest to get his input. "You come to these meetings quite often. What is your opinion of them? I'm not an Emissary, and I'm trying to figure out if what they say is heretical or some of the most brilliant spiritual insights in one hundred years."

He looked at me with a sincere, sober gaze. "To tell you the truth, it's not what they say that bothers me as much as what they don't say."

"What do you mean by that?"

The priest—in his black coat, collar, and hat, standing in the dark corner—could have been an informer from a Sam Spade novel. He divulged, "You never hear anyone talk about sin, redemption, Jesus's blood, heaven, hell, forgiveness, or grace. They talk a lot about what to do and what attitudes to have, but without these other things as a basis, it means nothing. They seem to want the results of salvation—peace, power, and purpose—without any atoning sacrifice."

I decided to start listening more carefully for the secret words.

The next meeting, the priest didn't show up. Had he finally cashed in his chips? It was a fairly small group, but that never bothered Mrs. D. She seemed in her element, sipping her tea and discussing sophisticated spiritual topics. She read from Cecil's latest talk as a starting point; the discussion was slow in beginning.

"Well, he brought up some interesting points, don't you think? I liked when he mentioned to focus on what is important in life," she said to get the ball rolling.

I felt my chance to flesh them out was coming. "Yes, and there were some interesting points on the here and now, but what about focusing on what's eternal?"

She seemed to be taken aback a bit. "Hmm…that's an interesting point. Eternal…yes, yes." She seemed off balance for a second but quickly got back to stable ground. "Let's think about that for a moment. Yes, we should consider the eternal. Can anyone here think of what 'eternal' actually is?"

She looked around. People started to look at each other and then down and then away. For about thirty seconds, there was an agonizing and ignorant silence. No one seemed to dare hazarding an answer. It was as if no one had ever thought of the concept of eternity before.

"I know!" she declared. "Humor. A good sense of humor is eternal."

Everyone nodded in agreement with her. Yes, humor was the lone eternal thing. With that pallid and limp answer, the group let me know it had absolutely no real and significant answers for me. Here I was with a blue-blooded royal family—with someone who was well bred, well educated, and living in the cradle of Western Civilization—and all she and her minions could come up with for eternal value was "humor"? The shallowness of their waters was frightening and disillusioning. This would be my last time at these meetings. I had to seek other paths to follow.

CHAPTER 26

A Different Kind of Roman Centurion

WITHIN A FEW MONTHS OF living and working in Rome, I was getting into the routine of the Italian life pretty well. I was starting to make a few Italian friends, and I was even dating some of the *ragazze*. I had learned the language pretty quickly through talking to my patients in Italian, through daily activities of living in Rome, and by going to American movies that were dubbed in Italian. Seeing James Stewart, Orson Welles, Woody Allen, and Marilyn Monroe speak in Italian is something that can only be experienced. My favorite was when Monroe's dubbed voice said, "Zucchero"—translated from her name *Sugar*—in *Some Like It Hot*. The source of my social life came through my office. I asked Rigel if it was all right to go out with the female patients. "How do you think I met my wife?" he incredulously answered. And that was that!

One day, a couple of attractive American ladies, about my age, came in as patients. I asked the first one, a strawberry-blonde, what her complaint was. "You're the doctor," she replied. "You tell me!" I was impressed by her moxie, and as I examined and treated her (she had a sore neck from an old whiplash injury from a car accident), I discovered that Joan and her friend Cathy were missionaries in Rome for a two-year stint. They had teamed up with a group of other college students to work as a group called the Centurions (or, as they called themselves, *I Centurioni*), whose goal was to start and establish one or two churches of Italian converts to Christianity.

"The fact is, if you've been here for any amount of time," explained Joan, "you realize everyone here is Catholic, but it's just a cultural thing. They have no real knowledge of who Jesus Christ really is."

This made sense to me, as the friends I had made—and the girls I had dated—would invariably tell me, "I'm Catholic, but I don't believe." Almost all the girls I met were amazed by the fact that I didn't expect to sleep with them on the first date, and the guys thought I was crazy because I wasn't trying to find girls simply to sleep with them. The fact that I was trying to live for something besides my animal instincts was akin to my telling them I came from a different universe. It was that uncommon to their way of living.

"Why don't you come to our church service on a Sunday morning, and then you can watch us afterward as we go out into the streets to share our faith."

I needed a church, so this seemed like an appointment from God.

That Sunday, I got on bus number forty-nine, which would take me to the Centurions' apartment complex. The bus driver drove that thing like a Maserati, doing a few hairpin turns, speeding through red lights as if they were merely suggestions, and even screeching to a halt for a quick cup of espresso at a bar. By the time I got to the center, my head was spinning in three different directions. A dark-haired, fairly thin, contemplative-looking guy was setting up the chairs by himself, getting the room ready for the service. He greeted me with a warm smile. "Are you George? I'm Jim. I was told you were coming. Welcome!"

"Thanks. I just got off the bus."

"You look like it. Did he run the usual number of reds for ya?" he said with a grin.

I knew I'd like this guy.

He explained how the Centurions were made up of college kids from all over North America and were overseen and managed by a couple of slightly older and married adults in their late twenties to very early thirties, Buck and Don. Jim introduced both of them to me as they came in. Don was a straightforward, open, friendly guy; Buck seemed like he wanted to be somewhere else. As I got to know him, he merely confirmed my initial impression.

The rest of the group filed in—about twenty of them—and I got to meet them all. I sat with Joan and really enjoyed her company, and Don gave a great sermon in English to us. It was nice to hear someone actually enthusiastic about the Bible and Christianity for a change. He ended the service with a recording of Muhammad Ali explaining why he was a Muslim. Ali sounded quite resolute in his conviction. As soon as Ali was done speaking, Don gave a great response: "Can't you feel Ali's sincerity? He really believes in his faith. But, you know, you can be sincere, yet you can be sincerely wrong."

That really hit me. I wanted both. I wanted to be sincere, and I wanted to be right. As I went with the Centurions to a street corner, I saw them sing songs in Italian about their faith and give moving testimonies of why they believed Jesus was God. They exuded sincerity. As I looked around, however, I noticed that very few of the locals were paying attention. Most of the men were quietly sitting and reading their Sunday sports pages, and the ladies were talking among themselves, sometimes giving the missionaries an occasional glance. Reflecting back to my experiences with the coed preacher in undergrad school, I couldn't help wondering if this was actually the best way to spread their message.

After a few of these Sundays, I started getting to know these people and to understand the inner dynamics of the group. I sensed there was a lot of internal tension between the leaders and within the team itself. Don's wife was ill, and Buck always seemed to be having some sort of digestive problem. The members themselves got into petty arguments and didn't seem to have any bond of affection toward one another. Usually when a group of diverse people get together, they become unified by working toward a common goal. This team, as a whole, seemed petty and disorganized.

I loved having some great discussions with Jim, who inspired me to read works by a midcentury preacher and writer named A. W. Tozer, and there was something about Joan's homespun quirkiness that attracted me, but the team as a whole seemed to be lacking any sense of inspiration or joyful duty. I felt at times that I was there to cheer them up. I never saw any Italians convert to Christianity, and I think the lack of any tangible results was taking its toll. What chance did a small group of believers have against the force of the modern Roman Empire?

As time went on, I felt like I was living two lives in Rome. One was my Italian life with my local friends, who had absolutely no interest in Christianity but were fascinated with their American and his entertaining way of living and outlook on life. The other was this ragtag group of dysfunctional but devout American missionaries, who saw me as a welcome distraction—or as a project, to get me involved in their team. I was enjoying my deep and challenging discussions with Jim, but I was developing an attraction for Joan that was palpable. There were a couple of Italian girls I was dating, but I didn't dare push the romantic envelope too far, as I could tell that those relationships were leading nowhere. With Joan, there was no envelop to push. Although I felt more and more drawn to her, I felt she was either blissfully ignorant of my affections or was just unwilling to consider the implications of a relationship with me. Would it jeopardize her mission trip? How about my trip through the Middle East and Africa? Would I still go? Would we wait for each other? All these things went through my mind, yet I had no idea if they went through hers. All the while, I felt that I couldn't jeopardize any hopeful future with her by pursuing any carnal or romantic desires with anyone else.

As time went on, I realized Joan just wasn't interested in me; while we talked about everything else under the sun, I would give hints about my feelings as a way of drawing her out, but she never verbalized reciprocal feelings about me. I realized that our friendship didn't seem to be going where I wanted it to and—without any faithful romance waiting for my return to the Eternal City—I'd eventually be moving on to Greece, Israel, and then to my ultimate destination: overlanding through Africa.

It was just another work day that warm May 13. I had only a few more months left to work in the clinic, and I was thinking about how the time had passed so quickly. Suddenly, Anna burst into my office as I was treating a patient. "Someone shot the pope!" she shouted.

Tom and I looked at each other in disbelief. "Are you sure?" we asked.

"It was just on the radio!"

Our office was only about half an hour's walk from St. Peter's, and you could hear the traffic and commotion. The panic in the air was horrifyingly electric.

"Was it the communists?" asked Rigel, who thought the Russians were so upset by Pope John Paul's stance against Poland's ties with Russia, and for Solidarity, that he might have been a target. We found out instead it was a Turkish Muslim named Mehmet Ali Agca, who was immediately thrown into prison.

The amazing thing was that, shortly afterward, when the pope had recovered, it came over the radio that the pope said he forgave Agca! The Italian world was stunned in rapturous and inspired disbelief. You could feel the hum of energy through the Roman streets that afternoon as everyone was buzzing about it. What kind of a man could forgive someone who had tried to kill him? The people of Rome shook their heads. "That pope, he's something special." They'd grin in admiration.

I had no desire to be a Catholic, but the pope was an inspiring figure. I had lived in Italy and was won over to his devotion to his faith.

CHAPTER 27

Three Coins in the Fountain: Addio, Roma

AFTER LIVING IN ROME FOR about ten months, I had been able to save about the equivalent of $6,000 in Italian lire, which would be the sum total of the money I would be living on for the rest of my trip through Greece, Israel, and Africa. I had a four-month job lined up in Israel, but Dr. Small—the chiropractor I was going to be working for—warned me ahead of time that the money I'd earn there was going to be just enough for room and board. "You'll live well in Israel while you're there," he told me on the phone, "but the 120 percent inflation rate makes the money absolutely worthless once you leave."

That was fine; I figured I had earned enough to travel and live on for the remaining year afterward. I had been reading books like *Africa on a Shoestring* by Geoff Crowther, and I figured I could make the money stretch pretty far. The immediate problem was how to get the money out of the country in some sort of viable currency. One of the major conditions of my working for Rigel was his ability to help me get the Italian lire I had been accumulating out of the country and into my own bank account in the United States. From there, it would be a simple matter of having my dad wire me $500 every now and then when I started running low, as I had no desire to travel around the world with that much cash. Being an American traveling alone put a large enough target on my back. There was no reason to paint a red bull's-eye by someone finding out about a stash of cold cash. About a month before I departed, I approached Rigel in his office about his strategy.

Reclining in his chair, he took a deep and contemplative draw from his filtered cigarette. "I have been giving this matter a lot of thought since I gave you that promise last year. Our first and most above-the-board way of doing this is to go to the bank where you have your money and see if we can negotiate something. Maybe I can be the person drawing the money out for you."

At the bank, we approached a teller Mario knew and conveyed our situation to him. He was a sober-minded, studious man in his early thirties, with dark, wavy hair and deep, dark eyes. He explained to us that no American was allowed to take more than $2,000 out of the country, so he could not be of any help to us. I couldn't change the lire into traveler's checks, as they were not in American currency, and besides, they were traceable. We left the bank fairly discouraged about the bureaucracy.

Back at our office, Rigel took a drag on another cigarette.

"What now?" I asked.

He blew a couple smoke rings. "We'll talk to Mario. He'll know someone."

The next day, a patient came to see us. It was the teller from the bank who had given us the thumbs-down. He talked in a low voice to Rigel, looked over to me, smiled, and sat in a chair in the corner.

"What's up?"

"This guy's got an idea," explained Rigel. "He knows someone in the money-transferring system in the bank. What he can do is—after hours—take your money, send it on an untraceable route through a bunch of countries, which hides it, and then have it end up in your account in the States."

"Brilliant!" I exclaimed, impressed once again with the genius of the Italian black market. "How much is he going to charge me?"

"Right now, it's one thousand two hundred ten lire to the dollar. He will charge you thirty lire per dollar."

"What do you think?"

"This guy's making under two hundred dollars on this. That's a pretty fair deal."

I smiled, went over to the guy, and shook his hand. "Let's do it!" I told him.

"What now?" I asked.

Rigel and the teller talked for a while.

"Go get the money out, and bring it back here in a couple of days. We'll discuss a place to drop him the money; he'll pick it up and let us know when it's been delivered."

This was sounding more cloak and dagger by the minute! Where did I leave my trench coat?

The next day, I headed to the bank with my backpack. The largest Italian currency was the equivalent of a twenty-dollar bill, so the lady at the counter brought out a giant container of money to pay me. She took me into a special room—"For your own safety, sir"—and she painstakingly counted off every bill until it added up to 8,531,200 lire in 50,000 notes. My backpack was stuffed to the brim! I had made a point of dressing particularly sloppy this day, so no one would suspect a haggard-looking backpacker of carrying around seven thousand bucks on the streets of Rome. That was definitely the most careful—and most paranoid—walk I'd ever taken.

I took the money to the office the next day. "What's next?" I fervently asked Rigel.

He went to his closet, put on his raincoat, sunglasses, and hat, grabbed the backpack, and looking like something out of the airport scene in *Casablanca*, deadpanned, "I'm going to go make the drop" and soberly left the office.

Two hours later, he came back, sat down, pulled out a cigarette, and silently lit it. "Now, we wait a few days. Call your dad in five days, just to be on the safe side."

The next week, I called Dad from the office. "How much is in my account, Dad?"

"What you had before you left: two hundred twenty-five dollars."

Rigel overheard. "Give it a couple more days."

Two days later, I called again. Still $225. Something was wrong. Rigel stared out the window, taking the cigarette out of his mouth very deliberately. "I'd better go see the guy at lunch. It's probably no big deal, but it's best to make sure."

Rigel came back around three o'clock, with his usual sober demeanor. "He checked with his friends. They made the money route so circuitous that it got stuck in Auckland, New Zealand. Give him a couple more days."

Three days later, I got a telegram from my dad: "Received $6,850 in your account today. Money from Rome, Geneva, Vienna, London, Auckland, Vancouver, and San Francisco."

"Gotta love the Italians!" Rigel sighed, sitting behind his desk, as he nonchalantly blew out a few rings.

The first major phase of my two-year trek was over. I had earned the money I required for the rest of my pilgrimage, and next on my upcoming itinerary was a few months in Greece to see my relatives and the home of my childhood faith. After that, I planned to spend a few months in the country that was the home of the *roots* of my childhood faith, Israel. I hoped that by seeing the Greek Orthodox church in action, in the country where the first Gentiles became Christians, a few of my questions would be answered, like "What does a country that defines itself as Christian look like?"

After spending ten months in Italy, I seemed to be leaving with more questions than I had arrived with. I was very disappointed by the short fuse and defeated demeanor of the Centurion mission group I had observed. A number of them had the right heart, but something was missing in all of them. Was it a peace? A sense of joy? They didn't seem as sold on the product as I thought missionaries ought to be. They appeared more interested in the Italian culture they were, in essence, preaching against. They seemed to have given in to the Italians, as so many other peoples had done hundreds—and even thousands—of times in the preceding centuries.

My feelings for Joan didn't make it any easier to leave. Was this the woman I'd someday marry? I sure would like to. I would have declared my intentions, but my innermost being told me this trip was more important than staying in Italy and forging a relationship with Joan. I was not spiritually or mentally ready to settle down until I was more at peace with my own conclusions about God. Besides, not once when we went out did she return the verbal volley that I'd serve regarding my feelings toward her. The answering silence was stultifying.

It alarmed me that Italy's Roman Catholicism, like so many other belief systems, couldn't be content with just Jesus. They had added a plethora of extra dos and don'ts that had very little to do with real, transforming, and personal faith. I never figured out the whole thing about worshipping the Virgin Mary—same with the pope. I liked him a lot, but I couldn't figure out why we couldn't figure out the Bible for ourselves. Why did he have the final authority on things like celibacy and fish on Fridays? And the Italians themselves figured that if you weren't Catholic, you were something akin to a Moonie. They just couldn't believe faith in Christ alone was enough for a right relationship with God. There had to be the beads, the smells, the chants, the rituals; I even saw "abracadabra" displayed on someone's wall over a picture of the Madonna and Child. Where was the simple faith that had once reigned in Ravenna?

I had purchased a Bible in an English bookstore a few months back and had become determined to read the whole thing through on the rest of the trip. A dear and gracious nun who was a patient of mine had given me a book of the Gospels that had put the life of Jesus in chronological order. I liked it a lot, so I figured—between these two books—I had God covered. During my whole time in Italy—no matter how estranged I had felt from God or allured by the ways of the Italian world—I had made it a point to pray in the morning and evening and read the Bible every day. I felt that God would honor my feeble efforts with guidance—both in spiritual things and in worldly things like travel and Joan.

I went one last time to the office—armed with my backpack to say my last good-bye to everyone. I wanted to weigh myself, as well as my backpack, to see how heavy my load was. The pack was twenty-six pounds; I weighed 176. When I had strategized about how I could travel as lightly as possible, I had chosen countries partly based on my ability to be in an area during its sunny and dry season. I had pared my belongings down to two T-shirts, two pairs of underwear, two pairs of socks, one pair of blue jeans, one pair of khaki shorts, tennis shoes, hiking shoes, my camera, my poncho, a sleeping bag, mosquito net, and toilet articles. I also included my Bibles and a few novels; I was determined to read everything by Steinbeck and then to pick off a few more authors along the way.

Armed with $500, I set sail from Bari to the land all four of my grandparents had left behind eighty years before. The traveling had begun again, this time to the country of my past.

CHAPTER 28

To Hellas and Back

THERE WERE THREE MAIN PLACES I wanted to see on this leg of my spiritual and geographic pilgrimage. Aside from the villages where my ancestors came from—and where my great uncles, uncles, and cousins still lived—I was intrigued by the Island of Patmos, the monastic peninsula of Mount Athos, and the gravity-defying monasteries of Meteora. All of these have special significance for Christians in general and for Greek Orthodox pilgrims in particular. I felt if I was going to get into the spiritual mind of my Greek heritage, these were the best places to start.

It fascinated me that the race of my ancestors were the first Gentiles to become believers in Christ's divinity, which occurred within the first few decades of the fledgling faith. Before us Greeks, there were only Jewish followers of Jesus Christ. That has become a source of great pride among Greeks—as if we had anything to do with what those people back then accomplished. But that's Greeks for you! (To show the extant of our ethnocentrism, while visiting the village of Neochori—the town my paternal grandfather came from—I discovered that the neighboring town was where Aristotle was born. Since then, I have made every opportunity to let people know the odds are very good that the reason for my mathematical acuity is my probable blood link to the ancient philosopher.)

I used Athens as a base for my excursions, as I had many cousins living there. From Athens, Patmos was an all-day boat ride away. When I arrived, I watched a beautiful sunset, while hearing dozens of little kids on the shoreline yelling, "Room! Room!" at the tops of their lungs in order to catch travelers' attention. I grabbed one kid (or did he grab me?) and was led through the crowd like a prize catch at the local 4-H club. He took me down a long and lonely street to meet the charming lady who ran a tiny family-owned hotel. For the privilege to stay there, I paid five bucks a day, which included a one-egg breakfast and enough Greek coffee to keep my nerves rattling for half the day.

My first morning in Patmos, I woke up from my cozy and Spartan bed and was startled by the most unearthly and piercing sound—completely unidentifiable. It was an eerie, metallic sound—like some distorted symphony. The sound shifted slowly, hovering by the window behind my bed—almost like a spaceship with half of its engine falling apart, searching for a place to land. Curious, and a bit bewildered, I leaned out the window to see what this alien looked like. To my surprise, it was a herd of two or three hundred goats with tin bells, grazing along the road, clanging along as they acquired their morning breakfast. Welcome to island life.

For those who don't know, Patmos is the island where the Apostle John wrote the book of Revelation. John was considered Jesus's closest friend, and he was the only apostle who was not martyred for his faith. Instead, he was exiled on this tiny, barren island near Turkey, where he wrote the last book of the Bible—which is essentially a letter to nine churches about their good and bad points, the fall of Jerusalem, and the final return of Christ in judgment, which results in the end of the world before the heavenly rewards for His people and punishment of hell for those who reject Him.

As one of my high school friends said, "The book of Revelation is something like a Christian acid trip." It has a *lot* of symbols, descriptions, and characters that we'll never really understand. (I'm sure many people have heard of the Beast and the number 666 from Revelation.) So, here I was at the place where it was all written.

If you're in Greece, you learn really fast that any place that has any spiritual value probably has a church built on it. In this case, the Church of St. John was close to the top of the island—a good hour's walk or a five-minute taxi ride. Trying to be a good steward of my finances, and wanting to get a feel of the island, I hoofed it up to the church, which was a stark-white building surrounded by white walls. Except for me, the church was completely empty of tourists. I was led into the cavern by a priest and was stunned by the room.

I thought that if you've been to one church, you've essentially been to them all. Protestant churches have a certain look, as do Catholic and Greek

Churches. This one, however, was completely un-church-like; it was a simple cave with a tiny altar, a couple of icons, and a few chairs. Over at one side was a kind of nook, almost like a bed made of rock, with just enough room for someone to lie down on. In this little petrous bunk was a giant crack that divided the rock into three huge pieces. "This is where Saint John stayed when he wrote the Revelation," the young priest explained to me. "If you notice, the rock is divided into three, to symbolize the Trinity."

I went over to examine the bed of stone more closely. It was smooth, as if worn down by many hands caressing it over the years. The room itself was dark and damp, with a single window looking out to the sea. What did John think as he looked out into the world? Hope? Resignation? Peace? Here he was completely separated from the rest of the world, writing or dictating a letter to people he would probably never see again. What was it like to have a vision of God? How did he know he wasn't flipping out in the solitude?

After spending so much time in Italy, where everything connected with God is overdecorated within an inch of gaudiness, the simplicity of this lonely and hermitic abode was peculiarly attractive. Suddenly, I realized the Bible wasn't written in some ivory tower or just put together by some religious institute. It was composed by people in peculiar situations such as this: a missive from prison for Paul, an investigative report for a doctor named Luke, and, here, a lonely letter from a Jew in exile. The fact that people are still reading this letter from a man who lived in this cave made me realize that either this letter is the biggest hoax and waste of time to read, or it's really God's word. There couldn't be any middle ground after seeing this place. Either John was really deluded, and a sad waste of a life or he was one of the wisest men around. I was gradually leaning toward the latter.

When I returned to Athens, I figured it was time to head north, to see a few more of the religious sites I wanted to visit. On the way up, I figured I could visit Livadi, a village where my paternal grandmother was born and raised. My dad had driven to it a couple of times and had filled my mind with stories through the years about how it was the quintessential Greek village. "The world could blow up, and this town would never know," he'd boast, meaning that Livadi lived in a timeless and self-sufficient society. Inhabited by hearty shepherds high up on a hill, where the road from down below actually ended, Livadi sounded like some mystical Shangri-La—where nothing had ever changed and you could lose yourself, never to be heard from again.

Not having a car for transportation, I figured my only hope was through the public bus system. Spurred on by the fact my dad had warned me, "you'll never get there; it's too far out of the way," I was determined to make it even if I had to hoof it. Another basic impediment to arriving at my destination was, at this point of my travels, my Greek was not exactly fluent, with having only taken a few "Greek School" classes as a kid and my parents feeling it was better that I never learned it so they could talk about me and my sister without our comprehending anything.

My dad had assured me this wasn't very important, as they really didn't speak Greek in the village anyway but what was called Vlachicko or "village language," which was a combination of Greek, Latin, and Turkish. Was this supposed to make me feel better about the trip, or was it my dad's way of again showing me he was "more Greek" than I?

Another difficulty was that I didn't know the names of any of my relatives (except that one of them was named Magdalena) and I didn't know what they looked like! My parents had never gone into detail about them while we were growing up. My only reference point was an old black-and-white picture taken from around World War II of a group of women sitting in front of a brick wall, dressed in traditional black widow's garb. That was it.

Still, I was not deterred. I went to the Athens bus station and, in broken Greek, figured out with the ticket lady how to *basically* get to this little village. Patiently, the ticket lady explained, "You take the seventy-six bus from here to Kozani, which is about seven to eight hours from here. After maybe five hours on this bus, you'll pass a town called Larissa. After that town, there's a big fork in the road. Tell the driver to let you off at the fork. The bus will go to the right. You'll have to wait there for some car to pick you up that is going to the left. Hopefully, it won't take too long. Tell the driver where you're going, and he'll probably take you there."

I was definitely in Greece—"hopefully, maybe, about, probably." A German would have had a heart attack.

Upon finding the seventy-six bus at the station, I explained as carefully as I could—and used a note that the lovely ticket lady had written for me to give to the bus driver—the instructions for my travel into the unknown. The driver looked at my message, listened to my imperfect explanation, and gave me a mixed smile of pity and camaraderie as he waved me into his vehicle. I figured this trip was just about to get very interesting or very disastrous by the end of the day.

The drive through this part of Greece was like cruising through Central California, loads of dry, open space with patches of trees scattered throughout the gently rolling plain. Sure enough, after about five hours, we come to a stop. I look around and saw nothing but dry, barren land.

The driver pointed to a small paved road on the other side of the road we were on. "That road will take you to Livadi," he confidently stated.

"How do I get there?" I asked him the same question I had asked the ticket lady, just one more time to make sure before walking off the gangplank.

"Just wait. Someone will eventually turn up that road. He'll pick you up."

And off he went, leaving me in a cloud of dust.

Standing there in the middle of miles of empty space, my mind flashed back to the famous crop-duster scene with Cary Grant in *North by Northwest*. That's exactly how I felt—like I was being set up for some sort of bump off. I figured I'd be better off if I crossed over closer to the road going to Livadi, so I grabbed my pack and waited for some form of transportation, or life form, to take me on the last leg of this trek.

Hours passed. Was this really a good idea to be here like this? Once again, my options seemed limited.

Just as I was giving up hope, a small truck turned off the main highway. Hey! Here was my lift! I jumped into the center of the road, with both arms waving. There was *no way* this guy was getting past me. He pulled over, and I walked up to him, simple and direct.

"Are you going to Livadi?"

The driver had a sun-beaten, craggy face, three days' of gray whiskers, and a dusty cap and coat. He could obviously tell my Greek was not ready to make me a UN translator. "Yes" was his simple reply. He waved me in.

For the next hour, we sat in complete silence, except for the ubiquitous Greek music on the radio. He had to be wondering what the heck a twenty-five-year-old American was doing in the middle of the armpit of Greece. He finally broke the silence.

"Why are you visiting Livadi?"

I had no knowledge yet of the words *relatives, family, cousins,* or even *vacation,* so I just pulled out my thirty-five-plus-year-old photograph and handed it to him. He stared at it, gave me a long, hard look, and handed it back to me.

"I'll take you right to her house."

It seemed that in small Greek villages, everyone knew everyone else, as people there had been living together since Socrates was in kindergarten. He dropped me off in front of a stone building with a slate-shingle roof. I was greeted by Magdelena, my great aunt's daughter-in-law. She was a sweet soul of a lady and graciously led me into her humble home. There was no running water except for the kitchen sink, and I quickly learned the Greek phrase for "We don't have it," which was the response in regard to everything, ranging from a cloth blanket, a spring mattress, a refrigerator, and even plumbing for a toilet. This place—with its outhouse, straw mattress, lamb's-wool pillow, goat-hair blanket, and stone walls with leaks for air conditioning—made a Spartan home seem like a Four Seasons Resort.

I spent a week in this wonderful village—not saying too much to my cousins who spoke as little English as I spoke Vlachiko, but we all appreciated that we are of the same heritage. I started getting a feel for this tiny self-contained village, meeting over and over again the butcher, the baker, the tailor, the clerk at the Communist Party office, the barber (where I got a wonderful shave with a blade each day), and the bartender, who mixed up the best Greek coffee I could ever experience each day at lunchtime, surrounded by men playing "tavli," which was what they called backgammon. This was a village where men still walked around wearing shoes with puffy balls on the toes and old-fashioned wool pants that were tight in the calf and wide in the hips. I got a pair of those pants specially made for my father, and I sent them to him, as a way of letting him know where I was. If nothing else, my time in this hidden oasis up in the mountains made me realize this was where I was from. The seeds that formed my roots in America blew from this area. This, in a great sense, was me. I felt excited that I could now envision the point on a map of the world and tell someone, "This is where my people came from." I was proud of this land that supplied my DNA.

CHAPTER 29

A Monastic Life

MY NEXT DESTINATION WAS A place that is to Greeks what the Vatican is to Italians: Mount Athos. The tradition holds that it was founded by Mary, the mother of Jesus, when she was on a boat with St. John (of the book-of-Revelation fame) and a storm took them off course. They landed on this peninsula. The monasteries were started around the third or fourth century, and in veneration of the founding Lady, they decided she should be the first, last, and only woman to set foot in the area. This tradition still holds, even to the point that no female animals are allowed, so the eggs have to be imported! All my life, I had been told by just about every Greek I had met that Mount Athos was *the* place to go, as "you really feel like a Greek" (the ultimate experience if you've got even a microfiber of Hellenistic DNA in your body) when you go there. Every relative I had known was considered a bit more special if he'd been to Mount Athos—sort of like winning the Triple Crown for a baseball player. My dad had visited it for one day back in the early '60s, and he had told me I'd really understand what it meant to be a Greek Orthodox if I ever went there.

As a kid and then once I started going to the Baptist church as a teenager, I couldn't help but think to myself, "What difference is there between being Orthodox and just a regular Christian?" As with the Roman Catholics, it seemed that each religious system had its own special shtick to add on to the simple, basic faith in Christ. I had to figure out what the special deal was with the Greeks and what market they had cornered.

For an American citizen, getting to the holy peninsula of Mount Athos back in the 1980s was essentially impossible; only Greek citizens were allowed.

The only exception to that rule was if you had a relative who lived there, and I actually did! My paternal great-uncle had been a monk at the monastery of Grand Karyes for all of his adult life. He wrote to my dad periodically before he died in the late '70s. I knew nothing about him, except for the fact that he had carved a beautiful wooden icon of St. George the Dragon Killer and had it sent to me when I was born. I've had it in my room ever since. I always thought it was pretty cool, a definite notch above the painted portraits in other types of churches. Before I embarked to Italy, my dad gave me a letter from my great-uncle that was dated 1977 and, in which, he had invited us to come visit him. Although he had died by the time I gave the letter to the proper Athenian authorities for permission to visit Mount Athos, the government agent was sufficiently satisfied with my connection to give me a ten-day permit.

I embarked in my journey from the port of Mount Athos in a small town called Ouronoupolis, which is an hour's drive from my paternal grandfather's village. It's a quaint, charming little fishing town that is known for some pristine beaches. Arriving there in the early morning for the only boat that would leave for the holy site, I was easily able to figure out where to embark, as I just had to look around to see where all the black-robed monks were. Boarding with me were also about a dozen Greeks who, I learned, were either hired to work at one of the monasteries or who just wanted to see what the place was like. Sort of like Jerusalem, Bethlehem, or Rome, Mount Athos is a place of pilgrimage; but the fact that only Greek men (and male animals!) are allowed to step a foot there keeps crowd control fairly easy. They told me that once in a while, some woman tries to sneak onto the place, but so far, the women's libbers had been turned away.

The boat took us to the dock at Grand Karyes, which was sort of the central hub of the area. There are about twenty individual monasteries in all, connected via a circuitous walking trail, with some connected right on the shore, giving them the additional option of using a boat for transportation. The basic way to get to each monastery is the same one that's been used for hundreds of years: simply by "following the yellow brick road"—essentially a small dirt trail from one site to the next. Most of the monasteries are between a four- and eight-hour walk apart, so it behooved me to start on any trek early in the morning. I had a ten-day pass, so I figured I could see quite a few of these places and learn a bit about the monastic life.

Before starting my walk to the first monastery, I wanted to find out if any of the monks who lived in the Grand Karyes knew where my great-uncle Demitriou had lived. Since he had died a few years before, I wondered if anyone would even remember him. (Many of the monks come and go after a year or so.) I found one man who remembered him, and to my amazement, he showed me my great-uncle's humble living quarters in the town of Grand Karyes. It was still intact! Things definitely did not change here very quickly!

The room was a tiny, Spartan quarters, about eight by six feet. There was a cot on one side that looked like it hadn't been touched since my great-uncle had died. All of the walls were of dark and aged wood, and there was a small desk opposite the bed. Across from the door I had entered was a dark wooden wall, empty except for a very large icon of Jesus and Mary. Above the desk were a couple of shelves and a bulletin board that had some letters and a few pictures. The photos looked pretty old but hauntingly familiar. They were of our family! There were a couple family portraits of us when I was about seven or eight years old, as well as a few individual ones of us, positioned right above a cross surrounded by candles. It was obvious my great-uncle Demitriou had spent a lot of time praying in front of that cross, with our family in mind.

Upon witnessing this insight into my heritage, a strong spiritual wave overcame me. All the years I was growing up, I had been surprised at how little my parents talked to me about religious things. As I was going through all of my spiritual journeys and quests, I had wondered if I was doing this sojourn all alone, without any advice, guidance, or direction from anyone. After seeing this humble domicile, I realized my great-uncle had been petitioning God on my behalf my entire life. I hadn't realized it while growing up, but I was never on my own; someone was praying for me. I felt tremendously encouraged; I now *knew* I was going to figure this whole thing out. I had over twenty years of someone else's intercession backing me up. I was ready to visit the place where my spiritual heritage originated.

The first monastery, Iviron, was a five-hour hike from Grand Karyes. I and a small group of fellow pilgrims who had come with me on the boat exhaustedly arrived just after the sun had set. Since there was no electricity, finding the place was a bit dicey, but after one thousand years of practice, these monks knew how to take care of us visitors. They were expecting us at just this time, knowing the general time it would take if one hiked from the dock. A simple bowl of lentil soup with some feta cheese, bread, and water, and I was ready for bed. There were about eight or nine other guys spending the night there. They were heading out the next morning as well to see how many monasteries they could see in their limited number of days; I figured joining them would make my trip a lot easier. My Greek was good enough to converse with these older guys—who were in their forties and fifties—while we were hiking, but I figured most of the hikes would consist of my silently walking alongside these gents, behaving sort of like an accompanying dog—lots of listening, but basically being seen and not heard.

Each day would start with an early-morning breakfast of tea, olives, lentil soup, and bread. Just as the sun was rising, we'd head off on the day-long journey through gorgeous hills, decorated with trees, rivers, rocks, and valleys. We took canteens, but the trickling rivers were fresh enough to drink from. The fascinating thing about each day was that by the time we had spent about six to eight hours of walking, we would be convinced we were hopelessly lost. As we trudged on, however, just like from a scene in *The Wizard of Oz*, we'd pass over a hill and suddenly get a glimpse of our Emerald City: a monastery, brilliant and awesome in its stern glory. As we'd get closer, we could see a monk at the entrance waiting for us, holding a tray in his hand. He knew what time the pilgrims usually arrived, and his ministry would be to greet us weary pilgrims with Greek coffee, ouzo, and pastries. By the third day, I was fantasizing about the powdered and gooey delights while trudging along on the trail.

Each day, a couple of my fellow hikers would peel off; they were just too tired and out of shape for this arduous trip. They would invariably find a monastery near the shore and get someone to take them on a boat back to the main port. The group was thinning out pretty quickly. At the Monastery of Great Lavra, one of the monks invited me to the midnight service. "It's something you'll always remember." Truer words were never said.

Growing up in the Greek church, I was quite used to the traditions, incense, paintings, icons, and chants that make up the Sunday liturgy service, but upon entering the doors of this particular church at the early-morning hour, I was overpowered by the foreign, fearful, and harrowing goings-on. First, the room was barely visible because of the mix of burning incense and candles; the two intermingling fragrances created an intoxicating smell, almost hallucinogenic. Quickly scanning the room, I noticed there were about ten rows of wooden bench seats, divided by a central aisle. The walls were lined with high-backed, chair-like edifices with armrests that people used to lean against during the service if they got tired from standing. No sitting was allowed, so the attending people would cheat by supporting themselves with these armrests.

At each corner of the dark, moonlit church was a priest. Each was reading aloud in a monotonous tone from the Bible as quickly as he could, and each one almost sounded like a Greek auctioneer. Each priest had at his disposal a select group of bones lying on a wooden podium in front of him. These were the remnants of venerated saints, and each time the reciting priest would mention either the name *God the Father*, the *Holy Spirit*, or *Jesus*, he would hold one of the bones, kiss it, and then use it while crossing himself three times (for the Trinity). Meanwhile, there were two lines of two priests rapidly walking up and down the aisles. Two were shaking incense holders, while the others were carrying the Bible over their heads, chanting something in a fearful and stentorian monotone. How they never crashed into each other, I'll never know, as it looked like a human figure-eight racetrack.

I walked up to the priests in the corner, and they essentially ignored me, too engrossed in their chanting, bone kissing, and crossing as they rapidly read aloud the Bible verses, turning the pages as if trying to break a speed record. As I gazed around, I felt surrounded by the Byzantine paintings of saints, with their detailed but otherworldly facial expressions, impressionistically drawn bodies, and their feet seeming to levitate off the ground. Above them were smoky stained-glass windows with solemn-faced apostles and saints gazing down at me, with the outside light from the moon eerily beaming through them. The burning candles, which created a luminous and smoky perimeter around the walls, made the scene complete; if I hadn't known that this was a Christian service, I would have thought I was in some sort of occult pagan ritual mixed with Mr. Toad's Wild Ride.

I had felt a lot of emotions during my years of going to various Christian churches and visiting Hindu temples, Jewish synagogues, or New Age meetings, but I had never before experienced fear, and that was what overwhelmed and ultimately overcame me. I felt like I was taking part in a witches' Sabbath, and I dashed outside through the ancient wooden doors to take in some fresh air. The moon was full, and the sky was perfectly clear; I felt like I had escaped.

This was why people came here?

By the next morning, I noticed a couple more people had dropped out, leaving only three of us as we left and headed to the Monastery of St. Paul. There, I met a regular Greek guy about my age who spoke excellent English. Nick and I hit it off right away; he was staying on Mount Athos for a couple of months "to do some work here, earn a little money, and save up something for the outside world." He was on a pilgrimage as well; while he had spent some time in the United States visiting relatives there, he had become a "born-again Christian, as you call it there." Intrigued, I had to ask him what his impression was of Mount Athos, since he had spent so much time there.

"Most of the people who come here don't come for religious reasons," he explained. "They come because the monks make a ton of money from growing and selling wine and olives. These places are loaded with money from their orchards and vineyards, not to mention all of the gold and silver from all of the relics. They could buy and sell half of Greece! Lots of poor farmers come here because their own places are failing financially, so they work for a while here for some free room and board while getting enough money from these guys to put back into their businesses. People come here because they can't handle the real world. It's crazy!"

"But haven't you learned anything *spiritually* here?"

"From these monks?" He laughed. "I ask them basic questions about Christianity, and they look at me like I came from the moon. Besides, they don't even believe it, anyway. This place is like your San Francisco, if you understand what I mean. I've been propositioned twice here by these religious guys, so watch it here, and as they say in America, 'don't drop your soap.'"

My head was spinning by now. Did other Greek Americans know it was like this? Was this just some disgruntled worker? The more I talked with Nick, the more sincere he seemed, and he didn't appear like some crazed loon. I felt like the foundation of my heritage was like the scene in *The Wizard of Oz* when they find out that the wizard is a fraud; I had looked behind the curtain, and I didn't like what I'd seen.

Now an incident made sense to me from the day before when we had stopped for water at a stream and had run into a priest and some day laborers. We had talked a bit, and the priest was very happy to know both of my parents were Greek.

"So, you are Orthodox?" he asked me.

"I'm a Christian," I replied.

He looked me in the eyes. "Are you Orthodox?"

"I follow Jesus."

"Are you Orthodox?"

I sighed in resignation. "Yes, I'm Orthodox."

"Wonderful."

All he had cared about was whether or not I was in the club, not whether I was going to heaven.

These monasteries had been here hundreds of years before I arrived and will probably be here hundreds of years after as well. I had seen enough of the monastic life. It was nice to get away, but as Jesus said, he didn't come to take me out of the world but to be the salt of the world. I had mixed feelings about Mount Athos: I was pleased beyond expression that this place existed where my great-uncle had dedicated his life to praying for my soul. But, at the same time, couldn't he have made the same, or a greater impact, some other way?

By the last day of my trek, all of my companions had taken boat rides back to Grand Karyes. That last morning, at the Monastery of Simon Peter, I woke up in a quiet and lonely dorm, and then I hiked the day to my place of origin at Grand Karyes all by myself. In one sense, I felt deserted by my fellow sojourners, but even more compelling was the internal euphoric realization that this long hike in solitude symbolized my entire spiritual quest; I'd have to do it alone with God. No one else could do it for me. It was one of the most blissful walks I've ever had in my life.

Upon arriving back in Ouranoupolis, I was struck by how much the week of first-millennial solitude had affected me. For those ten days, the only sounds I had heard were ones that had been in existence before electricity and the Industrial Revolution: soft voices, walking, cooking, and animal sounds. Suddenly, I was thrust into the world of radios, car horns, traffic, people shouting and yelling, and immodest dressing and behavior. I was thrown back into the harsh modern world. I could now understand why these people liked to escape, but that was not part of my destiny. I'd have to stay a part of this world and figure out how to deal with it while in the trenches.

The next stop on my trek through Greece was to the central area, with its major attraction the monasteries of Meteora. If you have ever seen posters that say "Visit Greece" at a travel agency or on an online advertisement, the odds are that a picture of these "monasteries in the air" is on it. Erected in the thirteenth century, they were built as a means for the Christian priests and pilgrims to be protected from the two major outside and destructive forces at the time: the Crusades and the Turks.

Setting down at a campsite outside the city limits, I hitched a ride to the base of the largest and oldest of these monasteries: the big Meteora. This monastery, as well as all of the others, was built on top of a group of fingerlike rock projections that were essentially inaccessible by foot once the ropes and drawbridges were pulled up from the buildings. It was sort of like Rapunzel in reverse!

As I walked up and around these amazing spectacles, I asked one of the monks, "What was the purpose of building something like this? I thought Christianity was supposed to go out into the world in order to make an eternal difference."

The gentle, patient monk explained, "You must understand those times. During the Crusades, the Greek Orthodox church was under terrible attack and persecution. Our holy icons were being destroyed, as well as our churches. The Muslims caused the fall of Constantinople in 1453, and the Islamic Turks wanted to wipe out any memory of Christianity. The priests felt the only way the church could survive was to become completely inaccessible to harm for a while so they could preserve the faith and traditions of the faith. In a great sense, it is because of them that we still have the Orthodox church intact today."

As I walked around and looked at these churches (or fortresses) that served as buildings of spiritual devotion and physical protection, I became awed at these men from hundreds of years ago. Right or wrong, they had devoted their lives to making these shelters in order to protect the faith they believed in and held on to so tenaciously. They literally dedicated their entire lives to this labor of love. How could you not be impressed by such focused and disciplined devotion?

"And, besides," I thought, "what will I have to show for my life once I'm dead and gone? Will anyone remember anything I'll have done? Has anything in my whole life been dedicated to anything besides making my own selfish monastery? Have I been serving anything other than myself?"

I realized that, yes, I could use my life for others; I could heal people with my hands through chiropractic care. After visiting this and another of the monasteries, I made it down the hill to my campsite, inspired to serve God as a doctor. Once, when I was just learning how to adjust my patients (the term we chiropractors use for manipulating someone's spine), I asked God to give me a special ability to heal people through my hands. As I lay down in my sleeping bag at the forested campsite that night, I lifted up my hands and stared at them for quite some time, thinking of all of the wonderful ways I could help people with them. With utmost sincerity, I thanked God for my hands and for the fact that I could use them for His work. I went to sleep with a peace and joy I had rarely felt before.

CHAPTER 30

Gimme a Break

THE NEXT MORNING WAS JULY 29, and I wanted to go back up to see the rest of the monasteries. There are about six, and I had only seen the three major ones. Feeling well rested and revived from my time with God, I had a nice, casual breakfast and started on foot up the road to try to hitch a ride to the Monastery of the Holy Trinity.

Traveling through Greece by thumb, I had been having a blast. I'd gotten rides to my great-grandmother's village up in the mountains of Livadi and my grandmother's village of fourteen people in Alpohori, as well as multiple rides to small towns from my great-aunt's home in order to get a day-old *Herald Tribune* to read something in English to figure out what was going on in the world. This day, I had the words from Vanity Fare's "Hitchin' a Ride"—a bubblegum hit from the '60s—running in my mind. I faced the upcoming cars and slowly backpedaled along the road thinking,

> A thumb goes up, a car goes by
> Oh, won't somebody stop and help a guy?
> Hitchin' a ride, hitchin' a ride

A solitary car whizzed by me, and as I looked to see if it was stopping for me, the next thing I knew I was falling straight down; there was no step behind me! I had fallen into a deep concrete ditch, right on my outstretched hand. *Snap!* My right hand took all the impact and made the sound of a dry branch breaking. I lay there wondering if anyone had seen me fall. How was I going to get out of there?

I was thankful the driver who passed by me and didn't stop to give me a ride saw me fall and turned back to help me. He and his wife carried me out of the ditch, with my right wrist painfully dangling at the end of my arm. "There's a hospital close by," he encouragingly told me.

We arrived, and he knocked on a locked door. A nurse came up to the glass and waved that they were closed for the day. Who knew why? This was Greece! They lifted up my limp wrist, and she opened the door. "I don't think we have anything for you here," she explained. "We are a very small hospital." She looked around the cabinets, went into the kitchen, and took the eggs out of a wire basket on the counter. Forming the wires around my wrist, she told me, "This will give you some support until you get to a big hospital. You must take a taxi to the closest city, which is Trikala."

They flagged down a taxi and explained the situation to the driver. My mind was racing with various scenarios. Would my wrist ever be the same again? Would I be able to adjust patients in eight weeks, when my job in Israel was to start? How was I going to pay for this? All my money was in the United States and I had no access to it.

And what about the doctors here? The doctors in Greece were notoriously terrible. My relatives would tell me that if you went into a Greek hospital and came out alive, you were one of the lucky ones. I'd heard dozens of scary stories from my relatives about questionable treatments for their problems by some Greek quack. Would I even recognize my wrist once it had healed after being treated by one of these illegitimate descendants of Hippocrates?

The taxi arrived at the hospital, and I walked in, expecting a long wait. The reception room was completely empty. I mean there was *no one*! Not a soul in the waiting room, in any of the labs, or in the treatment rooms. I went to a tiny reception window and peered through it to spot a lady in her late twenties sitting there reading a comic book with the TV on! She didn't acknowledge my existence until I shouted at her.

"What do you want?" she distractedly asked.

Lifting my arm, I showed her my problem.

"You need help. This is a bad day for you."

"I'll say. Where is everyone? Did a bomb go off?"

"No. Don't you know? Everyone is home watching Lady Di's wedding! I'm the only one here. I have to be here; otherwise, I'd be home as well."

"I need help!"

"Yes," she replied pedantically. "I will call the radiologist at his home. He'll be over here in a few minutes. He's not too far away."

I was not feeling too confident about this whole scenario, but what could I do? My options were extremely limited. All I had was my ability to pray, and I asked God that these guys—who would affect the future of my career in their ability to heal me—would perform their task with His miraculous healing power. In Greece, that is as close to a miracle as you're going to get.

The radiologist, an olive-skinned, happy-go-lucky, twenty-odd-year-old gent with two days' of growth on his face came strolling in after a few minutes, looking quite cheerful at the whole situation.

"How's the wedding?" I asked, trying to get on his good side.

"Boring. I was glad to get away."

"That's a good sign," I thought. "He's going to be slow and thorough."

After taking the X-rays, he took me to a waiting room. "The doctor will be with you shortly."

All I prayed was that this guy at least knew some English. That would be a good sign that he wasn't a total hick village doctor who was used to setting bones for sheep.

A short, gentlemanly, thirtyish fellow in a white lab coat came up to me and said in perfect English, "Well, young man, I've seen your X-rays. How are you feeling?"

Ignoring his question, I felt a sense of hope due to his speaking abilities. "How did you learn to speak such good English?" ("Please don't let it be from watching *Dallas* reruns!" I thought.)

"I went to orthopedic medical school in England, and I am now doing my residency here."

Bingo! The skies opened, and the "Hallelujah Chorus" with full choir was performed.

"You just made my day."

"You were concerned, maybe, that you would get a bad doctor here?" he asked with a sly grin. "I understand; I grew up in this town. You'll be fine."

He showed me the X-rays; I had a double fracture, which meant both of the bones of my right wrist were completely broken in two. He gave me a general anesthesia in order to make the setting go as easily as possible. The next thing I remember after the drug settling in was someone slapping my face. Groggy, I woke up in a stupor, lifting my arms in self-defense. I could feel my new companion, the cast on my wrist, as I tried to get out of bed.

"You can stay here a bit longer," the doctor told me. "Here in this town, visitors are treated for free for emergencies, but that doesn't include spending the night, so I recommend that you go back to your place for the evening."

"How will my wrist be?"

"Let it rest for about six weeks, and you'll be fine. I set it real nicely. You got lucky!"

I'll say! Taking the taxicab to my campsite, I just couldn't get over the fact that barely twenty-four hours ago, I was thanking God for my hands and now this! The sun was setting, and I still felt quite groggy, so I lay down in the exact same place and position I had been in when I was thanking God for these same pitiful hands, but now, one was permanently damaged and weakened. I could feel that I'd never have the same strength in this hand again. I'd had exactly one year of treating people without a worry about my tools of the trade. From then on, there would be a thorn in my flesh. Fatigued from the whole trial, I fell asleep very easily that night in the open...

Only to be awakened by...I couldn't believe it! A flash thunderstorm! And I had nowhere to keep dry! The warm rain was relentlessly beating my freshly made cast into a pulp, causing it to swell up like a giant piece of rice. It expanded and pressed into my thumb as if someone were standing on it. Of all of the crazy things to happen to me! Was this my reward for thanking God for my livelihood? Remind me to keep my big mouth quiet next time!

The next morning, I started my way back to my relatives near Athens with my swollen cast and wrist. I was to stay with my aunt and rehabilitate the best I could before my next adventures. I had Dr. Small organize a seven-day camping trip in the Sinai Desert (which still belonged to Israel at the time) before I was scheduled to head to Israel where I had his job lined up to start treating patients in eight weeks. Should I cancel my job and Sinai trip? Should I just pack up my things and head back home? Was this the way my trip would end?

I went back to Athens, but there was no one to nurse me there, so one of my aunts took me to the family summer home near the beach. She didn't know a word of English, which made the time drag by torturously, as every step I'd take to go around the village caused an agonizing throb in my arm. While staying and recuperating at my aunt's home, I had nothing in English to read in order to pass the time except *The White Nile* by Alan Moorehead, which detailed the story of the early English explorers who searched for the source of the famous river. The fascinating characters and exotic settings, with people traversing the cataracts while infected with malaria and dengue fever, made me realize that people had traveled in tougher conditions than I was presently in. I determined to keep going, cast and all, and make this just another part of the adventure. For better or worse, I'd forge ahead, like an embattled warrior. My quest had been detoured, but that was what made it a journey and not a tour. Better to be in Israel with one working hand than to be back home in American suburbia with two.

CHAPTER 31

L'chaim!

IN EXACTLY EIGHT WEEKS FROM the day I broke my wrist, I started working in Tel Aviv for Dr. Robert Small, who was leaving his practice for two months to visit his family in the United States. I had worn my cast for six weeks in order for my bones to properly heal; I therefore had one to two weeks of self-rehabilitation in order to get myself ready for treating Dr. Small's patients. While taking the airplane ride from Athens to Tel Aviv, I tried to work out the scenario. How was I going to meet Dr. Small and explain the situation without having him panic about the fact that his hired hand was literally just that—one hand—when he saw my weak and shriveled wrist just days out of a cast?

As my plane landed in Israel, I was overwhelmed by the fact that every passenger broke into a song and clapped along as soon as the wheels hit the tarmac. They were singing the Israeli national anthem! What a great feeling to experience people truly in love with their country. I was going to like it here!

Growing up in Encino, California, I was quite accustomed to American Jewish culture. It was simply part of my life. I had friends named Berg, Cohen, and Weiner, as well as German friends named Keller. This was part of living in LA suburbia. An Israeli business friend of my dad's, Benny Iron, picked me up from the airport and let me stay at his house until it was time for me to work at Small's office. A robust and enthusiastic man, he made me feel right at home, which wasn't difficult for me in Tel Aviv, since it seemed strangely reminiscent of my childhood days.

By this time, I had a couple of weeks until I began working for Small; Benny suggested that I go ahead and go on the ten-day camping tour of the

Sinai Desert. "We just negotiated a treaty with Egypt, and they are getting it back within a year. You'll never be able to see it like this again from our side," he explained with classic Israeli pride.

I decided to go. The camping trip took us to various Bedouin camps and seashores for snorkeling, as well as to Mount Sinai, where Moses delivered the Ten Commandments to the Hebrews after escaping from Egypt. Whether the mountain we stair-stepped to the top was the actual mountain or not was a moot point as far as I was concerned. What impressed me most of all was the fact that someone took the time to painstakingly make all the steps up this mountain in order for the rest of the world to have access to it.

At the base of Sinai was the monastery of St. Catherine. (Have you started noticing that monasteries and I kept running into each other?) It was built by the good ol' Greek Orthodox monks in the sixth century. These guys really got around! Once again, the monastery was filled from the floor to the ceiling with skulls and other bony parts of various saints, making you viscerally feel like your stay on this earth was quite temporary. These men felt that being here and maintaining this site, as well as the steps up Sinai, was a worthwhile use of their time. Who was I, some selfish twenty-something-year-old, to argue with them? What was I doing with *my* life?

The stillness of the serene and ancient Sinai Desert at night was something that had a mysterious allure to it. The Bedouins that I saw—walking their donkeys or camels, seemingly going in no direction at all, eating dates and fava beans, living a simple and basic life—had a timelessness about them that was fascinating. What was the difference between these people and the ones Moses met when he escaped to here from Egypt? I couldn't think of any. I thought back on the people in the Bible; so many of them met God out in the desert like this. There was a silence and quiet that would make it easy to contemplate God. There were *no* distractions here; I had plenty of time to think about myself, my life, and my God. God didn't reveal Himself in the busy traffic in streets; He seemed to work best in the open spaces, where you heard nothing else except His voice.

Returning to Tel Aviv after ten days and hearing the crashing and busy sounds of the city sounding like a great cacophonic intrusion was just like my reentry experience after Mount Athos. I almost liked the solitude too much;

I realized I needed the give-and-take of dealing with people to keep myself sharp and alert. I'd be getting a lot of that in just a few days once I met Dr. Small and his busy practice.

My apprehension about my introduction to Dr. Small permeated my every thought. What would he think about me once he shook my limp and wimpy hand? Would he cancel his trip? Would he be mad at me for not telling him about my accident? Would he just tell me to get lost and close down his office without me, since I couldn't treat the patients as effectively as I had promised?

When I got off the bus to meet Dr. Small, I could pick him out at the street corner, even though I had never met him before. He had told me he was in his early fifties, but he looked easily fifteen years younger: vibrant, wiry, with an enthusiastic glow. I had been practicing delivering a firm grip when I shook hands with Benny for the past week, so I hoped I could make a good, quick first impression on Small. I stuck out my hand and delivered a cold-fish handshake. "Sorry for the weak grip," I explained defensively, as he looked at my hand. "I just got a cast taken off a few weeks ago, but—"

"Ah, you'll be great!" he dismissed, as he led me to his car. And that was that, which is the essence of the Israeli attitude: Don't let anything get in your way. Keep moving forward, and you'll survive. I liked this guy; he trusted me!

"You're going to love it here," Small confided. "You're not going to be able to take any money out of Israel for the rest of your travels because, like I told you, the inflation is 120 percent here. Any extra money you get here will be worthless by the time you leave. So, just live well with what you earn! You can live in the back of my office for free, and since you'll only be working three days a week, you'll be able to see as much of Israel as you'll like." With that, he showed me the basic ropes of the office and set me free to make it work on my own. What confidence he had in me!

I jumped in with enthusiasm and found that working with the locals in Tel Aviv was a real treat. I was amazed how friendly everyone was toward me. "That's because you are an American," explained Benny. "We Israelis are always interested in the opinion of Americans."

After a couple of weeks there, I had started making friends with some people my age. Because of the diaspora return, there were people living in Israel who had come from just about every nation, making it a fascinating way to meet people from all over the world. At a Mexican restaurant called Taco Taco, I befriended Nehama and Nurit, two ladies who worked there. Nehama, a Yemenite, had deep, inviting, and penetrating eyes, olive skin, and curly hair that flew in a thousand directions, while Nurit had freckles and straight, flaming-red hair. They took me to all their hangouts and introduced me to the Tel Aviv nightlife.

I was attracted to Nehama, so I coyly asked her if she had a boyfriend. "Oh, I had one, but his parents didn't like me."

"What for?"

"I'm Sephardic."

"What do you mean? You're Jewish, aren't you?"

"Yes, but my boyfriend was Ashkenazi, which means his family was from Europe. We Sephardics are from the Mediterranean and Middle East— places like Spain, Morocco, and Yemen. They've never liked each other. We Sephardics are more religious and usually do all of the manual jobs here; the

Ashkenazi are more intellectual and educated. They are usually more secular, professional, and unreligious."

"But you're both Jews!"

"My boyfriend's parents wouldn't let me even set foot in their house. They said I was a 'dirty Jew.'"

Nurit nodded in agreement.

I just couldn't believe this.

"It's true," Benny somberly admitted when I told him I was seeing a Yemenite. "The fact of the matter is that we need the Arabs here to be our enemy. If it weren't for them, we Jews would have probably killed each other by now. The Arabs keep us unified by a common purpose, so we don't cut each other's throats!"

I started reading the *Jerusalem Post* and was amazed at the vitriol between these two classes of Jews. The Sephardic claimed they were the true Jews because they were more religious. They would taunt the European Jews by telling them God truly loved only them because Hitler only killed the Ashkenazi Jews. No Sephardic was affected by the Holocaust, as they hadn't lived in the areas Hitler invaded. The European Jews called the Sephardic backward and uneducated. If anyone in the United States—Jew or Gentile—had written or said the things I heard in Israel, they would be labeled an anti-Semite. The most anti-Jewish comments I ever heard were spoken by Israelis. So much for "shalom" meaning "peace"!

People in Israel greet each other with the phrase *shalom* and say good-bye with the same phrase as well, yet it seemed that everywhere I looked, there was everything except this elusive peace.

Because I was scheduled to work on only Tuesday, Thursday, and Sunday of each week, I had a lot of time to explore the wondrous and historic countryside. There was just so much for me to see, including sites of the Old Testament events like the walls of Jericho, where David slew Goliath, as well as a main point of interest for Christians—to be able to walk where Jesus walked. I was equipped with the Bible I had purchased in Italy, so I could read about all of the events while I was at the actual places they occurred.

As a Christian, I figured the first place I should visit had to be Bethlehem, the birthplace of Jesus. The bus from Tel Aviv delivered me to Jerusalem, and from there, an easy taxi ride took me to the bustling market of Bethlehem. After taking in all of the wondrous and exotic sights and smells, I asked a kid where Jesus was born. He pointed to a large church.

"He was born in that church?"

"Go inside," the young boy said. "You'll see."

I passed an armed guard. (Hmm...I'd never seen that at a church before, although I'd been to some where they probably needed guards to keep people *in*!) I entered through the large door and stepped into a dark, musty, and spacious Greek Orthodox church. The smell of the candles, the shiny icons, and the Byzantine paintings gave it away. Why was this big church here?

A young man behind the candles noticed my perplexity and came over to help. "You must understand," he explained, "when the Muslims invaded and took over this land, they wanted to destroy all memories of Jesus's birth, so the church built this fortress around His birthplace so it wouldn't be desecrated. This is not only a church but a guardian of Christian history. Please remember that way back then, very few people knew how to read, so the story of Jesus had to be shown through paintings and mosaics, which you see all around you."

As I looked around at the works of art, gave the armed sentry at the door a second look, and observed pilgrims coming and going, I realized that, once again, people had devoted their lives to preserving something greater than themselves.

Still, as I worked my way into the damp grotto where Jesus was said to have been born, I thought the site was not exactly like what was described in Matthew and Luke. The dark and cramped room was illuminated by a multitude of candles around the icons, which were accompanied by a myriad of incense holders that formed a circle. At the center of the circle was a multipointed silver star, surrounded by marble. Some adults were praying over it, and some were kissing it. I felt like I was in an old pirate movie and had reached the final place on my leather map, complete with an *X* marking the spot.

"Would you like to kiss the spot?" an open-handed monk asked me.

Repulsed at the arbitrariness of the whole scenario, I politely declined and left. The whole spirituality of Christ's birth seemed obscured and overshadowed by all of the church trappings. I just couldn't picture our Savior being born on a slab of marble, thank you. I had arrived there about two thousand years too late.

Walking around the town, I saw a small sign that said, "3 km to Shepherd's Cave." This sounded intriguing, so I walked down a dirt road to the quiet, out-of-the-way town of Beit Sahour, where I came to a small building that said something about this being where the shepherds were told by an angel that Jesus was born. Curiously, I walked into the museum, which was basically a tiny room no larger than an ice-cream parlor.

"May I help you?" a young Arab woman asked from behind a counter.

"Where am I? What is this?"

Her large brown eyes glistened as she sweetly smiled. "This is the place where the shepherds were told by the angel that Christ was born. Come. I'll show you the cave."

Mary (what else *could* she have been named) led me to a quiet, simple grotto where tradition says the shepherds stayed after visiting Jesus. Now *this* is what I expected a biblical site to look like: unadorned, dignified, and humble. I was the only one there, so I got a chance to soak it in without being hustled for a donation. As I left the cave, I straightened up and looked around at the hills of this area. This was where it had happened; people were going about their business, and these young men were chosen by God to bring good news to the rest of the world.

And here was a devout Catholic girl and her family in charge of protecting this site and its meaning. Embarrassingly hospitable, they invited me to stay for dinner and had me spend the night in their humble abode. They had never heard of California, let alone Los Angeles, and just wanted to share their lives with me. One of the brothers slept on the couch at night; he gave up his spot and slept on the floor beneath me. I certainly felt like there was room at the inn *this* time around. This family understood, and I wanted to as well.

This conflict between the Bible and modern reality kept coming up at every turn. I figured the next destination on my itinerary should be Jerusalem to see the Holy City for myself, so I planned a two-day trip there. By then, I was getting used to the bus system, and I walked from the central Jerusalem bus terminal to the Old City. As I approached the city, I was told there were seven gates to enter by, but the Damascus Gate would give me the best atmosphere. Upon arrival, I understood the advice; the amphitheater-like entrance was bustling with ad hoc sellers with their wares of herbs, fruit, trinkets, and linens. People were hustling and bustling, wearing all sorts of outfits. Standing along the crest of the entrance, I felt like I was at the top of a basin, about to slide into the center of a drain. Working my way down the steps, I threw myself into the Muslim Quarter, looking for a place to start my pilgrimage of Jesus's ministry here.

Walking along a small, narrow street, I noticed a procession of devout Catholics. A middle-aged man was carrying a cross, and others chanted something while working with their rosaries. They stopped suddenly at a spot that had a number on it, and the leader of the group started speaking in French. The sign next to him said, "Via Dolorosa No. 3." Curious, I waited until everyone had passed by and entered the building. It was a courtyard to a small Armenian church. I spotted a guy about my age sitting at a desk.

"Excuse me; what's going on outside here?"

"Oh, they're reenacting Christ's journey to the cross. That's what the Via Dolorosa is. There are fourteen stations that tell of the different things that happened to Him on the way to His crucifixion. Tradition says that at this spot, Jesus fell while carrying the cross."

I looked around at the plaster, concrete, and stone building and peeked up and down the cobblestone street. This just didn't seem like a first-century road. "How do they know it happened here?" I asked.

"Oh, they don't," he matter-of-factly replied, not even looking up from his desk work. "The Catholics just picked a bunch of spots in the Middle Ages and said, 'That's where this happened,' and no one's bothered to argue about it."

I started to wonder just what I was doing here. I could've easily watched a movie about Jesus's life and had a more authentic experience. This whole scenario started to seem like a Disney amusement park to me, with everything manufactured to make you feel like you were somewhere authentic—sort of like the Pirates of the Caribbean ride or the Jungle Cruise. Here were people making their livings selling access to religious sites that weren't even the real thing! Surely, the place where Jesus was buried and rose again would offer me some hope. With trepidation, I followed all the stations to the final destination: the Church of the Holy Sepulchre.

Upon entering the cavernous Byzantine church, my attention was drawn again to a giant slab of marble; this time, it was where Jesus was said to have been buried and resurrected. Once again, I had to fight incredulity to believe this was the spot that had been the center of Christian faith and history all these years. I mean, the Bible says the stone was rolled away…Why was this thing rectangular?

Even more disheartening was the site where Jesus was crucified. I approached what looked like a giant tent with four separate entrances, each one leading to the spot where the world was changed. Each entrance was guarded by a priest of a different denomination: Roman Catholic, Greek Orthodox, Eastern Orthodox, and Armenian Apostolic. They had been fighting over the rights to this real estate for years and had finally come to an agreement where the spot would be divided between the four of them. This made beachfront property in Hawaii seem like small potatoes!

As I walked around the structure, each priest—like a Times Square watch vendor—would lean over to me. "Psst! Wanna see the holy site?"

I felt like I was walking by some peep show. Simply due to ethnocentric loyalty, I picked the Greek Orthodox priest, who led me into his tiny, cramped space and pointed to a bunch of icons and candles. "This is where Our Savior died."

I used every ounce of discipline to refrain from asking him, "By which candle?" I simply nodded and gave some money to his already outstretched palm. What would Jesus have done if He came back just now? I needed to get out of there.

I headed out and made my way over to the Garden of Gethsemane, where Jesus prayed with His disciples before going to the cross. By the entrance to the garden, there were rows and rows of mobile souvenir carts, selling the tackiest of religious artifacts. I couldn't help but wonder if Jesus wouldn't have overturned these moneychangers. I was not exactly having a religious experience here.

Things got even more bemusing when I made subsequent trips to many of the sites of Jesus's ministry: Capernaum, Galilee, Nazareth, Tiberius. All of these places drew in tourists—and their dollars—based on the reputation of Jesus having visited there. The problem was that *all* of these sacred places had *rejected* Jesus. Some had tried to kill Him, and Jesus usually left these areas by condemning them. And now, all these years later, people were profiting from the rejected Savior having graced an area where He was hated.

It was like some carny at the local county fair bellowing, "Step right up and see the places Jesus cursed." This is how people feel more spiritual? By visiting the sites where Jesus and Paul dusted off their sandals upon leaving? The whole thing was not making sense to me.

What *was* making sense to me was the Jewishness of Israel. It seemed perfectly logical to me that this piece of real estate should be the Jewish homeland. I was impressed by the pride that the sabras (native-born Israelis) had in their heritage. How many Americans are proud of their own nation? How many Christians are unashamed of their culture? These Jewish people felt they were forthrightly continuing something important—something that began thousands of years before they ever appeared on this planet—and that impressed me deeply. I decided to start checking out the Jewish side of life.

CHAPTER 32

"Who Is This Moses?"

THE FIRST STOP FOR ANYONE interested in Judaism would have to be the Western Wall in Jerusalem, which is the only remnant of the Second Temple, built by Herod around 19 BC. It's actually not the wall of the temple itself, but a wall that was only one side of the peripheral wall around the courtyard, but who's counting? Going up to the ancient edifice, I observed lots of Hasidic Jews rocking back and forth as they faced the stone construction and prayed. In the cracks between the bricks that made up the wall, there were a lot of papers shoved in. I went up closer to have a look and noticed that people had written prayer requests and put them in the crevices, assuming that the prayer would somehow be answered better if it were sent from Jerusalem.

I flashed back to this morning when I had noticed something upon entering Jerusalem through the Dung Gate on the southeast side. As I was walking up the path, I could look around the surrounding hill and see hundreds of grave sites near the wall of the Old City, and the closer to the wall and gate I got, the more burial sites there were—including Muslim, Jewish, and Christian. A Sephardic storekeeper told me, "Rich people buy their graves as close to the holy sites as possible, so when God comes to judge the world, they'll be the first to get to heaven. It's like beachfront property for religious people. Crazy!"

Here at the wall, the same thing was happening. Young boys were being flown from their American homes to have an authentic bar mitzvah in Jerusalem. Guys who grew up in the Bronx or Los Angeles wanted to feel more Jewish, so they changed their name from Murray to Moishe and started learning to speak and read Hebrew. Here were people reciting prayers faster than any Greek Orthodox priest, swaying back and forth in order to work themselves into a religious fervor. It seemed so close, yet so far.

It was around 5:30 p.m., and the sun was starting to set at the Wall. I wanted to stay this Friday to observe the religious Jews welcome in the Sabbath. To the really observant Jews, the Sabbath is the highlight of the week, and everything they do is in preparation for this climactic time. Setting their clocks by the sun, the Jews begin their festivities right as the sun sets, which is the start of Saturday—their Sabbath and day of rest and something they've been celebrating since there have been Jewish people.

I leaned against a wall, checked my watch, and compared it with the setting of the sun. Anytime now *something* should start happening—what, I had no idea. Sitting and waiting, I start hearing something in the far distance. Something was coming up the side streets into the large square. I heard men singing! Lots of men! It was really a joyful sound, and here they came, all locked arm in arm, swaying in one another's arms in a casual walking/dance step. All were dressed in the traditional Hasidic black and white and wore the head coverings and all the accoutrements; they streamed into the giant, open arena and worked their way into the roped section where people had been praying. All I could make out from their singing was the word *Shabbat*; they were welcoming in the Sabbath with song and dance. I liked this!

Like a giant conga line, they wove their way to the Wall and broke into four or five circles—some were concentric, some were like cogs in a machine rotating against each other. The men of all ages locked arms and broke into some of the most joyful folk dancing I've ever seen. Watching, I was taken back to the days I went folk dancing with Evan at the Jewish Center at USC. I knew these dances! I wanted to get in on the action!

I plunged into the fray, got between two guys, and start dancing along with the human current. The singing built up in celebratory intensity and fervor. We dancers were stomping and shouting like there was no tomorrow. We were laughing, singing, and pulling at each other in a sweaty lovefest. This went on for over an hour or so. By then the sun had completely set, and every one of us had built himself into an excited and spiritual frenzy. Finally, after some climactic celebration, the singing and dancing gradually wound down, and the party started breaking up. By then, it was about 8:30 p.m. or so, so I had to figure out where I was going to eat. This is no easy task in Jerusalem, as the Jewish shops are closed on Friday night and Saturday, the Muslim ones on Friday, and the Christian shops on Sunday. A poor use of your map could find you ending up very hungry for the weekend.

Luckily, a tall, robust Jewish guy—who looked about forty and wore complete Hasidic attire—came up to me and asked, "Would you like a nice meal?"

This seemed like manna from heaven! "Sure! What do I have to do?"

"Nothing! Come join us! It's part of our tradition to have a guest at our house." He grabbed my hand. "Let's work through this crowd, and I'll take you to our home. You're going to have a nice Jewish meal."

Between the high from dancing and singing and now this offer of hospitality, I was just beaming with excitement.

"This is wonderful!" I gushed as he led me by the hand.

"I can tell you're not Israeli," he panted as we hurriedly worked through the masses of people going in a thousand directions. "Where are you from?"

"America."

"Very good."

"Los Angeles." I then pulled out my ace in the hole: "Encino."

"Yes! I know many people there," he puffed excitedly as we made it to the sidewalk.

I knew that would endear me to him.

"What are you doing here?"

"I'm a doctor." (I knew he'd love that, too, as the old joke from where I grew up is that if you're Jewish, you're either a doctor, a lawyer, or a failure!)

"I'm taking over the practice for a chiropractor in Tel Aviv who's going back to the States for a while."

"You're a doctor? Very nice!"

I felt I was *really* in now. I wondered what they were serving.

"I'm working here for three to four months. I love it here."

"Do you think you might live here?"

"Maybe! The people are so friendly here. Everyone has been warm and accepting. I'm making lots of friends. My patients in Tel Aviv are so kind to me, and even though I'm not even Jewish—"

Just then, he turned to face me, all aghast. "What do you mean, you're not Jewish?"

"No, I'm a Christian—Greek heritage and American," I answered defensively.

He immediately dropped my hand as if it contained a communicable disease and stepped away from me. He wiped his hands against his clothes and then raised them up as if defending himself against someone striking him in the chest. "I can't have you in my house!" he shouted in a panicked voice. "I can't be with you tonight! You're not Jewish! I have to find someone else!"

And just like that, he melted away into the bustling crowd, leaving me on a side street in Jerusalem, in the Jewish section, with no stores or restaurants open and nowhere to go. So much for helping out "a stranger in a strange land." Where had this religious system gone wrong?

When I was back at work, I kept thinking about my encounter with that man. The whole definition of what constituted a Jew perplexed me even more.

I talked to one of the girls who worked at my office; she said she had to join the army because she was Jewish.

"So, do you go to temple?" I asked.

"Oh, no," she demurred. "I don't believe in God."

"So, you can be an atheist and still consider yourself Jewish."

"Of course!"

"How about being a Buddhist?"

"Yes, I have friends who are Buddhists. They're still Jews."

"Can you be a Hindu Jew?"

"Yes!"

I pulled my ball out of my glove, slowly wound up, and threw her my curve. She swung at it just like I had hoped…

"What if someone is Jewish, lives here, and becomes a follower of Jesus?"

She gave a look of complete disdain. "Oh, no! They would no longer be Jewish."

"What would they be?"

"Nothing."

The idea of being defined as Jewish by a negative declaration (not believing in Jesus as Messiah) fascinated me—especially after I'd read about, and actually met, some American blacks who had come to Israel for free land that was intended for the Jews returning from the diaspora. Claiming to be members of the "lost tribe," they had left Detroit in the '70s and had settled outside of the Negev Desert to start their own little town. The man I met—who looked a bit like Sly from *The Family Stone*—said he believed he had Jewish blood and was therefore entitled to live there. "So, don't mess with us, man!"

Was being Jewish authenticated by blood, declaration, identification, or by simply signing on the dotted line?

Another place that was high on my must-see list was the area of Masada and the Dead Sea. These were landmarks that were very important in terms of Jewish history, as Masada was the site where the Jewish residents committed a mass suicide around AD 72 rather than live under the yoke of the Roman Empire. The Dead Sea/Ein Gedi area was the locale of many biblical stories—such as David's flight from Saul—and was near where Lot's wife was turned into a pillar of salt when she looked back to see the destruction of

Sodom. Seeing places like these was really impressive because the Dead Sea is *really there*, and the places where David slew Goliath and where Saul got defeated are actual places. OK, so maybe the pillar of salt by the side of the road I saw wasn't a real person at one time, but I think it was in a Mark Twain book where it said, "It's not a lie if it makes the story better."

Seeing all these places once again helped me more fully appreciate Judaism. This religion is really cool; it's got some great history, holds no punches in criticizing itself, and is still around. You've got to love a system that has survived after all of these millennia, especially after so much persecution.

Coming back from a full day at Ein Gedi and heading to Jerusalem, I was reflecting on all of these great facets of Judaism, when I noticed the public bus I was riding on started smelling funny. The driver veered over to the side of the lonesome two-lane highway in the middle of the desert and pulled over to stop. "Everybody off the bus; there's something wrong with the engine," the driver informed us. So, we all poured out into the late-afternoon sun.

We must have looked like a motley crew, standing around by the side of the road: a number of Hasidic Orthodox Jews, a bunch of secular sabras, some Arabs, and myself—the only obvious Gentile Christian of the lot. Sitting by the edge of the highway on some rocks, I noticed that each group sort of coalesced together, ignoring the others while they waited for either the bus to be repaired or for a viable replacement to arrive.

I was in no rush to go anywhere, as I knew—if worse came to worse—I could stay with my friends at Beit Sahur. As I watched, I noticed the dozen or so Hasidic Jews appeared quite agitated—walking and pacing about in a very nervous way—and they seemed to be inordinately harassing the driver about something while he was working on the bus.

"What's going on with those guys?" I asked the thirty-something sabra next to me.

"Oh…" he chortled as he pointed at them with his cigarette. "Those guys are all in a panic, as they want to get to the Wailing Wall to pray, but if the sun sets before the bus gets fixed, they won't make it there in time and will be stuck here, as they aren't allowed to travel on the Sabbath. They might have to stay here until sunset tomorrow unless they get a ride before the sun goes down."

With each passing moment, this group of men got more and more animated—and equally more belligerent—as they confronted the poor, patient driver. They started pacing up and down the highway, looking for someone who might drive by and get them out of this religious mess. They saw a car coming down the highway; about four of the men in black waved the car down. It slowed to a halt. An Arab Christian was at the wheel of the humble, dusty vehicle, and as soon as the Jews figured out the guy wasn't kosher, they jumped back, repelled from that car like a pair of opposing magnets! The driver said something in Arabic, and as the Jews backed away as if from a leper, a couple of Arabs got into the car and headed into the rapidly approaching sunset.

Now the Orthodox Jews were in *really* dire straits, as their chances of worshiping God the way they had intended seemed to be getting slimmer. Within a couple of minutes, another car was flagged down; this time, the driver was a Jew, and he got out of the car and said something to the Hasidic Jews. Obviously invited to hitch a ride, the entire dozen guys jump at the chance of reaching the Wall before becoming defiled by being marooned with vermin like us. They proceeded to push, scratch, claw, and pull at each other so they could win a place in the limited seating of the vehicle at the expense of someone else's bad fortune! It was like Friday night wrestling at the Olympic Auditorium, with more eye gouging and half nelsons than I'd seen in years.

"This is what they do to each other in order to be able to worship God," joked my sabra companion as he stared at the situation, patiently dragging on his cigarette.

Filled to capacity, but leaving a few bruised and disheveled Hasidim behind, the weighed-down Mercedes trudged on…hopefully in time to please God.

In the throes of that scenario—about ten minutes later—followed an old, beat-up flatbed truck that pulled up and offered anyone a ride. Since the driver and passengers were Arabic, none of the Jews were takers; the secular ones didn't trust them, and the Orthodox didn't dare get their hands dirty. With all of the other Arabs gone, I decided this was the best chance I had to get to Jerusalem, so I hopped in—the *fifth* guy in the front seat of a Toyota truck. Now I *knew* I was in the Middle East!

The drive was cramped, smelly, and sweaty but filled with the kindest men I could encounter. Our communication was limited, but we understood each other as fellow Christians, as well as members of the human race. The guy riding first shotgun pulled out a lime, peeled it, and offered me a slice. Polite and parched, I took a bite—*wow*. That hit the spot, if there was one to hit. They all laughed, taught me a few Arabic words, and made me realize there was just no way I could ever follow a religion that made me refuse a ride with kind souls like this. These people had been following God since those shepherds from Bethlehem. They were simple men, living a simple but hard life as farmers. I loved and respected the Jews, but I felt that these Christian Arab guys were my brothers, united by more than rituals.

CHAPTER 33

Give Me "the Letter"

I WAS WORKING MY USUAL Tuesday, Thursday, and Sunday routine at Small's office, earning my keep. Part of my daily routine was watching for the mail to arrive at the clinic early in the morning. No matter how important the patient or how long the line of people in the waiting room, I'd stop whatever I'd been doing to see if anyone had written me. The hope of news from someone in the United States—or maybe Italy or Greece—was this Bible verse in action: "good news from far away is like water to a parched throat." (Proverbs 25:25) My parents and I wrote each other weekly, and I still numbered my letters so they'd know if the letters arrived out of order or whether one got lost.

This particular day, I had received a letter from Italy, and it looked like Joan's handwriting! I had written her a few times, hoping I might be able to see her once I returned from Africa to figure out where our relationship was headed. Opening up the letter hurriedly, I shook with disbelief as I read the words she had written; she had just gotten engaged to a longtime friend of hers who had a ministry in France and would be married shortly. And if that weren't a kick in the face, the classic "I hope we can still continue as friends" closing line sealed the deal with the kiss of death. I was dumped with a capital *D* and had no relationship to look forward to—whether real or imagined. Just as I finished the letter, an old '60s song by the Tremeloes came on the radio:

Here comes my baby
Here she comes now
And it comes as no surprise to me
She's with another guy.

Here comes my baby
Here she comes now
Coming with a love, a love that's oh so fine
That never will be mine
No matter how I try.

This was going to be a rough day.

I went through that day in a depressed stupor, treating patients with my slowly healing and still painful wrist by rote memory and mechanics. My mind was spinning with questions about God's plan and judgment. I had imagined in my fantasy world that it seemed so right for Joan to be my wife. Everything I was doing, every decision I had been making in regard to my behavior, was done in order to be godly enough for God to bless the arrangement. I'd made a point of not dating any Greek girls, and I was keeping my friendship with Nehama platonic for this very reason. I wouldn't be back in the United States for another one and a half years. Would I need to wait to look for a wife until then? After being out of circulation for close to three years? Maybe I was destined for a lonely life.

An elderly lady came into my office for a treatment; she must've been in her seventies. She looked me over and asked what was wrong with me.

"Got dumped by a girl," I told her matter-of-factly.

She looked me in the eye, pointed her finger at me, and said, "Look, fella, girls are like buses; there's another one coming every ten minutes."

That truth hit me like a fresh aftershave. Yes! There was hope for me! Maybe Nehama—she was warm, friendly, smart, and attractive. I loved her ethnicity and her attitude about life. Could I—would I—marry someone who was Jewish?

I was so upset about Joan's rejection I began to feel that pursuing relationships the way God prescribed in the Bible was getting me nowhere.

Nehama and I had talked about Christianity—actually in a peculiar way. One time we were talking about sex and where our relationship might lead.

"If you want to make love," she stated, "of course we can."

For a guy who had grown up being accustomed to complete rejection from girls, her matter-of-fact reply was a startling and welcome invitation!

Pondering the relational and biological implications of her statement, I asked her, "Why do you say that?"

"Well, unlike us religious Jews, you Christians think it's OK to have sex before marriage. So, if you want, that's all right."

Her indictment hit me like an avalanche of guilt. She associated moral laxity with my Christianity! And I was trying to convince her of the truth of my faith! This was not a great foundation for any type of debate with her. I would have something to prove to her, and to myself, about the truth of Christianity affecting my behavior if this relationship was to have any future.

One weekend, Nehama suggested that we go visit a friend of hers in Jerusalem for Yom Kippur, the annual Day of Atonement for Jews. It consists of spending an entire day fasting and going to a service to ask forgiveness for all the sins you did that year. "You won't be allowed to go to the service," she explained, "but you can spend the day walking around the city during that time."

After arriving at the Jerusalem bus station the morning before Yom Kippur, Nehama and I walked along the sidewalk to the main street. I spotted a sign that said "Garden Tomb." I realized this was the traditional site where Protestants say Jesus was buried and rose from the dead, as opposed to the church-enclaved site I had previously visited. While she was chatting with some friends who had met us at the station, I felt an impulse to walk down to see the tomb and the stone that was rolled away.

"So, this is where it all really started," I said to myself as I stared around in the tomb and looked at the giant rock. There was no denying this place existed and that *someone* had been in there. There was a small scattering of pilgrims, humbly walking about, soaking in the significance of this place. Some were singing hymns, others were praying, but most were just absorbing and reflecting on their relationship with God. I walked back up the path out of the garden, and Nehama and her friends hadn't even missed me; they were all joyfully gabbing away.

I looked around at the amazing and contrasting panorama. Down below us was the place where a man claimed to conquer sin and death by dying on a cross and coming back from the dead. Just above us was a bustling bus station with people coming and going about their own daily business—as were the shop vendors nearby, hustling potential customers to make a living. Right by my side were scores of pedestrians, absorbed in their usual activities, and walking around my Jewish friends, who were here to try to receive forgiveness by some ritual not even prescribed in their own Bible.

I was witnessing the actual crux of existence—why Jesus came here and its implications. He died and rose from the dead, and since then, people have been doing for centuries since exactly what I was presently witnessing this very moment: ignoring, rejecting, or having His actions change their lives. There seemed to be no fourth option, and here I was with a group of people who had chosen options 1 and 2.

The next day was Yom Kippur. We were staying in the Jewish Quarter, and the streets were as quiet as a library on a Friday night. Everyone was at home either fasting or pretending to fast or at a temple service—everyone, that is, except me. I left the solemnity of the Jewish Quarter to partake of the atmosphere of the Muslim and Armenian Quarters. The sights and smells of these narrow and meandering streets led me back to the amphitheater of the Damascus Gate, which was fully crowded with activity.

Among the sounds of vendors, chickens, and engines, I could hear some choral singing at the top of the steps. I worked my way up there and discovered a group of people singing hymns. There were about four rows of about ten people each, led by a director who was quite focused and attentive. They were singing in a language I didn't understand; the sign behind them looked Northern European or Scandinavian. Their pale complexions denied any Mediterranean blood. These people were obviously pilgrims who had come all this way from their native land to see these biblical sites.

I watched them as they passionately sang a cappella renditions of hymns I had learned at the Baptist church. I glanced around the crowd; some people were mocking them, and some were looking at them with disdain. Others were trying to sell them some chintzy trinkets, while most of the pedestrians simply ignored them and went about their business. And here I was, watching them worship God and observing the entire scenario.

These singers were making a statement about their faith to the watching world, and I was simply a spectator. Was I always to be a simple outsider to committed pilgrims, or would I be identified with those who mocked or ignored them? Was I perpetually to be a member of what I would contradictorily call the Nonjoiner Society? I felt something stir inside of me; I had an urge that it was time to decide who I was going to be associated with. I worked my way through the crowd and stepped up to one of the choral rows, joining *my* people in "Amazing Grace." I realized that, even though we were singing in different languages and I knew absolutely nothing about these people, they were still *my* people. This was whom I had decided to cast in my lot with.

After singing a few songs, we all hugged each other, and one of them said to me, "See you in heaven." I felt rejuvenated; I knew I was being reunited with my spiritual family again.

CHAPTER 34

Star Eyes

—♫—

MY FIRST REAL EXPOSURE TO Islam came during the last month of my time in Israel. In order to see some of the sites—such as the tombs of Abraham, Isaac, and Jacob and their wives—I'd have to go to Hebron, a town that was a hotbed of contention at the time, as Jewish families were trying to establish settlements in this Muslim-populated area. It was not the safest of places to visit. During my first bus ride into the area, I had sat next to an intriguing Hasidic Jew who had emigrated from New York in order to return to the land of his people. He spoke earnestly of his desire to be part of this mission of resettlement in the homeland. A few days later, I saw an article in the *Jerusalem Post* that he had been shot by Arab militants. Just like that. Anger was in the air, and you could feel it as soon as you started walking the streets.

Being an American during the Reagan years, I seemed to be the focus of attention for both sides of the Arab-Jewish relations. Everyone wanted my opinion on the matter, with each person questioning me appearing to search for validation for his or her cause more than my opinion. I think the fact that my family was Greek made me even more of an objective source of information, as both opposing sides were on good terms with their Hellenistic neighbors.

As I walked along the meandering, narrow streets to check out the de rigueur and ubiquitous souvenir shops, an Arab guy about my age started a conversation with me. He wanted to show me around town and seemed genuinely interested in getting to know an American. I let Hassan be my guide for a while, and he even allowed me to go into a couple of mosques to let me observe the goings-on inside.

"I was able to visit the Dome of the Rock in Jerusalem," I mentioned to Hassan.

"You mean the place where Abraham offered to sacrifice Ismael? It's very beautiful."

"Ismael? I thought the Bible says that Abraham took *Isaac* to be sacrificed."

"Oh no!" exclaimed Hassan. "Your Bible may say that, but it is wrong. Your Bible has been corrupted over the centuries. That is why Muhammad had to get a new revelation of truth. That is why we need the Koran."

"But what about Jesus?"

"Well, He was the last great prophet before Muhammad."

"Then, why did He have to die on the cross?"

"Oh, He didn't die then; someone else took His place."

"Where did you hear this?"

"In our schools, of course. Everyone knows this. That's what's in the Koran."

"How do you know the Koran is right?"

"Why, because Muhammad said it is, of course!"

In just these few swirling moments of conversation, I understood the eternally wide gap between Christians and Muslims. How could I approach the topic when we had such opposite opinions? Either the Bible was true or the Koran was; there was no room for compromise. So, you have the Jews stopping at the Old Testament, the Christians adding the New Testament, and the Muslims adding on a further edition with the Koran. I recalled something one of the Centurions in Rome used to tell me: "You can be sincere, but you can also be sincerely wrong." Somewhere, someone's got to be on the wrong side of this equation. For me to sit there and explain the historicity and accuracy of the New Testament to a guy who was surrounded by a web of culture and customs that declared the exact opposite of what I believed seemed like putting an eyedropper full of red dye into the Pacific Ocean; the impact would be infinitesimally small.

As I departed from my friend, I realized that at least I knew where I stood with the Muslim world, and I decided I'd have to get a Koran and read it for myself. I felt like I now had another dragon to slay before I could enter the reward of knighthood.

My time in Israel began to wind down, and I was starting to look forward to my next stage. I would finally enter the continent of Africa, with Egypt being my port of entry. I realized my time with Nehama was drawing to an end, and we were both at peace with our status. We figured that after this trip, if there was something between us, I'd come back, and we'd see what we should do about it. The maturity of our departure seemed strange, but after traveling for over a year, I had gotten used to saying "hello" as often as "good-bye." In fact, I realized that at this stage in my travels, one would invariably lead to the other. Was I destined to be subjected to a series of short and transient relationships? I realized this was part of the package of traveling; my concern was that I would get used to this setup and never be able to strike up a long-term relationship again. It's sort of like when you're used to interrupting someone, you never learn to hear a complete conversation. I saw the initial stages of an acceptance of transient relationships creeping into my psyche and behavior.

I reflect once again to lyrics in the Tom Waits song "A Foreign Affair":

A foreign affair, juxtaposed between a Stateside
And domestically occurred romantic fancy
Is mysteriously attractive due to circumstances
Knowing it will only be parlayed into a memory.

Two days before I was to leave, the news blasted through Israel: Anwar Sadat—president of Egypt and the initiator of the elusive peace accords between Israel and Egypt—had been brutally assassinated by Muslim terrorists who were against any friendship between the two countries. During the whole time I stayed in Israel, I never could fully comprehend the deep level of hatred among everyone: Muslims and Jews, Sephardic and Ashkenazi, secular and religious Jews, moderate and radical Muslims. This land, where everyone greets one another with the phrase "peace," reeked of everything except that quality. The Jews were aghast, the Muslims were angry, and I was sure the border between Israel and Egypt, which I was about to cross, was going to be a nightmare. I checked my blood pressure before I left. When I arrived—at the beginning of August—in Tel Aviv, I had been a James Taylor mellow 110/62. Living in this hotbed of hatred, I departed October 31 at 142/88. The Middle East had not been good for my health!

CHAPTER 35

It's a Pyramid Scheme!

THE PART OF THE TRIP that had actually motivated me to start this whole series of plans, mini-trips, letters of correspondence, and even traveling to Italy, Greece, and Israel in preparation had finally arrived. My initial goal was to travel through Africa by myself for a year. Having no money to initially get there, the whole plan and process of getting a job in Italy was to save enough money to traverse Africa. I had also purposely planned my itinerary by slowly traveling through countries that were progressively less sophisticated and more primitive than the previous ones in order to slow down the culture shock of living in a third-world country, which many people had warned me happened to travelers.

After ten months in Italy and a few months each in the villages of Greece and in Israel, I felt I was getting acclimated fairly well to traveling on the cheap. I had cut down my traveling weight to around twenty pounds, a workable amount. Since I would be in Africa during its sunny and dry season, I discarded my sleeping bag in favor of simple mosquito netting.

During this part of the trip, I'd have to figure out when to travel alone and when it would be advisable to link up with another traveler for safety, companionship, or cost reasons. My eyes had been opened to the pitfalls of small-group traveling when I had been hitching a ride in Central Greece. A guy in an old VW van picked me up. Impressed with the van (since I had a similar one back home), I asked him how long he'd been using it.

"Oh, about four months—two since the deal."

"What was 'the deal'?"

"The one I made with my best friend when we started traveling together," he replied.

"After about two months together, we decided we would either kill each other, continue traveling together—but as bitter enemies—or split up as friends and see the rest of Europe by ourselves, continuing to consider each other as friends and acting, upon our return back to the States, as if nothing had happened. We chose the last option."

This guy looked and appeared fairly normal, so I didn't feel like I had to jump out of the van or anything like that. I guessed that just traveling on the road for a while, especially with the duties of daily finding a cheap place to sleep and eat, must take its toll.

As any traveler quickly learns, there are basically two ways to travel: quick and expensive or slow and cheap. Most people who go to Africa for just two weeks of vacation spend more than I did the entire year I was there. Why? Because they chose comfort over experience. This is not either good or bad, just a trade-off. Because I had time on my side, I had to think of the trip in terms of a marathon—never spending too much and conserving as much money as possible. Each dollar I saved meant I could travel that much longer. If I lived on five dollars a day, I could travel twice as long as if I lived on ten dollars a day. Saving a buck fifty by living in a fifty-cent fleabag dump instead of a two-dollar hostel for over a month meant I could travel an extra month.

The same went for food. Since there was no middle class in Africa, eateries were geared to either well-heeled Europeans or dirt-poor locals. There was nothing for the average guy, as there *was* no average guy. The wisdom and necessity of a middle class in society was abundantly clear. This was no demographic lecture; this was real day-to-day living. In order to fulfill my traveling goals, I'd eat in the cheapest of the cheap diners, where for two to three dollars a day, I could have three meals that, while not being exactly square, were at least perpendicular. Armed with my guidebook *Africa on the Cheap* by Geoff Crowther, I found a way to sleep, eat, and travel on not just a shoestring, but on the tips of the shoestrings. The challenge to travel with more and more frugality became intoxicating—and at times almost deadly.

I soon learned that every traveler who comes to Africa has one of a few basic reasons. Many come simply looking for adventure; they want to go on a safari, see some exotic sight, or travel on some *National Geographic* type trek. Others come just to get away from Western society. They want to escape from something or someone—usually themselves, but they haven't realized that part yet. The last, and certainly not smallest group of travelers, are looking for either the best drugs in terms of hash, marijuana, or whatever or the most sex with the largest selection of African (or fellow traveling white) women who could be found. Most of the people I linked up with were predominately Australian, with their motivations comprising a mix of the above. The collection of adventurers, hedonists, sociopaths, and potheads in whose hands I would place my hope, faith, trust, and fate on these travels would be fascinating, exciting and eye-opening.

CHAPTER 36

Arabian Nights

"Vultures, vultures everywhere," warned the debonair Moroccan as he picked the pocket of the unassuming and naïve Englishman in the movie classic *Casablanca*. That one short scene typified my entrée into the Egyptian world of gypsies, tramps, and thieves—or as Aladdin said in the Disney movie, "It's barbaric, but hey, it's home!"

My residence in downtown Cairo was a fifty-cents-a-night place called the Golden Hotel, which included a mattress, shower, and seatless toilet. Besides its usefulness as a place to sleep, these quarters were where I could meet with other travelers who would come and go and, therefore, give me the latest news on where to eat in town, what the best sites and cities were to visit, and what to watch out for in terms of safety. The general rule slowly emerged that the more cheap and funky the dive, the better the environment for finding good advice from travelers who knew their way around the sketchy side of the world.

"The buses here are *nuts*," advised one Aussie in the adjoining room. "First of all, all of the numbers are in Arabic, so you have to stare at the front of the bus just long enough to figure out if it's the number of the bus you want before it runs over you. Then, the buses in town never completely stop; they just slow down to a roll, while people jump off and on."

Sure enough, as I walked through the streets of Cairo, I witnessed people pouring out of and into the moving buses. Once I even saw a poor guy in a flowing white galabia catapult out of the bus, vainly try to control his breakneck pace, and ultimately crash into a streetlight. Poor guy!

"What you've got to watch out for," my confidant, whose name was Jeff, cautioned, "is that when you jog along the bus in order to hop aboard, some guy will run alongside with you. Just then, as you're about to get sucked into the vacuum-packed sea of humanity, this guy will slide his hand into your pocket and steal your wallet or passport while you are being driven away from him. You'll be too tightly stuffed to get out and follow him. It happened to a guy I traveled with."

I learned quickly to put toilet paper in my front pockets while keeping my essentials safely tucked in my pant legs. I suckered one guy as I got on a bus, and I caught another pickpocket red-handed as I was in a crowded falafel bar. The fascinating part of that whole scenario was that the little punk whose hand I grabbed and bent backward (a nice, painful lesson) showed absolutely no sign of shame or regret. He had a sheepish expression that seemed to say, "Oh well, better luck next time." Those guys were pros!

It seemed all of the Arabs viewed me as a target of some sort. If I asked anyone for directions, I'd immediately be asked for *baksheesh*, a bribe, to appease whomever I talked to. Countless times, I'd be welcomed into a kiosk for tea or conversation, only to be lulled into either buying something or at least paying the guy for spending time with me.

One day, I decided to take a trip through Alexandria to the historic town of Mersa Matruh, where the famous World War II Battle of El Alamein occurred. I arrived at the train station early in the morning to catch my ride up north to Alexandria, from where I'd take a bus ride along the Mediterranean coast.

With ticket in hand, I went up to the train, where I approached the man at the cabin and asked, "Alexandria?"

"Yes, Alexandria! Come in!"

I worked my way in and found a seat. Not quite sure the guy at the entrance understood me, I asked my fellow passengers, "Alexandria? Yes?"

"Yes! Yes! Alexandria! Sit down! Sit down!"

They all smiled.

As the train started rolling, I settled into the comfortable seat, gently catching up on the sleep I had missed to make this early-morning train ride. About an hour into the ride, the train glided into a stop. It was some town on the way up north, and people started getting on and off.

Just to satisfy my traveler's paranoia, I leaned out the window and asked the first guy I saw, a young and pleasantly smiling Arab boy, "Hey! Is this train going to Alexandria?"

Beaming with delight, he pointed ahead and said, "Hello, American! Yesssssssss! You are going to Alexandria! Good morning."

Just then a Westerner walked by. He turned to me. "Did I hear you say you want to go to Alexandria?"

"Yes!" I answered with joy and relief to hear a familiar accent.

"Well, good man, you're going in the wrong direction. You've got to get off and take a train going north. This is going to Luxor!"

Five Arabs and one Westerner later, I learned that—in opposition to Christianity—in the Arab world, a man's word means nothing...at least if talking to a non-Muslim.

"Life is cheap in Casablanca," I thought.

All of these lines from one of my favorite movies were popping into my mind as I witnessed the Arab worldview and lifestyle firsthand.

What grabbed my attention was the fact that the Middle East still used the donkey, that perennial beast of burden, as a major tool. While in Alexandria, Mersa Matruh, and even down in Luxor, these animals were used to pull carts, carry human passengers, and lug cargo, such as corn, wheat, boxes, and even cages of birds. Taking mincing steps, they'd trot up and down the roads, with their riders continuously beating them with a stick or whip to go faster and faster. Never complaining, they simply and stoically did their job, just as they had for the past five thousand years.

Walking along a road in Mersa Matruh as the sun was setting, I came across a couple of donkeys tied to a tree. Emaciated from a life of toil, they looked weary from a hard day's labor. Their owner was a man in his midfifties, casually sitting next to a tree, sipping his tea. I looked over the animals, nodded my head to them, and asked their owner, "How much does a donkey cost?"

"About one hundred dollars." (That was about three months' wages.)

"Why do you have them, instead of a car or motorcycle?"

"I can't afford a motorcycle. I need something to do my work for me."

"They must be very valuable to you."

"They're all I have!"

I glanced at these pitifully tired animals, standing with their eyes closing in fatigue, too tired to even eat.

"How do you reward them for their work?"

"I let them sleep at night."

"I let them sleep." That was the reward for twelve hours of slavery. I looked again at the tired beasts of burden. Each one had a horizontal line across its shoulders and a vertical line along its spine. It looked just like a cross! No wonder Jesus rode one of these through Jerusalem. He was the humble servant of humanity! Why else would this be here?

Not only is animal life expendable, but so is humanity. While using a donkey-cart ride as my taxi to the battlefield of El Alamein, with a young boy as my driver, another lad started running toward me. With postcards in his hands, he was trying to sell me a couple souvenirs or at least get a little baksheesh for his troubles.

Jogging alongside us, he raised his cards and trinkets. "Mister! Mister!" he yelled at me. Armed with a rubber hose, my driver whipped the donkey harder to outpace him, but the boy kept up. "Mister! Mister!" he kept yelling at me, grabbing the side rail of the cart. This kid was a hard sell; he wanted me to buy something. Not only did he want my money, but he really didn't care if he got it through a sale. Undeterred by my lack of funds, he started grabbing for my camera and day pack! Suddenly, my driver stopped whipping the donkeys, and without breaking stride, turned around and whipped the junior salesman. After about four or five hits, the young lad fell away into the dust.

People thought differently here.

After about a month, I started feeling worn down by always being the local target. As soon as I'd enter a main street, I'd be surrounded by a crowd of locals, each holding some treasure wrapped in newspaper. Very meticulously and ceremonially, they'd unwrap a dirty and chipped alabaster carving of some god or insect, shove it up to my face, and start to bargain: "Very rare! Thirty Egyptian pounds."

"No, thanks."

"Ten."

"No, thanks."

"Two."

"No, thanks!"

"You want to exchange moooney? I give good price."

I'd just keep walking…

"Want to buy good hashish?"

It's easy to feel like you have a giant target on your back that says "steal from me" when you're a Westerner. You hear stories from other travelers of locals planting joints or other drugs in travelers' jackets, pockets, or backpacks, and then reporting them to the police for a reward. Meanwhile, the unsuspecting sojourner gets thrown in jail for who knows how long. I decided it was time to start being a bit more wary and travel as inconspicuously as possible so as not to look like a rich American.

I started taking the absolutely cheapest means of transportation, both to save on my expenses and to not stand out among preying Egyptians. I took the third-class train from Alexandria back to Cairo and sat on a wooden bench among the Bedouins with chickens and vegetables. A young boy with a tray of soft drinks would come through the doors every once in a while, yelling "Peps! Peps!" as he tried to sell us a lukewarm soda.

About a third of the way along the ride, I took a look outside my window. In the distance, I could see the whirling of a dust storm, slowly twisting in our direction. By my calculations, it looked like in about five to ten minutes, our train and the flying sand were going to be intersecting, and the prospects didn't look too pretty. Since I was wearing contact lenses at the time, I figured my best chance was to put on sunglasses for at least some protection and push up the window next to me to give me the best chance to save my eyes from the irritation of a lifetime.

I immediately started trying to pry loose the window that had probably been in the down position since Nasser was president. Looking in the distance, I could see the storm slowly working its way to meet with us. Time was running short, but I continued persistently shaking, jiggling, and jimmying the levers.

The storm was maybe a minute away from hitting our cabin. The other passengers didn't seem at all interested in raising the windows; they just put shawls over their heads and huddled over their animals, with the soft-drink guy coming through yelling, "Peps! Peps!" one last time.

I kept fighting as hard as I could with the stuck window; just as the storm was about to impact, I could feel the levers give way…I was able to push the window all the way up! The only problem was the window frame had absolutely no glass in it! No wonder no one else bothered! Time to hit the floor along with everyone else…

The storm hit the train and spun around inside the cabin like some giant sandblasting machine, used to get rid of paint on the side of a building. For one split second, I dared to look up while I covered my face with my hands; I couldn't see the people in the bench right across from me. All I could hear was the rapid-firing sound of the sand pummeling the train, yet still barely audible through the torrential attack was the sound of the persistent young capitalist, still yelling, "Peps! Peps!" A Fellini movie was definitely in the making on this return trip.

We finally made it back, and it took me little time to recover from the journey. Soon, I was back walking around downtown Cairo, looking for an

English bookstore where I could load up on some literature for my travels down into Black Africa. I figured the deeper into the third world I got, the harder it would be to find literature to stimulate my mind.

"What are you looking for?" the voice behind me inquired. I turned around, and it was a young, handsome Egyptian, beaming and friendly, just about my age."

Waiting for the setup of some sort of sale, I just mumbled, "I'm looking for a bookstore."

"Oh! I'll show you a great one! Come follow me!" And he took me through a maze of narrow avenues, down some stairs, and into a store. This wasn't a bookstore; it was a perfume shop!

"Let me bring you some tea."

"No, I don't want any tea, thank you, but I could use a bathroom. Do you have one?"

"Yes, my friend. Right down that room."

What this gent described as a bathroom was packed wall to wall (and to ceiling) with old car batteries! The stench of the fluid was overwhelming! What did all of those batteries have to do with perfume?"

"See, my friend," my new host said as he brought me a brochure, "this store is a member of Rotary and Kiwanis USA. Very good reputation."

"Yes, but I'm looking for a bookstore, not perfume."

It didn't matter. He spent twenty minutes showing me various types of perfumes, refusing to take no for an answer. Finally, he shoved a tiny jar of some stuff into my hand.

"Take it."

"I don't want it."

"Only thirty Egyptian pounds."

"I *really* don't want it."

"OK, five."

"I have no use for it!"

I put it back in his hand. "Thank you, but I can't take it with me, as I'm traveling down Africa and can't carry it with me." I started to leave, but my host grabbed my arm. The smile vanished from his face.

"You must pay for using my bathroom."

"I only had to go because you filled me up with your tea! I almost choked on the battery acid."

"So, you refuse to buy any perfume?"

"No! This whole thing started when you said you were going to show me where to find a bookstore, and you haven't done that. Are you going to help me?"

He led me up the stairs, out of his store, and onto the busy street, filled with cars and pedestrians rushing back and forth. He waved his arms across the streets at all the buildings, as if conducting them, and dismissed me with "The streets are filled with your bookstores," and left me as he had found me.

I decided all interpersonal interaction would have to come from the fellow travelers I'd link up with. In Egypt, my fellow traveler consisted of one New Yorker who wanted to get away from everyone, once shouting at an intersection, *"I hate angry people."* As I'd mentioned before, people travel to the third world by themselves for unique, strange, and peculiar reasons. I stayed with him for my two weeks along the Egyptian Mediterranean, as meals and rooms tended to be cheaper for two than one. After a while, the monetary benefits started being outweighed by the aggravation of two mavericks traveling together. And we amicably went our own ways.

CHAPTER 37

My Position on Missionaries

⌥

I MET MY TRAVELING PARTNER for Kenya at the Nairobi terminal after having flown from Cairo over Sudan. (There was a civil war in Sudan at the time, and no one was allowed in.) John—who was about five foot four and was scrunched like a squinty and squatty leprechaun—was originally from Brisbane, Australia. Because they are so geographically separated from the rest of the world, Aussies around my age tend to travel for one to two years, as they realize this may be the only chance they get to see anything before they settle back into domesticity on a distant island continent separated from the rest of humanity. This fact tends to make them the best people to travel with, as they know how to stretch their money by living on a shoestring while on their sojourn.

I knew he was my kind of guy when he said he took the same flight as I did "because you nevah want to arrive somewheah when it's dahk." He'd already been to South America, "but it was too civilized fo' moiy tastes," and he was looking for a bit more "adventcha" in Kenya. Like me, he wanted to go on a safari, so while we were on the bus from the airport to downtown, we developed a plan to exchange money, find a cheap place to sleep, and locate a safari company.

We learned quickly that the best way to exchange money was through the black market, which gave 25 to 35 percent more money than the bank. Most of the exchanges were done in shops run by Indians, who tended to be the middle-class merchants of Eastern and Southern Africa. Good old President Reagan was making the dollar strong, and these countries with monopoly money wanted our currency to send home to their families in India, or they'd keep it in a safe in case they needed to make a quick escape back to their homeland if some domestic coup d'etat made their present existence perilous.

The trick to finding a good place to sleep was to discover what kind of people stayed there. If an establishment was for European travelers (which we were considered), the prices could be pretty high. If it was for locals, the prices could be dirt cheap, but these places could also be relatively unsafe, as a white guy can be considered a target for a little nocturnal mugging. We'd try to find places that were hangouts, but we would avoid those that had drugs or booze—as a fight would usually break out at those places where, as one local told us "they drag a body out once a night."

We found the perfect place; the Iqbal was where guys would meet with the local prostitutes for a hookup. The rooms themselves were fifty cents a night, without the extra fringe benefits. We stayed there long enough for us to get enough money exchanged, arrange a two-week safari, and for John to spend the night with a couple of the ladies in a prearranged rendezvous. Obviously, he was out for a different type of game than I and had a bigger budget! Not that I wasn't tempted, mind you. Here I was, far removed from my home and frustrated over the end results of my dead-end relationships with both Joan and Nehama. I had moral, societal, and relational reasons for not pursuing intercourse with those ladies. But here, having been dismissed by the former and who-knew-what-ed with the latter, many constraints were removed from my overt pietism and outer layer of spirituality. Eyeing the beautiful Kenyan and Somali women, the mix of availability, exoticism, and anonymity seemed strangely attractive. As Billy Crystal asked so well in the movie *City Slickers*, "If you could cheat on your wife without anyone ever finding out, would you do it?"

If I could give in to my sexual desires, without any of my friends, associates, or fellow church members finding out, why not? Who would know? Well, there was still one Person who would, and after wrestling with Him long enough, I came to the sobering and somewhat physically disappointing conclusion that He would not reward my quest for a happy marriage, let alone a safe trip through Africa, if I compromised on this test—for that was what it was. So, it wasn't for exactly righteous reasons, but there was enough faith there somewhere in the equation to get me past the immediate carnal temptations...at least the sexual ones. The one thing about traveling is you get down to basic daily functions and duties. But besides eating, sleeping, and transportation, you start getting fixated on the most peculiar things. In Italy, I was fixated on local signs, to the point where I started collecting them (keeping them in storage until I figured out how to ship them home once I returned to Rome). My favorite was one I saw on a bus that said, "No Spitting." During these African travels, I became fascinated by many of the local crafts. Makonde carvings made of ebony wood, wildly decorative cloths, fascinating batiks, and unique bracelets and chess sets started becoming an obsession with me as I tried to figure out which ones to buy and send home. Even the whole safari thing was a variation on a similar theme: fill all of your desires, be they material or adventurous.

About a week into the safari (I'll try not to bore you with the touristy parts of my travels), John sheepishly sauntered over to my tent. "You're a doctah, George, roight?"

"Well, yes, a chiropractor."

"This isn't exactly your specialty, but I need yo' help. I think I've got the clap."

Sure enough, those lesions you either laugh at or gag at when you see them in your pathology-class slides were right there in living color. John definitively had gonorrhea, so I told him that after the safari, I'd walk him over to a local free clinic for a shot of penicillin. Suddenly, I felt God looking over my shoulder, with His arms folded like Mr. Clean, smiling the exact same way: "Follow me, and I'll take care of ya, kid."

The safari in itself was enjoyable in the sense that I finally got a chance to see so many animals in their home environment. They had a hardier and leaner look than the domesticated ones that we see at the zoo. Something about the hunt makes you stronger. I could relate to that.

One time while driving around, the van got stuck in the mud, and we all had to get out and push. The van spun out of the muck, and all of the guys got back in, except me, having taken a spare moment to relieve myself on a nearby bush.

"Get out of there, Harris! Get in here! *Now!*"

I couldn't figure out what the fuss was all about, but I meandered back to the van. Just as I passed the bush, I saw two panting lions taking in the shade!

Our guide told us that if a lion has recently eaten a big prey, it may not eat for several days. Judging by their satiated look, I realized that it was not my time. Further pressing my luck, I took a couple of pictures and quietly scurried past the king of the forest.

Postsafari travel with John consisted of journeying along the coast to Malindi, up to the northern border, and enjoying the pleasures of the Indian Ocean and Indian food. We met up with a pair of Dutch girls our age and were impressed by their hearty attitude about traveling.

There are a number of ways of creating a pecking order with fellow travelers. One is by what you'll eat. As John would say, if a novice sees a fly in his bread, he'll take the fly out; a seasoned traveler will eat around the fly; a veteran will just eat the fly with the bread; and a hardened traveler will ask for the fly in the bread for the extra protein!

The other criterion of your traveling caliber is the weight of your backpack. Obviously, the heavier the weight, the more you need, and therefore the less of a real traveler you are considered. John and I had gotten into a contest to see how light we could each get our loads to be. We had gotten rid of everything that wasn't absolutely essential. Before my trip to Africa, I had replaced my sleeping bag with a mosquito net, but now I got rid of my washcloth, and we'd each even broken our combs and toothbrushes in half in order to get the weight down. No matter where you are, and no matter what the circumstances, pride is still there!

We were pretty impressed with ourselves, as we'd gotten our necessities down to fifteen pounds each. (My Bible and camera were my biggest weights.) That was until we met the two ladies. They had twenty pounds of baggage *between* them. Knowing what it had taken to get to our weight, we felt completely outclassed and stood in awed admiration.

After the safari, I took John to the local free clinic, and then I invited him to stay with me and visit my missionary friends in the suburbs of Nairobi. "No, thanks, mate." He smiled. "Gotta keep movin'. Maybe we'll meet up again. Ya never know."

I was excited to finally meet up with Les, Ron's friend, who was a member of the missionary group the Navigators. We had corresponded by mail, and he seemed enthused about having me there. I felt I had seen all the sights of Kenya I wanted to see, having done quite of bit of overland traveling with John, and I was ready for a change of pace.

I grabbed a local bus to a small suburb on the outskirts of Nairobi. The bus system, like Egypt's, consisted of slow, rolling pauses, with people jumping on and off at the right time (or else!). I was let off at a little apartment and was greeted by a couple of Kenyans about my age, Karega and Matu. Warm and sincere, they led me into the living room where I saw firsthand an example of what the Navigators believed. They used a term I had never heard before, called *discipleship*.

"I became a follower of Jesus Christ through Les and his friends Greg and Steve, who live here," Karega explained. "We've lived here with them since we became Christians. That way, we learn what it means to live day to day as a believer in Christ, and eventually I will move out and do the same thing for someone who I will bring to faith in Christ."

I was stunned by the simplicity of this concept: sharing one's life in every aspect so others could catch what it really meant to be a Christian. Les and his friends modeled what it meant to live the faith in all its practical terms. This made much sense to me, as what bothered me about most of the Christianity I'd been accustomed to was that it was taught—well and good—but never seemed to be lived out and shared. This Navigator thing seemed to make a lot of sense. I wanted to be like Karega and Matu, people who were filled with the love of God and wanted to pass it on through being a living example and embodiment of Christ to someone else.

Greg and Steve eventually entered the room and explained that neither one of them had set out to be long-term missionaries, but after going on a few similar trips for two to three months, they felt they wanted to dedicate their lives to "making disciples for Christ."

There was that word again, *disciple*. I'd gone to church a long time, and by this time, I had read a lot of the Bible as well. In fact, I had started reading all the way through the Bible a few months earlier and was determined to complete it before returning home. No one Stateside had ever made a big deal about being a disciple of Jesus. I was always just told to get people to believe in Jesus and then get them to church. Fascinating.

Even more interesting was my first meeting with Les—and subsequent ones as well. Since getting to know his buddies and with him being an acquaintance of my longtime buddy Ron, I had expected him to be a similar type of guy: friendly, passionate, and winsome. Instead, I found someone who seemed a bit distant, perfunctory, cold, and self-absorbed. It seemed like every time I brought up some topic concerning Christianity, he would get into an argument with me. After a few sessions like this, I was surprised to admit to myself that I just didn't like this guy!

He was kind enough to let me stay for a couple of weeks in his home and use one of the bunk beds, but I rarely saw him, as he was always off to a meeting or something. The other American missionaries helped me figure out how to get around town, while Karega and Matu wasted no time in befriending me. They took me to the movie theater to see movies like *Raiders of the Lost Ark*, while giving me the lowdown as to what parts of town to stay away from at night. What was bewildering to me was that these converts seemed to exemplify the love of Christ embarrassingly more fully than the missionary himself.

I didn't dare say anything to these guys about my opinion of Les while staying with them. All I could figure was that he must be an incredible teacher, able to separate his disagreeable personality from his lessons, or that maybe something was just wrong with me.

CHAPTER 38

The Magic Bus

ONE DAY, I DECIDED IT was time to buy some souvenirs to send home before I moved on to my next destination. I was in the downtown area looking at all the trinkets, carvings, and paraphernalia when I became aware of a peculiar struggle within myself. I was suddenly struck with the irony of how my spiritual pilgrimage was turning into a shopping spree. It just seemed to be the antithesis of what I had initially intended. However, I shrugged off the feeling and kept purchasing various local crafts that attracted me.

On my way out of a shop, I walked beside an enclosed apartment complex, one that had a central patio surrounded by three sides of a two-story building. As I looked up, I was drawn to the beauty of a lovely young lady. Her high cheekbones; large, luminescent eyes; light-brown skin; and lithe build told me she was from Somalia. Fascinated, I found myself walking up the stairs to her place as she was putting up the laundry on a clothesline.

She glanced at me when I approached and gave me a shy, sweet smile before quickly turning back to her laundry. Strangely attracted, I easily struck up a conversation with her, as if we had been friends all of our lives.

I found out Mailiki had been born and raised in Somali but had to move to Nairobi when the civil war broke out the past year. She worked and was struggling to make ends meet. I was captivated by the gentle lilt of her voice, her sweet gestures as she put each garment on the line, and how she graciously carried herself. Observing her, I felt strong animal instincts; I was strangely attracted to this exotic lady.

As the remaining clothes dried, we went into her apartment to fold and put away her laundry. Her place was clean and spare and had an enticing simplicity to it. As I looked around and listened to her subtle, light voice, I felt a strong pull toward her. Strong feelings of lust boiled inside me, and I unapologetically enjoyed the sensation as we timidly sauntered toward each other and gently embraced and caressed each other.

In the midst of all this, I realized this was the opportunity I had previously decided against. Here was a beautiful and willing lady wanting to fulfill the desires of my rapidly warming flesh, and, what the heck, I was a man and here was my chance for a real African experience. I was enjoying every minute of the chase when I felt the gleaming look of God—in the form of Mr. Clean again, looking at me with his arms folded. That—along with the image of having taken John to the free clinic for a venereal disease treatment—quickly sobered me up, causing me to break off the completion of our afternoon delight like I had been doused with a bucket of cold water.

Gathering myself and my purchased articles together, I walked with Mailiki to the balcony of her apartment. As we parted, her veneer of charm and sweetness disappeared; she suddenly exuded a harsh, pouty, disdainful aura. I was startled by the sudden change in her demeanor, and I wondered if I was simply suddenly seeing her with a more sober eye. I gently grasped her hand and falsely promised to see her again, as she sneered a farewell.

I suddenly flashed back in my mind to my days in chiropractic school when I carpooled with Wayne, a true ladies' man. Often was the morning when, picking him up on the way to class, I'd knock on the door for him, wait a few seconds, and he'd finally open, pie-eyed, disheveled, and wrapped in a sheet whispering, "I'll be ready in five minutes," while in the background, I could see in his bedroom his latest conquest still asleep.

One time while driving to school, I couldn't contain my curiosity. "Wayne, you seem to sleep with every woman you meet. Young ones, older ones, blondes, brunettes, tall, short…have you ever slept with a woman that was just plain ugly?"

He soberly looked me right in the eye for a split second while driving. "I've never slept with an ugly one, but I sure have woken up to a lot of them."

Wanting is always greater than having.

Still reeling from the mix of passion, lust, sobriety, shame, and regret (for the temptation or for not completing the equation?), I wobbled over to the bus stop that would take me back to my Christian mission—the irony of which was not lost on me at the time. With my hands loaded with purchases and my blood still hot from the pursuit, I contemplated what this trip to Africa had degenerated into: a self-serving expedition.

As the bus pulled up, I took my wallet out to pay the bus driver and returned it to my waist belt. This belt was an early version of a fanny pack. It was a small pouch with a thin strap to tie around my waist, and it contained my recently converted money, along with my passport and other ID that I had used during the day and had been too lazy to return to my pant-leg pocket.

I climbed into the sardine-packed bus, standing in the crowded aisle, as the bus rumbled on toward my destination. Holding onto my bags of souvenirs with both hands, I suddenly felt something strange and foreign; someone's hand was feeling around for my pouch, trying to untie it while my defenseless hands acted as helpless observers. The bus was so tightly packed I couldn't put down my parcels; I was trapped and hamstrung in this squeezed mass of humanity. As the hand clawed along my belt, I kept hammering my elbow against the pickpocket to try to dissuade him. After a few hard hits—even tightly pressing his hand hard against my hip—I felt I had finally chased him away.

The bus slowed down for one of its semistops, and while I was observing even more passengers climbing aboard, I suddenly felt my belt whoosh off my waist. I'd been lifted! My entire collection of money, tickets, and ID were gone with the Nairobi wind.

All of the blood rushed out of my face. Within the wink of an eye, my trip was over, having left me at the last bust stop. It was agonizing; I had known all the warnings and had been prepared for them. Still, I was impotent to stop the theft and had been completely and irrevocably robbed of all of my important possessions. What could I do?

"Help!" I shouted out for anyone to hear. "Someone just robbed me! *Somebody here help me! Help! Help! Help!*"

The sea of ebony faces stared at me. At first, I couldn't discern whether anyone was listening to me or cared about my predicament. But as I kept yelling, I could sense a gradual growing tide of concern.

"What happened to you?" a man a few feet away asked.

"*Someone stole my wallet. Please help!*" I screamed with all that was within me.

Completely helpless and vulnerable, amid the sea of confusion and humanity, I cried out, "Oh, God, please help me! I really need you!"

A slow hum started drifting through the bus, and the energy of agitation was filtering to the front. The bus driver looked up to glance at me through his mirror. "Who took your wallet?"

Exasperated, I tried to be patient and helpful. "I don't know! I just know someone took it, and he left at the last stop."

Or had he? Suddenly, like an urging from God, a thought came to me that maybe the thief *hadn't* made his escape yet. There was one way to find out.

"Sir!" I shouted to the bus driver. "Ask the people at the doors if anyone got off the bus at the last stop." The driver shouted something in Swahili, and a rumbling of voices answered. Suddenly, the mumbles grew into a series of declaratory shouts.

"They say no one got off! He's still on the bus!" pronounced the driver. He spoke in a forceful voice, in Swahili again, to all the passengers. Immediately, the front and back doors were slammed shut by the driver's simple push of a button, and all the seated passengers leaned over to close the windows with militaristic and determined efficiency. The bus driver shouted something again, and this time, the people started to howl with joy.

"What's going on?" I asked hopefully.

"I'm taking the whole bus to the police station!" the driver joyously declared. "We'll have the police frisk every passenger one by one until we find who stole your wallet." With that, my ingenious driver made a 180-degree hairpin turn and floored the pedal toward the Promised Land of justice.

I couldn't believe what was happening. Inside the bus, the crowd of passengers was vociferously ecstatic over the justice of finding and punishing a criminal. Building up into an ecstatic frenzy, the people started chanting in unison, "One by one! One by one!" The fervor was infectious; their pent-up hostility and frustration over living in this crime-ridden area was about to be released on this thief. The pitch grew in volume, intensity, and speed as we headed up a side street. We were arriving at the station!

The entire bus exploded like a football crowd cheering a game-winning touchdown as we pulled into the parking lot. A pair of policemen, gently tapping their billy clubs against their palms, seemed to be waiting for us, as the driver turned off the engine. He turned to all of us. "I'm locking everyone in here while I go talk to the policeman," he feverishly explained as he jumped out of the bus onto the pavement.

The policemen, sharply dressed in khaki shorts and short-sleeved safari shirts, nodded and smiled with approval, tapping the clubs more rapidly as they started understanding the situation.

The front door cautiously opened. "Each person comes out one at a time to be examined by the police," warned the determined patriot. As the first few people descended from the bus to be frisked, someone shouted, "Look! The wallet is on the ground!" A circle gathered around the precious treasure. The frightened pickpocket had obviously dropped the evidence. In joyful but hesitant belief, I stooped down to grab the prize.

"Open it up! Make sure your money and passport are still in there!" The man next to me shouted. As I unzipped my pouch and saw my unmolested wallet and passport, I knew God had showered His grace on an unworthy sinner. "*Praise God!*" I shouted out loud, as the whole bus again responded with celebratory joy.

The bus was vibrating with a victorious cheer as we returned to our regular route, and people got off the bus with beaming good-byes, as if they were departing after a World Series victory. As I was stepping off at the stop by my apartment, the setting sun seemed to shine brighter and the color of the sky seemed clearer; I felt like life was brand new, with a fresh beginning.

My friends inside were simply amazed at my experience; Matu was beaming with joyful praises, and everyone else was smiling in happy bewilderment, while Les was being his usual unemotional self at the whole scenario.

That night, as I lay in my bed and wrote in my journal of my day's affairs, I numbly stopped writing down my thoughts, put the notebook aside, and rested in thoughtful meditation. In the silence of the evening, an uncontrollable sensation slowly and gradually came over my entire body. I was building up a vibrating sweat, only it wasn't from a fever or food poisoning. I was experiencing an overwhelming sense of guilt, regret, remorse, and dread, and it was consuming my entire body.

On this cool, dry night, I was shaking with febrile intensity because of the my conviction over how I was mocking God's love, grace, and provision. All I had been doing on this trip was striving for myself, and this shaking that I was experiencing was telling me that God thought that enough was enough. During this half-hour experience, I felt an indescribably deep and intimate closeness to God, yet simultaneously I felt a regretful alienation because of the darkness of my evil and self-seeking thoughts, desires, and deeds.

Like Jacob, who wrestled an evening with God and ended up walking with a limp for the rest of his life, I felt I was being pierced with conviction. It was an intimacy that was both frightening and thrilling in its sorrow and forgiveness. There was no way I could continue on my previous selfish path after feeling that experience with God. It was like I was seared with a hot iron in order to clear away the infection. All of the things that had happened that day of emotional, physical, and spiritual highs and lows happened to me for a reason, and I prayed to God, then and there, to not let me forget this searing lesson.

CHAPTER 39

Come Sunday

THAT FOLLOWING SUNDAY, I WENT with Karega to a local church. After that ordeal at the bus, I felt like I needed to get back in the spiritual swing of things, since I hadn't found a church to visit since hitting Africa. We had walked from our apartment for about three miles to a large, nondescript building. Entering the cavernous room, I notice that the place was pretty filled up. Good sign. The pastor—a white, lean, and slightly hunched man in his midfifties—greeted the congregation: "Let's worship today as if Jesus Himself were standing right here."

For the next hour, the band and singers led us in a series of passionate musical pleadings. I had been to diverse churches in my lifetime, and I could pretty well tell when the worship was contrived (which many of the times it was) or when the music was almost manipulative in its attempt to get the congregation in the right mood. This congregation sang and prayed as if they really meant it. I could feel this powerful, energetic tidal wave flow through the church that mixed love, reverence, and joy. I didn't want it to end, and I wished I could somehow bottle it and use it another time as a pick-me-up. Once again, I felt that combination of conviction and cleansing, just like I had the night of my wild bus ride.

By the time the worship part of the service had finished, I felt both spiritually exhausted and rejuvenated. No one had rolled down the aisles or done anything like bark, jump, or fall over. It was just people coming face to face with the God who loves them.

Just as gradually as the praise erupted, it now slowly calmed down, and the pastor returned to the podium. I have absolutely no recollection of the topic of his sermon, except that he was just as passionate about it as the musicians had been about the music. Shorter than a half hour, the sermon was almost an epilogue to the main novel of worshipping God.

Walking back home with Karega, I was curious about what had attracted him to Christianity.

"Before Jesus became my Savior, I had hatred toward people from other tribes: the Luo, the Luyia. Once I learned how much Jesus loved me, I can now love them. Matu, my roommate, is a Luo, and before I became a Christian, I would have hated him. Now, I love him because he is my brother."

I was fascinated by this admission. I had figured that blacks had hatred only for whites, but there were a myriad of tribal conflicts and differences that gave root to hatred between the various black groups. This was alarmingly similar to the racism between the various Jewish groups in Israel, as well as the fraternal hatred between the different sons of Abraham, which had led to the millennial fighting between Arabs and Jews. I was slowly starting to see that only a spiritual change in a person could overcome these racial and tribal differences.

Returning to my bunk in Les's room, I perused his bookshelf to see if there were any Christian paperbacks I could delve into to get me a bit more grounded in the faith. I had been reading the Bible, but besides that, my only Christian literature had been C. S. Lewis's *Mere Christianity* and *The Screwtape Letters*. I had gotten frustrated with trying to have a discussion about spiritual things with Les, as he seemed to answer everything with a Bible verse. I had mixed feelings when he kept returning my serve with a Bible forehand. I was impressed that someone could know so much about the Bible, yet I felt frustrated that I couldn't answer him. I didn't know enough of the Bible to determine if the verse he was quoting was in its proper context or was simply being used to manipulate the conversation—a technique I had seen in my old Baptist church and with the Centurions in Italy. I was determined to memorize some core verses and chew on them for a while.

I knew if I could memorize all of the members of Duke Ellington's 1941 orchestra, the starting lineups of the 1965–66 Dodgers, or the lyrics to Tom Waits's songs that my mother had mailed me, I could get some of the Bible down. But where to start?

The first book I picked up from Les's bookshelf was by the author Hal Lindsey, *Countdown to Armageddon*. I had heard of Lindsey before, as he had written the largest-selling nonfiction book of the seventies, *The Late Great Planet Earth*, which predicted how and when the world would end. Not exactly a bad conversation starter! I figured *Countdown* could be interesting, and it was. It talked about various scenarios that were going to soon take place that would result in an all-out war, which the Christians would avoid by being taken away to heaven while the rest of the world blasted away at each other. It was quite fascinating; yet the whole thought of having special future information felt a little elitist to me and the idea of being secretly and divinely escorted out of worldwide difficulty seemed like a Bible-sanctioned coward's way out.

I recalled the high-school room at my church in Inglewood; there was a painting of Jesus standing high above the world on a cloud with His arms raised, with Christians being raptured out of their cars, homes, and offices while cars and planes crashed at the absence of any drivers. The rest of the world could go to hell, but the Christians got on the one-way escape bus. That picture, and this book, just seemed a bit too much like a lazy worker who just wanted out of his job and to get home early.

Though it felt like the middle of summer to me, Christmastime was actually approaching here in Kenya. Greg and Steve invited me to a Christmas dinner with the rest of the Navigator staff. (I never figured out why Les didn't invite me.) There would be about twenty people in all, and the meal would be held at the humble home of a guy named Ron Wyatt, who was the director for the Navigators in Kenya.

I didn't know what to expect, as I'd never met an older adult missionary before. Usually I'd hung around the ones my age in Italy. I was simply stunned at how relaxed and gentle—and yet focused—this guy was when I met him. His kids seemed normal, well mannered, and obedient; he had no chip on his shoulder and nothing to prove. He seemed completely at ease with what he was doing. In essence, he was exactly what I wanted to be: completely comfortable with his faith and his life's calling. After traveling for over a year, I had finally met someone I wanted to emulate.

Ron was very interested in my travels and was patient with my questions about the Navigators. After a few minutes, he went over to his bookshelf, pulled out a paperback, and handed it to me. It was a plain-looking orange book called *Essentials of Discipleship*.

"What's this for?" I asked.

"I just think it's something you'll like. It just goes over the basics of Christianity," he responded. "One thing you'll really like about it is that it has a lot of Bible verses for you to learn, since you seem eager to do that."

I felt that I was finally on a good start with some solid guidance from the Bible. I put the book into my day pack and continued with the festivities. At the table with the desserts was a married couple about my age, Bill and Susan Green. I felt an immediate kinship with them, as we discussed our spiritual journeys. We compared notes of where we had traveled. Their eyes lit up when I told them I'd lived in Rome.

"We have a friend who did missionary work in Rome. Did you ever meet a girl named Joan Johnson?"

My heart skipped a beat. "Are you kidding? I thought at one time that I wanted to marry her!" I blurted out so loudly that just about everyone turned to look at me.

"You know she got engaged to someone, right?" they asked with trepidation.

"Yes, I know about that."

"Did you hear she had a nervous breakdown and had to leave Italy and the Centurions?"

I stopped cold. "This is news to me! What happened?"

"I don't know all of the details; I just know she had to leave and go back to the States. I know nothing about the relationship."

Why would God have these people meet me here in the middle of Africa to relay this information to me? Was this God's way of offering me a glimmer of hope about Joan or was this information closing a chapter in my life? I couldn't figure it out and told Bill and Susan how confused I felt.

"Well, if it will do any good, next time we write to Joan, we'll mention we met you and put in a good word for you." Susan smiled.

This had been an interesting Advent season. While the climate was nothing like an American (or Israeli) Christmas, I felt like God was showing Himself in ways I needed to see. I'd experienced great and deep spiritual conflict by observing part of my temperament that frightened me in its shamefulness. Materialism, sensuality, selfishness, and pride had all been manifest this past month here; yet, there was also cleansing, forgiveness, grace, adoration, and a pursuit of holiness. I'd met people who truly had a life-changing experience by meeting with God, and I felt like the Navigators had inspired me and pointed me in a positive direction.

I was ready to move on toward my next destination. Les drove me to the station as I headed toward Malawi. As I got out of the car, he extended his hand. "Even though we didn't see eye to eye on anything, I hope you have God's blessing on your trip." Impersonal to the end.

I left Kenya closer to God, thanks to some Christians, but also—once again—in spite of other Christians I had met.

CHAPTER 40

The Heart of Africa: Choose Your Partners

AWAY FROM THE SAHARA AND Islamic Egypt, as well as the well-touristed Kenya, I felt I had truly arrived in the heart of Africa when I reached Malawi. Everything here seemed like I had imagined a subtropical country should be: slow-paced, lots of cheap food and places to stay, inefficient transportation, and genteel residents.

With a place on the floor at the Government Hostel going for about twenty-five cents, a breakfast of two eggs for another quarter, mangos at a penny each, pineapples for five cents, and a chicken meal for a dollar and a quarter, I figured I could live here for well under five bucks a day. This trip was going to work out just fine. I had my dad wire me some money in Kenya just before I left, so the three hundred dollars he sent me should easily last me for a month or two, if I traveled cheaply enough.

The key to making this work was choosing to accept cheap accommodations. I'd scrimp for about a week or so, but then I'd splurge on a deluxe place (that had an actual bed) for one dollar once in a while so I wouldn't go stir crazy. For twenty-five cents, you got the privilege of sharing the floor with about fifty to one hundred other guys; if you were lucky, you'd get a foam cushion to lie down on, but you couldn't count on it. You also learned to quickly tune out the sound of a roomful of guys snoring!

The bathrooms were as Spartan as they were sticky. The first night I arrived at the house, hot and dusty from a bus ride, I walked into a shower stall, only to be greeted by a pair of green flying something or others heading straight for my face. As I bent down to avoid getting hit in the face, I looked at the floor; the welcoming committee of lizards greeted me with their split tongues jutting in and out at my naked body. I was definitely in Africa!

Still traveling as lightly as possible, I had no mirrors at this stage in the trip. Using the bathroom—or just a spigot outside somewhere—to wash myself each day, I used my fingers to guestimate where my sideburns were when I shaved. Why even bother doing things like shaving, showering, and flossing your teeth when you're in the middle of a dirty, poor third-world country where everyone looked about two weeks overdue for a good bath? Because as George Burns said in *Oh, God!* when everything around you is abnormal, do something normal. These daily routines helped me keep a sense of stability, which helped when everything else around me was completely foreign to my senses.

The goal of my stay in Malawi was to travel up to Zomba and take a trip along Lake Malawi in a steamship, visiting various villages at each stop. The gent at the house told me that the bus to Zomba came to town about three o'clock in the afternoon. I figured I'd get there about a half hour early, just to be ready in case there was a problem.

Three o'clock…half past three…a quarter to four…I looked around and noticed the bus stop wasn't too crowded. Had I arrived too late, or was this standard procedure for Central Africa? At four o'clock, I sauntered over to one of the people sitting on a bench.

"Excuse me. Is this the station for taking the bus to Zomba?"

"Yes, sir, thank you."

"Was the bus supposed to be here at three o'clock?"

"Yes, sir, thank you."

"So, it is usual for it to be late?"

"Yes, thank you."

"How late is this bus?"

"Two days, sir. Thank you. But I think it is coming today."

Sure enough, right on time—at 5:30 p.m.—the bus rolled up. Hot and sticky, I got on and looked around for a place to sit.

"Hey, George, ol' boy!"

I looked down the aisle and saw John, my traveling companion from Kenya! "Hey, ol' mate! Good to see you!" I hurried down the bus and sat next to my Aussie buddy.

"We meet again." I beamed.

"Yah neveh know, do yah?" he said with a smile. Looking at the seat across the aisle, he nodded his head at a rough-looking guy with a shaved head, covered with a bandana. The guy had high cheekbones, a hooked nose, and a giant feathered earring dangling from his right ear. (This was about fifteen years before the day this look became part of the mainstream, to say the least.)

"George, I want you to meet our traveling companion, Dave, the mad dentist! Another Aussie!"

We exchanged pleasantries. He seemed like a very agreeable sort of guy, a bit rough around the edges (who *wasn't* in this neck of the woods?) but a really gentle spirit. Like most other Aussies I'd met, he'd been traveling well over a year, so he had some great stories to tell. He'd spent most of his time in India and Central Asia. This guy looked like a perfect traveling partner.

"What brings you to Africa?" I asked.

He smiled. "We know why John's here. He got another case of the clap already!"

John blushed. "Ah, I got a shot already! I'll be as good as new in no time!"

"Back to, Dave. You've been on the road for a long time. Aren't you ready to go home yet?"

"You bet!"

"So, what are you doing here in Malawi?"

"Well," he explained as he looked out the window, "after I became a dentist, I decided to travel to Turkey, India, Pakistan...all that area. I had a great time there. Really good hash, let me tell you. I sent some home in some boxes to my girlfriend in Brisbane. The police came to her door with the packages. The dogs discovered what was in there and asked her about it. She wrote to me and said there's now a warrant out for my arrest. As soon as I set foot back home, they're going to put me away for smuggling the hashish. I'm here traveling through Africa to try to find some way to sneak back home so I can practice dentistry and get back to my girlfriend."

An STD poster child and a druggie for companions...these were the guys who were going to keep watch over me, on whom I'd depend for safety on my travels. I was ready for anything! Actually, things worked out great, as while they were smoking the local vegetation, I'd use that time for Bible reading and studying the *Essentials of Discipleship*. Once in a while, they'd ask about the Bible, but it seemed more out of a drug-induced paranoia than anything else. Anyway, the traveling accommodations worked quite well.

One of the benefits of traveling is that you end up with a lot of spare time. When I'd arrive at a town, I would search out the local bookstores for something to read. Through Africa, I worked through phases of Steinbeck, Dickens, Stevenson, C. S. Lewis, Wouk, Tolstoy, and Hemingway, while still doing my daily Bible readings. To keep my mind active, I memorized lyrics to songs my mom was sending me—mostly traditional country like "Red River Valley" and "Tennessee Waltz," as well as early rock from The Drifters and Coasters. Armed with the *Discipleship* book, I embarked on memorizing certain verses in the Bible, such as "the fruit of the spirit is love, joy, peace, patience, kindness, goodness, and self-control" (Galatians 5:22-23) or "the fear of the Lord is the beginning of wisdom" (Proverbs 9:10)

By this time, I'd also worked my way through most of the Old Testament. So far, I'd read lots about rebellions against God, people getting punished and asking for forgiveness, and then those same people reverting back to rebelling against God. Hmm. I could relate to this! The only question I had was how many times could one rebel before God said "Basta!" (to use the Italian word for "Enough!") and left you on your own…to be truly God-forsaken? I really didn't want to find out, so I figured I'd better not test God too much on that one.

After traveling together for a while, Dave decided to head in a different direction in order to get back to Australia. John and I headed up Lake Malawi in a boat to the town of Chilumba, determined to explore the inner tropics of this tiny country. Having done this a few times before in Kenya, we had learned that the best strategy was to slowly go further and further from civilization, hang out there for a while, and then find the fastest way back to the major town of transportation, which in this case was a boat to take us to the town of Zomba.

By the third day, John and I had hitched and hiked until we felt we had arrived at the outer reaches of civilization—so much so that we started wondering if we'd run out of places to find something to eat. By late afternoon one day, we were getting pretty hungry, but as we strolled along the dirt road, we couldn't find a shop of any kind. The mix of oppressive heat, humidity, hunger, and thirst was getting on our nerves; you start wondering if you should keep going forward or just head back, but you still keep going, always hoping for something.

We finally spotted a small wooden shack up ahead cozily tucked under a bunch of shady baobab trees. Approaching it, we noticed a stocky man in his fifties or sixties (I never was able to size up the ages of these Malawians), sitting in a chair, just hanging out. He warmly greeted us.

"Hello!" he shouted as he stood up. "Where are you from?"

"Hi! I'm from America, and John here is from Australia. Say, we're awfully hungry and thirsty," I said as I looked around at the vast subtropical brush and red clay. "Is there any place around here where we could get something to eat? I think we're hopelessly lost."

"You just relax right here, thank you." Our friend beamed as he went into his tiny thatched hut. "I will take care of you."

Incredulously, we strolled around the area a bit more, wondering what was in store for us. When we turned around to head back to the front of his abode, we spotted our host, standing next to a very well-laid table that he had set up, complete with chairs, a red-and-white-checkered tablecloth, plates, silverware, and a bowl full of rice and fruit. This jungle had turned into a three-star hotel—and who were we to argue?

Watching us feast on our entrée of mangos, our host smiled with pride. "How old are you?"

"I'm twenty-five, and John here is twenty-eight."

"Where are your wives and children? "

"We aren't married yet."

"Not married yet? At your age?" he asked incredulously. "Who's going to take care of you when you get older?"

John and I looked at each other quizzically. "What do you mean?"

He sat down to join us, with his elbows on the table—one hand holding his chin and the other pointing at us. "Listen, my friends," he advised. "I have five sons and two daughters. When I get too old to work, I am going to need them to support me and take care of me. I have given them life, and it will be up to them to give me a nice end of life, like I did with my father. You men are fools for not preparing for that now. You're getting too old!"

I'd never met a man before who taught me about preparing for the future like this. My own father never had. The churches I had gone to were so obsessed with the world ending within the next ten years that they seemed to feel that planning for the future was akin to "rearranging chairs on the *Titanic*" (as one of my pastors would say). Here in the middle of Nowhere, Africa, was a guy who was making a lot of sense to me. Instead of indulging myself, I needed to plan for my future, and a wife and family had better be part of it, or I just might end up alone and dependent on who knows what (or who). I felt even more determined to figure out this life so I could marry someone I could grow with and raise children with—"equally yoked" as the Bible taught.

I had seen a lot of farms throughout Africa, and all of them still used the same procedures that had worked since Moses was found in the Nile River. Get a pair of beasts of burden, hook them up to a wooden yoke and a trowel, and lead them into your field to make some rows to grow vegetation. As our host was talking to us, I pictured the contrasting scenes I'd observed. Some

farmers had a pair of oxen that moved through the dirt quite easily; others were pulled unequally by two different animals—an ox and a mule, a cow and a camel, a cow and a burro. They were all the farmer had, so he had to use them, but it sure made for difficult farming. I wanted to be pulling the load equally with my future wife, so I realized I had better know what I wanted in myself, so I could know what I wanted in a partner.

CHAPTER 41

Alone Again, Naturally

JOHN WANTED TO GO DEEPER into Central Africa, but I wanted to head back south, so we parted ways once again. Back in the town of Chilumba, I spent a couple of nights in a tiny village, strewn with mud huts and thatched roofs.

By the second day in town, I had found the local diner. For $1.50, I could get a decent meal of chicken and rice. The place always seemed to have its dozen tables packed with customers, and it seemed like a nice way to take in the local atmosphere. I was enjoying this calm and peaceful country. It was one of the very few that had been stable since gaining independence in 1966, having the same president, Hastings Banda, since its inception. I had noticed that a lot of the people here wore a button with a picture of Banda on their shirt, displaying their reverence for their venerable (born in 1896) leader. I was impressed with the citizens' loyalty; they were content working on their farms instead of driving their country into the ground with the failed social-ist economies that had killed off so many other countries, like Tanzania and Uganda.

When the waiter brought me my meal, I expressed to him my enjoyment of his country. "Mr. Banda has done a great job making this country success-ful," I pointed out as a compliment.

"Thank you, sir," the waiter politely answered.

"It's amazing he's been able to run the country so well for so long, even into his eighties!"

"Yes, sir. It's very nice. Thank you."

"Tell me," I asked, while cutting up my chicken, "is there anyone next in line to be president? What would happen in case he died?"

As if on cue, every voice in the diner suddenly stopped, all activity ceased, and I could feel every eye focused on me. All of the warmth immediately left the room, and an oppressive fear suddenly replaced the previous calm. The waiter, his face blanched, blankly stared at me with shock. A man from another table got up, came over to where I was eating, and leaned over to me while looking right into my eyes, "We are not allowed to discuss politics in this country. Please do not ask these kinds of questions ever again. Thank you."

I sincerely apologized to everyone in the tiny restaurant and finished my meal in uncomfortable silence. I had obviously hit a raw nerve. These people—surrounded by countries that had had multiple military coups, civil wars, or oppressive regimes—were trained never to discuss anything that could rock the delicate balance of their boat. Sometimes, what looks like freedom is actually a guise for a different type of subjugation. I still had a lot to learn about life. I went back to my room and rested in solitude the remainder of the day. Once again, I felt being by myself was the best option.

The next day was a Sunday, and I hadn't been to a church service since I had arrived in Kenya, so I started looking around to see if there was a church nearby.

I went up to a couple of teenagers and asked, "Is there a Christian church service here?"

The young man looked at me and blithely responded, "We'll be starting one soon." He then went around to the different huts, just like a shepherd gathering his sheep, and within about five minutes, about thirty to fifty people were gathered inside a hut with rows of wooden benches, obviously serving as pews. I couldn't tell if they had a regular service in this town or not, but by checking out this hut, I could tell that someone had obviously laid some groundwork here, and these kids knew enough about Christianity to know they should be meeting together on Sunday.

After filling up the room, he came back to get me. "We'll be having our service right now." Was he doing this just for me? The collection of teens and adolescents sang some lovely hymns in their local Chichewa language; genteel and lilting refrains lulled my soul. Then, one of the older teenagers got out a Bible and gave a subdued and straightforward reading. His sermon was understated and calm, and the kids nodded their heads in agreement.

I couldn't understand a single word they were saying. What was impressive was the fact that on this given Sunday, all over the world, people in different countries, different geographies, in different languages, with different musical styles—some in giant, fancy churches; some in humble homes; and some in thatched huts like this one—were all meeting together simply because Someone rose from the dead in order to set us free from sin and death. The universality of Christ's act and meaning struck at me like a sharp knife. Someone from somewhere in the world had cared enough to come out of his or her comfortable home all the way to this nothing part of Africa, tell the people about Jesus, and then help establish a church. And here I was just trying to see the world, for some crazy, selfish reason. What was I contributing, besides feeding my insatiable sense of adventure? Was I adding anything to this creation?

Part of me wanted to head straight back home to the United States and get on with my life. However, even if I did that, how long would it take for me to make it home? It seemed it would take almost as long to take all the buses, trains, and planes to get to the United States from this remote location as it would to continue on my adventures. I seemed destined, or trapped, into finishing this course of my life.

My next stop would be South Africa—via a railway to Blantyre, Malawi—and then I would take a plane to Johannesburg. Nothing happened immediately in this part of the world. I couldn't just travel through Zambia to get to South Africa, as they were having a civil war of their own. So flying over Zambia would be the only option.

CHAPTER 42

The Train Kept A-Rollin'

BACK IN ZOMBA, I LEARNED that a train left for Blantyre (the only town with an international airport) at six o'clock in the morning. The 180-mile railway trip was scheduled to take six hours on a steam engine—good old African transportation! This was one train trip I did *not* want to miss, so I spent the whole night at the station, sleeping underneath the ticket station. Unfortunately, the booth was nearby a government building that was hosting one of the rowdiest parties in Malawian history, so getting any sleep that night was going to be a pipe dream.

Groggy and edgy from a poor night of touch-and-go sleeping, I purchased my ticket and plopped myself into a booth on the train. Getting a few winks of sleep here and there, I figured I'd arrive in Blantyre around one to two o'clock in the afternoon, with plenty of daylight left to make it safely to the local hostel and get a much-needed night of sleep before flying out.

The train slowly chugged along, and I do mean *slowly*. Just about every thirty minutes or so, we'd stop for some unknown reason and linger around for about a half an hour. Was something wrong with the train? Was this just standard Malawi procedure? Even by African standards, things seemed to going by with an extra dash of sluggishness. I was passing the time by reading my Bible. I was still working toward my goal of reading the whole Bible while in Africa, and I figured this train ride would help me put a big dent in 1 and 2 Chronicles.

Four hours later, I looked up from my reading and glanced out the window. We didn't seem to have gotten very far. A ticket conductor walked by— an Indian, very stately in attire and serious.

"How far have we gone, sir?" I queried.

"Oh, we have a few more hours to go," he replied. "Just relax and we'll get there."

A couple more hours passed. It was about 2:00 p.m. We should have arrived by then. I flagged down the ticket man.

"We're about halfway there," he assured me.

"Shouldn't we have been there already? I'd like to get there before dark."

"Don't worry; you'll be fine," he replied as he efficiently moved on to the next car.

I'd never seen a train move so slowly in my life. I saw people walking outside, selling mangos or pineapples alongside my car, who were moving faster than we were! Was this some sort of a great practical joke? I looked around inside. I was just about the only one in here. Maybe everyone else had gotten smart and decided to abandon this heap of iron and find a speedier mode of transportation, like crawling on your hands and knees. My only problem was I had no idea where I was or how to get from here to Blantyre, so I was held hostage on this locomotive.

Late afternoon! Just how long does it take to go 180 lousy miles? The shadows were starting to lengthen. This was not a great scenario, and odds were that I'd be arriving in a bad part of town well into the evening. That could be dicey; something had to give.

With the train crawling along, my ticket man waddled up to me. "Good news!" He beamed.

"What? We're going to start moving faster than one mile an hour?"

"Very good news, sir. Another train is coming to meet us at the next station. It can take you to Malawi in just over one and a half hours, as this one has four more hours before we arrive. For just seven kwacha [seven dollars], I can sell you a ticket for that train!"

That was it! I couldn't hold back my frustration. "You mean to tell me that after already paying fifteen kwacha for a train ride that was *supposed* to have already taken me to my destination, you are now telling me I have to pay seven *more* kwacha for the privilege of arriving eight hours late?

"What is this? Some extortion racket? I've been up since five this morning and paid for a first-class train ride in order to guarantee my safe and timely arrival into Blantyre, and now you're telling me I have to pay even more money—almost half the cost of my original ticket—in order to get there at all? This is ridiculous!"

The ticket man dropped his grin and pointed his finger at me. "Sit down, and just be quiet," he sternly replied. "During this trip I have walked by and noticed you were reading the Bible. I assumed you were a Christian, and that made me very happy, as I am also a believer. I was looking forward to sitting down here with you and having a nice time of fellowship with you sharing what God has done in your life."

He looked right through my eyes. "But now, here you are making a monkey out of yourself by complaining in front of these passengers and making self-ish complaints about how uncomfortable you are. Everyone is looking at you and wondering what kind of an impatient and whining person you are. And they know you are a Christian because they see your Bible. Yes, I wanted to sit down and talk to you before, but now, because of your immature display, I want you to get away from me. You embarrass me!"

I looked around, and the passengers were all gazing at me. I felt the actions of my self-absorption cutting the bond between myself and this forth-right believer like a searing poker. I humbly apologized to the passengers and then to the ticket man. He forgave me, but he was visibly disappointed in my behavior. I felt like an ugly, spoiled American.

I changed trains and arrived just as the sun was setting in Blantyre. I threw my pack on the floor and fell into my tiny cot. I was disgusted with myself; I had let a fellow Christian down because I had demanded what I perceived as my rights. Just what *had* I learned on this trip so far? It felt like nothing had changed in me.

CHAPTER 43

Apartheid, Post-apartheid, and Just Apart

MAYBE I WOULD FIND A few more answers and some guidance in South Africa. I had a connection in Cape Town, some Emissaries about my age who seemed enthused about seeing me. Also, Tubby lived somewhere around Cape Town; this was the guy who had called me on the phone, out of the blue, a number of times when I was back home. This could be good!

The tricky part, as always, was actually getting there. As I mentioned, I couldn't go directly through Zambia and Zimbabwe via rail to South Africa, as Zambia was having some internal war going on. It was just flabbergasting to me how often this occurred in various countries. I had already learned that it was absolutely forbidden to bring outside literature into certain countries—things like *Time* or *Newsweek* magazine...let alone a newspaper like the *Herald Tribune*. Most countries' leaders did not want their citizens to know what was really going on where they lived.

I was able to figure out a way to learn about world events, though. Just about every country had a Christian Science Reading Room, and their paper, the *Monitor*—while technically a religious paper—actually had some intelligent and objective news reporting. If I could find one of these places, I'd periodically go into one of their rooms and scan the latest events, sometimes even taking the paper along (with the blessing of the people who were working there). The luxury of having outside information was immeasurably helpful, as the daily political events in the area I was traveling through sometimes changed how I'd get from point A to point B.

I was able to get a plane ticket from Blantyre to Johannesburg—picking an early flight so I could arrive in the city and have plenty of light to find a safe place to stay and change some currency. J-burg was notorious for having one of the highest murder rates in the world, and I was in no mood for dealing with dangerous situations. Besides, South Africa was still under the apartheid leadership of the white ruling government at the time, and the racial/political tensions were quite high. Zimbabwe had just gotten independence and had achieved black rulership a little over a year before, and a lot of the white diehards there subsequently emigrated to South Africa as the last bastion of their privileged life in a "fool's paradise" (as more than one white citizen called it). These Europeans (as they called themselves) were not going to let go of their lifestyle without a fight. I was warned to get in and out of J-burg as quickly as possible and head for the less dangerous west coast.

Unfortunately, after we had taken off and had been flying for about three quarters of an hour, we noticed the plane was changing direction. A voice came over the speaker and explained one of the airplane's propellers wasn't working properly and the only hangar that had the part to repair it was back in Malawi, so we had to head back to get it fixed! Nothing like flying with one prop not working on a four-prop plane to test your faith in God!

Three hours later, we were back in the air, headed in the right direction. My biggest concern, however, was the fact that I'd now be arriving in J-burg well after sunset, with no idea where to stay, how to get there, and how to get any money to pay for the place. I quickly scanned through "Places to Stay" in my *Africa on a Shoestring* book, and nothing looked promising at all. Searching through my mind for inspiration, I finally realized "I'm going to be staying with someone on this plane! I've just got to figure out who that lucky person is! Time to start trolling..."

Making as much noise as possible but trying not to look too obvious, I pulled out my trusted map of Africa and rustled it as much as I could while folding it to where just southern Africa was showing. No bites from anyone yet. I got out of my seat and opened the overhead compartment to pull out my day pack, letting things fall out around on the nearby passengers before apologizing to everyone, picking everything up, getting a notebook out of my pack, and returning to my seat. Closing the map didn't get enough attention, so I opened it up all the way to its eighteen-by-twenty-four-inch size, almost like I was sending up a signal flag for passing ships to see. "Hmm." I loudly sighed. "South Africa—"

"Are you traveling by yourself?" a man's voice in the chair behind me asked.

Bingo! Got one on the hook! I looked behind me, and there sat a kind-looking white South African businessman. He looked like he was somewhere in his fifties, sincere and serious. Within a few minutes of conversation, I knew I had my quick airplane prayers answered. "I have a place where you can stay tonight. You'll like it."

We landed, and as we went through customs, I politely ignored the remark of one of the Afrikaner passengers, who turned to me and said, "Welcome to the holdout, as the world's last fascist country." My businessman, Mr. Barnard, whisked me through the lines (just who was this guy?) and helped me with my backpack into his cab. We rode for a while, and he explained the difference between the tribes in South Africa.

"You see," he explained, "there really isn't a white-minority rule here in South Africa. There are two groups of whites—us Dutch settlers, the Afrikaners, and the British, who mostly live along the West and the Coast. The blacks have about ten different tribes, so if either of the white groups stop running the government, one of the black tribes will take over, and then it will be a black-minority rule by that tribe...Here's where you'll be staying."

We pulled up to a giant shopping mall, where he led me to a gorgeously furnished penthouse apartment. I hadn't seen a real bathroom, let alone a hot shower, in months.

"I own this mall and have this apartment for when I need to spend the night here sometimes," he explained. "Just leave your stuff here. I want to take you somewhere and show you something that I guarantee you'll never see anywhere else."

Intrigued, I followed him into the elevator and down to the mall's basement. He took me to a conference room, filled with about twenty well-dressed men sitting around a long table. I sat in the corner while Barnard gave a short speech to the men. These guys were all obviously local businessmen, called together to meet with the host. The topic was over my head, as I knew nothing about South African politics, but my eyes and ears were opened when the lights went out, and a movie was projected on the screen. Its title put a lump in my throat: *A Private-Business Response to Urban Warfare.* The film methodically and seriously went over, point by point, how each business owner should prepare himself for the inevitable civil war between "Capitalism and Communism." These men had noticed how Zimbabwe had come under the sway of the socialist president Robert Mugabe, and they did not want that to happen to them. The film showed blacks working together with whites in uniforms and helmets to prepare for the onslaught by the "agitators."

I looked around after the lights came back on. The men seemed fairly nonchalant in their response...just another long day at the office. I couldn't believe what I had just seen: a preparation for an inevitable local bloodbath. Welcome to South Africa!

After months of staying in places that even Spartans would reject, I thought the feeling of a hot shower on my body was like coming out into the light after living hibernation. The clean sheets made me feel like I was being teasingly reunited with modernity. After a good night's sleep, I found my way to the nearest highway and started thumbing toward Cape Town, about twelve hours away. I figured one good ride could do it, as the Johannesburg-Cape Town highway was a major travel artery. On this Sunday morning, I got lucky when a guy stopped and agreed to take me as far as Kimberly. "It's still before noon." He smiled. "So you could get lucky with one more lift."

Outside Kimberly, I stood on the on-ramp, staring down each occasional car, waiting for a break. Hours passed by. How come there were so few cars? And the ones that came by gave me the signal that they were only going a short distance (the thumb and forefingers squeezed together). Of course! It was a Sunday! These people stayed with their families all day and went to church. And here I was, with my thumb out and my face getting blistered by the relentless sun. It was at moments like this that I delved into my reserve of information and started memorizing in order to pass the time.

I repeated Bible verses, over and over, like "I can do all things through Christ who strengthens me" (Philippians 4:13).

Then there were Tom Waits lyrics:

A foreign affair
when juxtaposed with a Stateside
and domestically occurred romantic fancy
Is mysteriously attractive
due to circumstances knowing
It'll only be parlayed into a memory.

This seemed to summarize my thoughts on all the relationships I had been involved with during these travels. Maybe it was the excitement of the exotic that made foreign women attractive…and knowing that nothing would come of it because I'd probably never see them again. Could I ever make a relationship really and truly last, or was I destined for a series of transient and frustrating dalliances?

More hours passed. I was getting that hungry, tired, weary, and desperate feeling I had experienced in Ravenna, Italy. What could be worse than this? I could feel the sun blisters forming on my face! I still had no South African currency, as the banks had been closed that day, and I had eaten the bananas the driver of my last ride from so long ago had donated to my cause. I just had to get out of there.

The sun was starting to set. This situation was getting a bit serious and just a tad on the unsafe side. Finally, a large Mack truck (or lorry, as they called them) pulled up. A wiry Indian guy rolled down the window. The first thing he asked was, "You got a pistol?"

"No. Do I need one?"

"You going to Cape Town? Hop in the back."

I opened the sliding door to the van, and there was nothing inside—nothing, that is, except three of the seediest-looking tough guys I'd ever seen in my life. None of the three black guys smiled at me, appearing as if they had been weaned on Sterno. There was stone silence as they stared right through me and leaned against the front inside wall of the lorry. I was going to spend twelve hours with these guys? I'd be jumped, rolled, knifed, and thrown out of this thing within two hours of falling asleep. Images of the film *Treasure of the Sierra Madre* flashed in my mind—particularly the scene where Humphrey Bogart and Tim Holt glaringly stare at each other all night long by the campfire because they know the first one to fall asleep will get killed by the other.

My options that evening, however, were quite limited. I could die out there on the highway waiting for the perfect ride, or I could take my chances with the three Pep Boys. I climbed aboard and staked my claim at the far end of the long cabin.

There's a freeing feeling one gets when one realizes this could be one's final hour. If I fell asleep, one of these guys could easily take me. I was, after all, outnumbered. Well, if I died in my sleep, I wouldn't know it anyway. I actually said good night to my three companions and said my prayers. The childhood prayer I learned years ago popped into my mind: "If I should die before I wake, I pray, my Lord, my soul to take." I closed my eyes, thanked God for my life, and cast my life into His hands.

What a wondrous feeling to wake up the next day! The vehicle was still moving along; I was alive! I felt I had a new lease on life! Rarely have I been so enthused about waking up. It felt as close to forgiveness as I had ever experienced before. God believed in me and had let me live! My three partners were still asleep. Maybe they were afraid of me! Anyway, I'd slept about ten hours, and we were almost on the outskirts of Cape Town. My face felt funny as I rubbed the sleep out of my eyes. I could feel blisters all over my lips, as well as places on my face that were sunburned from hitchhiking in the unforgiving heat.

My driver stopped just outside Cape Town's city limits. I jumped out, and the three guys smiled and waved good-bye. Maybe they were afraid of me? Maybe we should exchange addresses and become pen pals? Didn't want to push my luck.

Now what? Whom should I contact? At least it was morning, so I had all day to figure this thing out. I pulled out my trusty address book. I had the Emissaries' address and phone number, but I was not sure if that was my best bet. Hmm. Maybe I would try Tubby!

I bummed some change off of a few people and found a pay phone.

"George! Where are you?"

"I'm in your town. Come pick me up!"

Within an hour, a big, round, jovial half-Indian, half-white slug of a guy came to my rescue in an old, beat-up blue Toyota. Tubby ran up to me and gave me a giant hug. "I'm so glad to finally meet you!" he exclaimed. "Get in the car, quick. I'll take you to my place."

"Can I stay with you for a couple of days?" I asked.

"Not really."

I was a bit disappointed. Was he not as friendly as he seemed?

"Maybe I can sneak you in for one night, but after that, you'll probably have to leave. Someone could report it, and I'd get in trouble."

"What do you mean?"

He reminded me of one of our early phone calls. "You're white. I'm what's called a colored. I'm not allowed to have a white stay at my house. That's the rules of apartheid. You wouldn't get in trouble, but I would if someone told the police I had a white person spend the night."

"That's crazy."

"That's not crazy. What's crazy is that it's all politically motivated. For example, when the black American Arthur Ashe played tennis here, he could stay in the nice hotels because, since he was from the United States, he was considered white. A Japanese person is considered white, but someone from Communist China is colored. What do you make of that?"

I had no answer. I just had to process this information.

Tubby let me spend a couple of days with him until I got coordinated with the Emissaries. He took me to different parts of town and told me that a person could actually swim in the Indian and Atlantic Oceans at the same beach.

"That must be fantastic. Let's go there."

"Well, I've never been there, as I'm not allowed at that beach. That one is only for whites."

"Look. Let's just pretend you're an American as well. Then you can be there with me."

"But what about my South African accent?"

"You've got a point. Hmm. Let's work on it a bit. Say 'Boston.'"

"Boston."

"Now, pop out the *B*, roll out the *O*, and slide it into the *S*. That's how people from Boston say it." For the rest of the drive, we worked on giving Tubby a New England dialect, figuring this was the best way to beat the system.

What a gorgeous beach it was. With the gently crashing waves and white sand, I felt like I was back in California. This was a true paradise, and a fool's one, indeed. Within about twenty minutes of lying down and taking in the relaxingly beautiful scene, I felt the tap of a billy club on my shoulder.

"What are you doing here?" the policeman asked.

"We're Americans visiting on holiday here, sir," I answered in all seriousness.

"Where are you from?"

"Los Angeles, California, sir," I soberly replied.

The cop tapped Tubby. "And where are you from?"

Tubby blurted. "I'm from Bwa-ston!"

Satisfied, the cop sauntered away, leaving us two linguists lying in the balmy sun, with Tubby particularly savoring the moment. I could go to the beach anytime. This was a once-in-a-lifetime pleasure for Tubby. How did I get to be born in freedom, while this guy was subject to bondage? How much of my life was I really in control of?

Tubby dropped me off at the Emissaries' home, and I saw him a couple more times, but the logistics of meeting were too difficult for people who were labeled as being of two races to meet very often. It was amazing how the system perpetuated itself.

Two college students, Ken and Amy, lived at the Emissary home. Amy was gone at work most of the time, but Ken was exceedingly gracious to me, letting me just get myself back together after traveling on the go for so long.

During this time, I spent the mornings trying to memorize the Bible verses that were mentioned in the *Discipleship* book. "Whatsoever things that are true, noble, righteous, pure, loving, excellent and of good report, think of these things," it said in the book of Philippians (4:8). I liked that thought.

I went to a couple Emissary meetings and tried to make a point of spending time with the leaders of the local group. One guy, Don, was gracious enough to spend some time with me and answer a few questions.

"I just can't figure out if this group confirms or denies the Christian faith," I told him.

"That's because it doesn't matter what your religion is. The Emissaries don't espouse a faith per se. It's more like a tool you use. A Christian can use it, a Buddhist can use it, and a Catholic can use it."

"Could you please point me to someone here who is a Christian? I'd love to talk to him or her."

Don put his hand to his chin in silence. "Can't think of one offhand. Sorry."

This was not getting any easier. I was starting to get the feeling this group was simply comprised of people who were turned off by "organized religion" (as they so often disparagingly called it) yet wanted a set of good morals to live by. I had noticed that all of the Emissaries I had met in the United States, Italy, and Africa were Caucasians. There were no blacks, Hispanics, or Asians, and my Mediterranean features stood in complete contrast to 95 percent of the other attendees' looks. Hmm. How could a faith that purports to give universal truths be reaching only those of Northern European descent?

The best and most lasting part of my stay in Cape Town was the music. Ken had two record albums that I played every day of my time there: Gershwin's *Rhapsody in Blue/American in Paris* and Stan Getz and Charlie Byrd's *Jazz Samba*. The living room was filled with that music until I had memorized every nuance of those two LPs. Ken hadn't even known he had them; they must've been left by some other Emissary. But after a week, he started humming along to the strains of Gershwin as well. Spiritual quests never had a better soundtrack!

It was time to move on, so I started hitching back up to J-burg. I stopped at Port Elizabeth for a few days of the most beautiful waves I'd ever experienced. While I was there, I stayed with some Emissaries in their seventies, and I must've worn out their Glenn Miller album. I finally memorized the words to "Chattanooga Choo Choo," which helped pass the time as I waited for a willing ride. And, once again, Tom Waits's lyrics helped keep me distracted while I was waiting for a merciful driver to stop for me.

> Well, you've gassed her up, you're behind the wheel
> With your arm around your sweet one in your Oldsmobile
> Barreling down the Boulevard
> Looking for the heart of a Saturday night.
> —"(Looking for) The Heart of a Saturday Night"

My mind started wandering, and I thought of my trips driving through the United States a few years before.

> Diamonds on my windshield
> Tears from heaven
> Pulling into town on the interstate
> The wind bites my cheek through the wing
> Fast Flying, freeway driving
> Always makes me sing.
> —from "Diamonds on My Windshield"

Up pulled a yellow 1980 Honda Civic—up to that time, one of the tiniest cars built. It was essentially a tin can with an engine, and it pulled over with two guys already squeezed into the front. The driver, a stocky dark-haired guy about my age, popped his head out the window. "It's a bit tight, but we'll make it if you wanna join us."

How could I turn down an attitude like that?

I squeezed my six-foot-four frame into what was laughingly termed the "backseat" and sat for about six hours with my knees giving me the ultimate facial massage through the gorgeous drive through the Free State. Tim, the driver, and I hit it off really well, while the other passenger just occupied his seat in silent, abject boredom. I got to sit in the front passenger seat after a few hours, as Tim let his friend off in some small town. Ahhh, so that was what uncramped hamstrings felt like!

"So, why are you hitching through this area of the world?"

The thing that struck me most about that simple question was that, up until this time—sixteen months into my trip—no one had asked me the reason I was on this quest. People had asked where I'd been, what I'd seen, and what it was like, but there had not been a single query about my motivation! I sat in silence for a while to put my thoughts into words.

"Well, I'm just trying to figure out this thing we call life," I started. "Here I am. Why am I here? How do I fit in? What do I believe about this world that I'm in? I was twenty-three when I became a doctor, and after all those consecutive years of education, I had to get out and figure out what I want to do with my life. I had no girlfriend, no responsibilities, just a piece of paper that says I can treat patients.

"So, I used my one possession to see different countries with different religions and ways of life and to figure out if any of those beliefs that are fighting for supremacy make any sense. So, here I am in the continent that seems to have Christians, Muslims, Jews, and Hindus all vying for their place, and I wanted to see them working side by side to see which one is the truth or if there's some other truth or if there's *no* other truth."

"I wish I could do that."

"I think that's the reason I'm doing it, too. So many people just don't have the time, energy, or enthusiastic stupidity to do this kind of adventure. Who knows what I'm going to do with it once I figure it out, but I'm determined to do so."

"What have you learned so far?"

That was another good question. I had written down snippets of insights in the diary I had been keeping all this time, so I thought through the most salient points.

"Well, first, you can be sincere, but you can be sincerely wrong."

"What do you mean?"

"Hindus, Jews, Christians, Muslims, atheists, and even the most whacked-out New Agers all have an opinion on who Jesus Christ is. They all can't be right. They could all be wrong, or one of them could be right. The entire world is divided into what, or who, Jesus is and what He did. They're all sincere, but someone's got to be wrong."

"What do you think?"

"So far, I'm on the side of Him being God in the flesh, who died for our sins and rose again. It just makes the most sense."

"I'm glad you said that. I've been thinking about who He is as well, and it's nice to meet someone who believes it. What else?"

"Well, the second one is sort of like your statement, 'He who stands for nothing falls for anything.' In other words, if you aren't firm in your faith, you're going to get run over by someone who is confident in what he or she believes, even if that person is dead-out wrong."

"Ya know what, George? Look how simple life is. Faith. What a simple word, but you need to have it. Look around at this great earth; look at all of these wonderful people in it. Look at how we're having a great conversation. We ate food today, and we're going to be able to sleep tonight. Life is sweet."

The look in his eye as he confessed his hope for both himself and me was a deep confirmation of my travels. I had met someone who understood. It had taken almost two years, but the pat on the back was worth it.

CHAPTER 44

The Delta Blues

FROM SOUTH AFRICA, I TOOK a side trip to Botswana to spend a couple of weeks in the Okavango Delta. Tubby had shown me a picture book about it, and its exotic beauty called me to see it. The Delta is essentially a game reserve; in order to see it properly, you have to rent a canoe, but it had to be a certain type. The water in those narrow and winding tributaries was so shallow in some parts that the canoe had to be able to float with the tiniest amount of aqueous support, or you'd have to get out and push. That might not seem like too big of a problem, until you realized the area was heavily populated by crocodiles, just waiting for an opportunity for a free meal.

"But you really don't have to worry about that too much," the canoe renter assured me. "Crocodiles are *very* lazy, and if they just see you do something one time, they won't think it's worth the effort to go after you. Only if you go into the same place again will they become interested in you."

He walked me over to his zoo, a walled-off area containing about fifteen crocs lying around as if in a dazed stupor. "See, they aren't interested in you, even though they know you're here," he pointed out.

I couldn't help but notice that one of the crocs had half his tail missing. What had happened?

"Oh, during the feeding time, it gets pretty intense, and one of the other crocodiles got so excited he ate this one's tail."

Cannibals!

"Watch this," he said as he went into his office and then came back with a bucket of meat. He banged the wall; still just a minimal amount of stirring around. The meat was thrown into the middle of the area, and as if someone had just given them an electric shock, all fifteen reptiles made a disgustingly savage dog pile for the food, fighting with pure, cold-blooded instinct for their daily piece of flesh. Yeeesh!

"So," he calmly stated, while the leviathan-like feeding frenzy took place, "you have to be careful about keeping an eye and ear open for these animals. They make a high-pitched chirp at night, so if you hear that, be careful. When you find a place to camp, shine your flashlight around to look for their eyes. If you see a pair of red dots, you've spotted a croc!"

"Anything else?"

"I highly recommend that you not go out alone. You should rent a poler. He's a guy who will take you through the delta and show you where to stay each night. He only costs five dollars a day."

"Does everyone take one?"

"No, but I think you should. The last guy that didn't take one a couple of weeks ago never came back."

Good salesmanship!

I decided that about four to five days should be enough time to go through the gorgeous, reedy aviary called the Okavango Delta. We started bright and early, and I sat in a dug-out log and was guided through the circuitous water trail by my poler—a tall, thin teenager whose eyes would get as large as saucers when we'd get stuck on the sand and be forced to leave our safe craft to get out and push, under the watchful eyes of the crocodiles! Between all the solitude while traveling and hitching across the continent and tending to avoid most locals, as they'd simply ask me for money, I started to become more and more accustomed to the silence of my surroundings. While gently gliding along the waters, I'd hear nothing but the delicate clipping of the pole diving into the water and the delectable sounds of the gurgling lily pads. I remembered my record-store manager and friend, Bob, telling me that record companies actually made complete albums of natural sounds, without the intrusion of human or mechanical interference competing with the rustling of leaves or trickling of water.

During the evening, just before the sun would completely set, I'd pull out my trusty map of southern Africa to try to figure out, literally, where in the world I was. I'd pass the last moments of the day staring at that map, figuring out where I'd been, where I currently was, and where I hoped to go. The thing that struck me the most was the realization that absolutely no one on God's green earth who really knew me actually knew where I was right then. No one around here knew my name; the last contact I had had with a familiar face was weeks ago in South Africa, and any letters that were being sent to me were being forwarded to some Emissary in Zimbabwe, my next major destination. For the moment, however, I was living in complete anonymity. Only God knew where I was. It wasn't a sense of loneliness or insignificance that I felt; it was something deeper: complete and absolute nonexistence.

A part of me really liked and soaked in the sensation; I was in this world, but I was completely off the radar. In this present modern day of GPS systems, computers, drones, and cell phones, it's essentially impossible to be completely alone. I was able to experience true solitude, and I treasured that sense.

On the other hand, after traveling for as long as I had, I started feeling that it would be nice to contribute something to this world God had made for me to live in. My thoughts went back to the missionary in Kenya. He was making his mark, sharing his faith with the young locals and making disciples of Jesus. Whether they were right or wrong in their zeal, the fact was they were essentially trying to make a dent in this world and for eternity. Could I ever do something like that? It seemed that most of my time traveling was filled with figuring out how to satisfy my own desires and instincts—finding a place to stay, a place to eat, and then, of course, the pictures I was taking and the local souvenirs that I'd buy and ship home, so I could show off where I had been to people Stateside.

I had purchased some beautiful wood carvings, soapstone carvings, semi-precious stones, batiks, cloths, local chess sets, and various woven baskets and things, all to be sent home on the slowest and cheapest boat. Sometimes on this trip, I felt like I was exploring the wilds of nature and other times like I was in the ultimate Pier 1 Imports store. Was this really why I had come all the way around the world?

CHAPTER 45

How Much Does a Zimbabwe?

On arriving in Bulawayo, Zimbabwe, I was struck by a T-shirt that a white guy about my age was wearing. He was obviously someone who lived there. On the front, the shirt read, "Rhodesian War for Independence," and on the reverse, it said, "Second Place." This pretty much summed up the attitude of the indigenous whites concerning giving up their tenuous power. I was to stay with a middle-aged Emissary couple who people in South Africa had referred to me, Roger and Sarah Stillman. They had grown up there and had lived in their humble home throughout the entire war from 1964 to 1979. Roger picked me up at the station in a late-forties-model Ford. Was this guy a car collector?

"Oh no!" He chuckled. "Once the war broke out, there was a worldwide embargo, so it was impossible to get any new cars. We just had to make do with what we had and repair these things ourselves."

Their cozy, clean house was Spartan and simple. Since it was out in the suburbs, there was a quiet peace that flowed through with the daily breeze. The only sounds I would hear in the morning were the tick-tocks of all the clocks in the house. And there were a lot of them—three or four in every room! There were all kinds too—windup, electric, cuckoo, and even a grand-father clock. Every fifteen minutes you'd hear a few of them chime away, and on the hour, well, it was not something you heard as much as something you felt. What was the big fixation with clocks?

"Well, yes, we're a bit overboard now." Sarah blushed. "But you have to understand that for so long, during the war, we were unable to get parts for anything, so after a clock would break down, we just couldn't get it fixed or replaced. We went for years without knowing the time here, so we're sort of compensating for that now."

Just as gentle a soul as Roger was, Sarah was sweet and fiery. She played the accordion almost every night I stayed there, and she showed me her vast catalog of sheet music. My memorization needs were set for the rest of my trip, as I copied the lyrics to every standard from the *Great American Songbook* written from the 1930s through to the 1950s.

We had some excellent discussions about spiritual things. One time, while we were sitting around the porch, Sarah blurted out, "Do you really believe that if someone lives a completely selfish life, and on his deathbed, he simply says, 'Jesus, forgive me, and come into my life' that God is going to let that scoundrel into heaven? Is that *really* fair?"

The way she asked, I knew she was sincere, and her question caused my eyes to open as to the Emissaries' blind spot. They had no concept of God's power to change a heart in order for it to ask for true forgiveness and lead it to repentance. They thought a person should simply reap what he or she sowed.

By the way Sarah's eyes looked piercingly at me, I could tell that someone not getting what he or she truly seemed to deserve just didn't seem fair to her.

"Sarah, do you *really* want to get from God what you deserve?" I asked her.

"Oh, *yes!*" she defiantly answered.

"Do you *really* want to get what you justly deserve for *everything* you've done?"

This time, the answer was a bit more restrained. "Of course."

"Do you mean for *everything* you've *ever* done in your *whole* life. You want God to perfectly judge every thought and deed you've done?"

She thought about it and slowly started playing the accordion.

"What about Cain and Abel?" she returned. "What did Cain do that was so bad that God rejected his offering? He seemed to have gotten a bad deal. It just doesn't seem fair."

"Cain didn't offer his gift with faith. Abel did."

Sarah became incredulous. "How can you say that? Just by saying the secret words 'I believe,' you can make God happy?"

"Look at the thief on the cross. After living an entire rotten and self-centered life, he saw the light and asked Jesus for forgiveness. Jesus could tell he was sincere and gave it to him."

"I never liked that story," she mused, as the accordion sighed away into the night.

CHAPTER 46

The Price of Freedom

IT WAS FASCINATING TO STAY in a newly independent country; it was definitely still going through its growing pains. An election was about to happen between the two major parties, which were essentially representing the two major tribes, the Shonas and Ndebeles. Roger said that Robert Mugabe was probably going to win because there were more Shonas, but his opponent Joshua Nkomo was very popular because he was "very fat."

"What do you mean by that?"

"Very simple," he said over his breakfast cereal. "People here in Zimbabwe are mostly very thin, if you've noticed, simply because of the lack of food. So, if someone is fat, that person must have had a very successful life and have God's favor. That's how the people here see it."

One day, the Stillmans took me to the home of one of their friends. A group of Emissaries was there for a meeting. My eye latched onto a tall, dark-haired lady about my age with large eyes and an even larger and more engaging smile. I went over and introduced myself.

"Hi!" she warmly replied. "I'm Liz."

We spent the rest of the day walking and talking, and before we'd known it, we had spent the whole evening together. It was the same the next day. This was getting interesting. I was attracted to her enthusiasm about life and her zest for just about everything that came her way. I was hesitant to push too far, since I still felt the urge to keep traveling. Also, since she was associated with the Emissaries, I had no idea what she really believed deep in her heart. I told her I enjoyed our time together and that I'd probably be leaving in a couple of weeks to continue my trip.

"Take me with you!" she exclaimed as her eyes lit up.

"What are you talking about?"

"I have no family here. I've grown up in this area and have never seen the world. You keep traveling for a while, and I'll fly up and meet you in Morocco. We'll see it together!" She beamed.

I felt overwhelmed at the thought. Why not? She seemed physically and mentally strong enough to handle it. I liked her, and after we talked about my beliefs about relationships and sex, she seemed even *more* enthused by the prospect. This could work out! Traveling as a sole trekker was a bit wearisome at times, and we would only be traveling together for a month or so anyway, as Liz would be going on to Spain and then to the United States to visit some Emissaries there. Why not?

Liz worked in an office, and I'd go visit her at lunch. I had to hitch a ride to get there, as Roger was already at work. The daily commutes were always a fascinating and educational affair.

One time, a truck pulled up to give me a lift. "You're not from here, are you?" the driver asked as I hopped in.

"How could you tell?"

"No white person from this area would ever take a ride from a black man. You must be a European."

"No, I'm American."

"No, I mean, you're a white but not from this area. If you're not from Zimbabwe or South Africa, you're a European."

I felt like I had just been categorized into a subgroup—almost like a tribe similar to the Shonas or Ndebeles. I tried to explain to him that we really don't have tribes in the United States, but as I started doing this, I realized we actually did. Just like here in Zimbabwe, the politicians in the United States coerced us to be loyal to certain tribes; they made voting blocks out of blacks, whites, Hispanics, unions, and white-collar workers just like they did here. The similarity of the two types of tribalism haunted me.

"Who are you voting for?" I asked him.

"I'm a Ndebele. I'm voting for Nkomo," he proudly declared. "Mugabe... those Shonas...aren't they ugly? They look like monkeys! They really are a stupid group of people. They don't want to work. They're just a bunch of socialists."

While we were driving to town, I considered what would happen if someone in the United States, like George Wallace or David Duke, said something like this guy's rant. I reflected back to the villages in Greece when the people in the tiny towns showed disdain for the city people and vice versa. Here, two blacks—whom the average American couldn't tell the difference between—made racial comments that would bring down the house.

As I returned home that evening, the TV was on. It was a week before the election, and there was a lot of shooting between the two tribes out in the bush. Several people had been killed, and a mass grave had just been found that day. A news reporter from the BBC reported on this carnage. He walked up to a Shona soldier and asked him point-blank, "After all these years of fighting together with the Ndebeles for independence against the white minority and finally achieving your goal, how can you go around now shooting each other?"

The solder bemusedly looked at the reporter and blithely replied, "Hey, who do you think we were killing before you white people arrived here?"

"It's like President Reagan once said," I told Roger. "He said if we all woke up one day the exact same color, by noon, we would have something new to be prejudiced about."

Racism, prejudice, greed—you don't have to be American, or white, to succumb to them.

I was having a great time with Liz, but I also wanted to move on with my trip. While she might be an excellent companion in Morocco, I was glad she would not be trudging through the rough terrain of Mali for her first trip out of her home country. Mali was the home of the famous Timbuktu and also of the austere and time-forgotten Dogon Cliffs of Bandiagara. I had read about them in the *Shoestring* book, and it seemed like seeing them could be the culmination of the entire trip. The mystery, primitiveness, and otherworldliness of this area beckoned me. I kissed Liz et al. good-bye and set out for the last solo part of my continental journey before I would reunite with my female companion…maybe not only my partner for the final leg of the trip but for my life as well.

CHAPTER 47

From Here to Timbuktu

MALI! NOW I WAS GETTING into some *real* Africa. Sure, I'd been on a few safaris, done some trekking, seen Victoria Falls, climbed Mount Kenya and other, lesser mountains—like Table Top in South Africa—but the more you travel, the more you want to up the ante in terms of adventure. So far, most things I had experienced had been on professional tours or with another traveler or two. Here in Mali, I was completely alone, with no guide except my faithful *Shoestring* book, which made special mention of the exoticism of Mali's Dogon Cliffs. Sure, there was also the famous historical town of Timbuktu, but people only went there to get that city's official seal stamped on their passport. It was sort of a way to show off to your friends when you returned back to your hometown. That wasn't my style.

The real attraction of this landlocked country was the primitive cliffs where people lived the same way they had for hundreds (thousands?) of years, in mud and straw huts embedded on austere rocks in the middle of nowhere. I had traveled from Côte d'Ivoire to Mali's capital city of Bamako and had received a three-week tourist visa. This was a Marxist country, so everything was regulated by the government. In every town I'd visit, I'd have to go to the local sheriff's office to have my visa stamped. Talk about control!

The only way to get to the Dogon villages from Bamako was to find a taxi to take me to the nearest connecting city, Bandiagara. Bamako was the only town in the country that had both running water and electricity, which meant that anything I might need for this adventure had better be purchased there, as the accommodations and facilities from here on out were going to get rougher and rougher. I found out the taxis (basically either an open-bed truck or a station wagon) left just before sunup—around 6:30 a.m.—as the drive to Bandiagara took about twelve hours. Once you arrived, you were supposed to hang out for a couple of days until you could find a guide who would take you on the five-to-seven-day hike to and through the cliffs.

I took a couple of days to rest and build myself up for what promised to be a fairly exciting, yet arduous, trip. I had read all I could about the area in the *Shoestring* book, so I felt I was prepared for all that could come my way. I was staying at a convent and was lightening my load so my hike through the Sahel Desert could be as easy as possible. I had been reading Leo Tolstoy's *Anna Karenina*, and since the book was so large, I wanted to finish it before embarking on the next stage of the trip, so I would have that much less weight to carry around.

I felt an immediate kinship to Tolstoy from the book's opening line: "Happy families are all alike; every unhappy family is unhappy in its own way." That line caused me to reflect on all I had seen so far on this long trip through the United States, Canada, Europe, the Middle East, and now Africa. All the people I had met thus far that I wanted to be like had similar qualities: a deep and unwavering faith, a sense of peace with their lot in life and in the direction they were going, and a focused contentment that they were doing the right thing with what they had been given by God. In contrast, all the people I had met who were bitter, sad, wayward, or just plain whacked out had a myriad of excuses—something bad had happened to them, or they had too much pride to listen to anyone else or were argumentative, self-absorbed, materialistic, or just looking for something to satisfy them that they'd never find...and wouldn't recognize even if it hit them on the head.

As I turned each page of this classic Russian novel, I felt like the main characters were all different and competing parts of my own psyche. There was the wife, Anna, and her dutiful—if stiff and perfunctory—husband, Alexei. Mixing up the arrangement was her attraction to the dashing and exciting Vronsky, who kept tempting Anna through the entire book to leave her husband and create the true, promising, and seemingly destined relationship she deserved with him but could only achieve by leaving her staid husband. Lastly, the character Konstantin was simply a young man trying to figure out what in this world could give him lasting peace, happiness, and purpose.

What struck me most of all was the attraction of the forbidden fruit that Anna and Vronsky had for each other. They kept thinking that once they consummated their affair, all of their problems would be over. Tolstoy described this visceral allure in such a poetic way that it was easy to identify with Vronsky—a seemingly romantic and dashing fellow. That was how I felt every time I wanted something. It seemed so important before I had it. Then, just like in the book, once I had achieved the object of my lustful desire, I saw it for what it really was and was distraught that it hadn't brought me the joy and satisfaction I thought it would. Instead, these instances brought misery to me and just about everyone I was connected with.

I thought back on all of my desires—whether they concerned relationships, personal experiences, or material things. How many of them were like that Tom Waits song, "Foreign Affair":

Most vagabonds I know, don't ever want to catch the subject
That remains the object of their long-related quest
The obsession's in the chasing, and not the apprehending
The pursuit you see, and never the arrest.

Or as Spock succinctly said in a *Star Trek* episode, "Most times, wanting is better than having." We think that we know what we want, but once we get it, we wonder what in the world we were thinking about in the first place.

Anna and Vronsky bore the seeds they had sown. What seemed so attractive beforehand ended up in tragedy. Meanwhile, Konstantin found the elusive peace in his life through Christ's Sermon on the Mount. So simple, yet so true:

Blessed are the poor in spirit, for theirs is the kingdom of heaven.
Blessed are those who mourn, for they shall be comforted.
Blessed are the meek, for they will inherit the earth.
Blessed are those who hunger and thirst for righteousness, for they will be filled.
Blessed are the merciful, for they will be shown mercy.
Blessed are the pure in heart, for they shall see God.

Blessed are the peacemakers, for they shall be called the children of God.

Blessed are they which are persecuted for righteousness' sake, for theirs is the kingdom of heaven. (Matthew 5:3–10)

Pete, one of the missionaries I had befriended in Rome, had given me a copy of a book before I left for Greece—way back when—called *The Pursuit of God* by a pastor named A. W. Tozer. It was a collection of chapters based on the Sermon on the Mount. I had left it in storage in Bamako, but as I read Tolstoy's book, I wanted to go back to it and study Christ's sermon even more.

There's nothing like finishing a good book; that sense of satisfaction mixed with inspiration is one of life's joys. Through Tolstoy's simple, insightful, and inspiring writing, I had been motivated to be content with the simplicity of the Christian faith. It seemed easy to follow Christ's teachings here, all by myself, in Western Africa, but could I continue living this way back at home in modern America?

I thought back on a song I had memorized by Bruce Springsteen:

And them South Side sisters sure look pretty
The cripple on the corner cries out, "Nickels for your pity"
And them downtown boys sure talk gritty
It's so hard to be a saint in the city.
—from "It's Hard to Be a Saint in the City"

At the same time, I amazed myself anew at my materialism. Here I was, in the middle of the second-poorest country in the world, where the average annual income was two hundred dollars, and I was checking out street sellers and market kiosks that were selling intriguing wooden Dogon carvings and wool rugs. I couldn't figure out if I was fascinated with them just because they were African and therefore exuded the exoticism of my trip or if I liked them for their own artistic sake. Either way, I felt like I had to possess something to show to my friends upon my return or at least to remind me of my sojourn. So, before heading off to one of the most remote and primitive parts of the world, I was negotiating with some salesmen over man-made crafts, packing them into a box, and taking them to the local government office to ship back to the United States.

As I carried this box over to the post office, I felt like Jacob Marley, carrying the burdens and accumulated chains of his life that he had made for himself to bear for all eternity.

I needed to deliver the box to the post office that very day, as it was the last day of the month and a couple of the locals had told me that the government workers didn't do anything until they were paid the first and fifteenth day of the month. Sure enough, as I entered the building, I saw the disinterested clerk standing behind a dingy counter. Behind him were a plethora of randomly stacked and collapsing boxes that had obviously accumulated over the past weeks and hadn't budged an inch. I settled my box on the counter, but I was unconvinced that the mass of cardboard behind my civil servant was ever going to reach within a thousand miles of its respective destinations.

"Will this package arrive in America?" I asked in my broken French.

Blank stare. Slowly, as if programmed to a time-delayed relay system, the deadpan response came. "Yes, sir."

"When will it be sent out?"

"Tomorrow. The first of the month."

My Malian tax dollars at work.

The next day, in preparation for my trip to the Dogon Cliffs, I needed to extend my visa for another two weeks. Sensing that the lack of efficiency at the post office portended future dealings with the local government, I decided to get up early and make sure I'd be the first in line at the Bandiagara Government Center to get my paperwork done. That turned out to be a good call.

I arrived at 8:00 a.m., an hour before the building was to open. No one else was in front of me. Ah! I had half a chance of getting taken care of! Slowly, a few people started trickling in behind me, obviously in need of some official government bureaucratic action. No one said a word to anyone else; everyone was just patiently waiting. Nine o'clock arrived. There was no sign of life inside. A quarter past nine…twenty past…

"What time is this place supposed to open, sir?" I ask the genteel middle-aged man behind me.

"Nine o'clock."

"What time do you have, please?"

"Nine thirty."

No one seemed too concerned. "What time do they usually open?"

"Anytime."

When you had nothing else to do, this was the way things operated.

Finally, someone in a drab gray uniform started silently working through the accumulated crowd, came up to the door, unlocked it, and let us all in. Politely, the people let me remain as the first person in line. If this were Israel or Egypt, I'd have been trampled underfoot.

Once inside the office, I saw a handful of civil workers silently milling around—seemingly without direction or purpose. Every now and then, one would jut his head out of a corner office to see how many of us were in line, but essentially nothing was going on. Meanwhile, the size of the civilian group on my side of the counter had grown to Frank Capra-sized proportions—only no one was nearly as animated. Everyone there passively accepted the situation. Was this resignation a result of the government's Marxism or the fatalism of the prevailing religion of Islam? I didn't know enough about the latter yet to make a conclusion. I realized I still needed to get a Koran and check it out. How could a nation be so gelded?

Around 10:30 a.m., a lackluster government agent finally came out of the office. With half-opened eyes, he blithely took my passport, listened to my request for an extra two-week stay in his sub-Saharan Xanadu, and lifelessly stamped my passport, telling me to hurry up and get out of the way so he could blandly service the next citizen. Would capitalism really change this place's norms, or would something have to happen before that? As John Adams said, "Democracy only works for moral people." Would these people know what to do with any type of freedom if it were suddenly handed to them?

CHAPTER 48

Well, I'll Be Dogoned!

Travel day! I had my game face on! There was nothing like the excitement of starting a new journey—new sights to see, connections to make, transportation to organize, and destinations to arrive at. Just like my *Shoestring* book said, there was a collection of station wagons at a dusty lot by the Niger River at 6:00 a.m., ready to take any and all passengers on the twelve-hour journey to Mopti. I climbed in the front seat with *three* other people, making a fearsome foursome, while the rest of the vehicle did a pretty decent impersonation of a sardine can as well. Off we headed on the long and dusty road.

Twelve hours! How did the driver know where we were going? The only thing I could see out of the cracked and smudged front windshield was a bunch of dust flying around us and what looked like a corrugated-cardboard-like surface posing as a dirt road. The only thing that prevented me from thinking we were on a "Road to Nowhere" was the fact that every two to three hours, the indefatigable boredom of the drive was relieved by a government checkpoint, proving we were actually on some sort of highway.

Stopping at these stations, I couldn't help but wonder just what these soldiers were looking for. More than anything else, it seemed like their activity was a way for the government to create jobs for some of its citizens, keeping the subjects happily occupied. The only people with any initiative seemed to be the kids who sold iced drinks. A cold drink in a place where electricity is at a premium is like manna from heaven. I had never craved ice as much as I did in that dust bowl of a landlocked country. The local soft drink, called a Yukki Soda, tasted amazingly terrible at room temperature, but it was somehow tolerable if slightly chilled. The cola industry would definitely shrivel up if refrigeration were taken out of the equation. I had no need for a government-ordained checkpoint, but a cold drink purchased from an enterprising young man in this sub-Saharan purgatory was essential.

Twelve hours and a mind-numbing collection of checkpoints later, we arrive as the sun was setting at the edge of the town of Mopti, where we were to make our connecting bus to Bandiagara. We couldn't enter quite yet, as the entire town (at least all of the men) were performing one of their five-times-a-day rituals of praying toward Mecca—all, that is, except the driver, who was more concerned with making a living than anything else. After a while, it became pretty easy to tell which of the Muslims took their religion seriously and which ones were just along for the ride. The committed ones had a bruise or callous on their foreheads from praying on their knees with their heads touching the ground for so many years. No way can you fake that mark!

The closest thing I saw in comparison was a Maltese nun in Rome, a patient of mine who had lost her patellar (knee) reflex from kneeling so often. What would I have to show for whatever faith I had at the end of my life? Enough friends to carry my casket? A roomful of grateful acquaintances and other close-knit lives I'd touched in a positive way? A wake of disheartened ex-friends and girlfriends? A house filled with useless artifacts and collections?

My first day in Mopti, I met a guy about my age who was working for the Peace Corps. Pete's job for his entire two years of service was to build a well for his designated neighborhood. This process would be fairly simple in most other countries, but here—in the land of "Ob-La-Di, Ob-La-Da"—there was a lack of a) electricity, b) water pressure, c) transportation, d) human initiative, and e) hardware to get the job done. He'd already been there almost a year, and he was still in the phase of getting everything coordinated to start the well. "When I come back here in twenty years," he boasted in hope, "they'll still be using this well."

Speaking of water, as I prepared for my trip into the Dogon Cliffs, I read in my *Shoestring* book that I'd better purify the local water with iodine tablets here and in all the villages I'd be visiting. While in Bandiagara, I could survive on drinking lukewarm soft drinks (no refrigeration here, folks). It's amazing how you can convince yourself that a room-temperature, lemon-lime Yukki Soda can actually refresh you. Everything had the same temperature: the water, the soft drinks, the rice, the chicken meal, the mangos, the bed...

The entire trip through the Dogon Cliffs would take about a week to accomplish. From Mopti, I would get a ride on a truck (taxi) to the outskirts of the cliffs, which would be about a four-hour ride, to a small town called Bandiagara. From there, I would look for a guide to take me along the cliffs. We would do a series of twenty- to thirty-kilometer hikes (fifteen to twenty miles), down the cliffs, along the valley, and back up the cliffs, in a pattern of an elongated horseshoe—each day traversing farther away from the truck that had originally carried us. When we reached the most distant point, we would be at a village, and a truck that took food to the local market every fifth day would meet us at the center of town and take us back to Bandiagara. This area was so remote and cut off from civilization that the week was divided into five days instead of the usual seven. I was definitely traveling out of the norm. How much further into obscurity could I embark?

I figured if I wanted to start the trip the next day, I should troll around town today for a guide. There was a local diner where I had hung out and where most of the town congregated sooner or later. I figured this was the best starting place. I soon learned that the people best suited for the trip were the youngest kids—anywhere from nine to twelve years old—as they had the most time, physical stamina, and knowledge of the area and the least reason and strength to bump me off in the middle of nowhere.

After about five or six informal interviews, I picked Jos, a wiry ten-year-old kid who seemed enthusiastic enough to lead me through the villages and yet smart enough not to try to cause any problems. I made sure to ask if his parents said this was all right, and he gave me a look like I was from another planet. Permission to walk around for a week? What was the big deal?

We determined a fair price—ten bucks—to be paid once the trip was over. I left most of my pack at the hotel I had been using (if you want to call the roof of a restaurant a hotel) and put just my camera, iodine pills, canteen, and a few other essentials into a day pack. There really wasn't anything worth stealing in the pack; I wasn't too worried about any thieving Tolstoy fans. I was ready to head off with my young guide into the world of prehistory.

There are really very few times in life when we are able to do something truly different. In the United States, we think we're adventurous if we go on a computer-controlled ride at Six Flags—maybe whitewater rafting on a class

IV or V river or hiking the John Muir or Appalachian Trails. But even those experiences are usually well guided by someone experienced. While hiking through this barren, dry, dusty, brown desert, with just a few grayish trees that served as markers like battlefield tombstones, I felt like I was trekking through a completely different world. A mauve-tan haze hovered under the sun, taking away any sense of shadows and further adding to the dimensionless atmosphere.

We hiked in silence for hours at a stretch. Somehow, Jos knew where the all the wells were situated, and we would stop to refill my canteen. The water was beginning to leave a tinny iodine taste in my mouth, but my options were limited. As Crowther wrote in *Shoestring*, you either protect yourself from every potential hazard and starve to death or you take a few chances once in a while, drink the water, eat the food, and live another day—albeit with a few more guests in your system than you may have wanted to invite.

Toward the sixth hour of the first day, we reached the edge of the cliffs, which were harsh, sullen, and unforgiving. There was only one way to get to the valley, and that was through a series of steep and jagged switchbacks that descended back and forth for about four hours. I had done my share of hiking this past year, but this stretch was a really tough one.

Just as I was wallowing in my agony, I spotted a line of about twelve young women, down below me, who were weaving their way up the spindly trail. Each one carried a large earthenware pot on her head, balanced with a towel and supported by one hand, as the other hand kept balance against the rocks. These ladies were going up the hill at a faster clip than I was going down it! And barefoot! Any notions of being a hardened world traveler were quickly dispelled by these quiet, gentle, and gracious ladies.

We spent our first night in a mud hut about an hour's walk from the base of the cliffs. The boy took us to the chief of the village, which is what custom dictated for visitors. We were entering his domain, and we needed to introduce ourselves so he would know we weren't some marauding invaders. Once welcomed, we were treated as guests; he asked us what we would like for dinner. With the clucking of benevolent chickens serving as a backdrop, Jos told me that all they had was rice and chicken. I therefore told him, "I'd like some chicken and rice." The chief went back behind his hut, and within a few seconds, I heard a blood-curdling *bwaack* and saw a few feathers floating through the air. It sounded like one chicken less back there; Jos went to check and informed me that dinner would be ready in about fifteen minutes.

Soon, a bowl was brought to me: a mixture of rice and various parts of the chicken. At the bottom of the bowl, just as I was finishing up, I saw the head of the chicken—mouth agape with its claws shoved through the throat. Was this the garnish or something?

The next few days consisted of walking through some of the most otherworldly scenery my eyes had ever encountered. I saw thatched roofs on mud huts, each one with a small wooden door—around three feet by three feet—through which the people crawled in and out. Other huts had simple drapes as doors, just something to keep the sunlight or dust out. A small cot would be inside, with a place for a cooking fire. Jos and I would sleep on the ground, and I saw some of the most gorgeous night lights I have ever encountered. When I was in Egypt, I would look around and realize that some of the farm scenes there hadn't changed in hundreds of years. As I looked around there—in this vast expanse of sand, haze, bare-branched trees, sparse vegetation, and people subsisting on and wearing next to nothing—I felt as if nothing had changed since Noah first got out of the ark. Had time completely passed by this part of the world? Did they know anything about a world one hundred miles away, let alone about a country like the United States?

It was now the fifth day of our journey, and according to Jos, it was the day for the market, which was supposed to be our last destination. We needed to get out of the valley, back up the cliffs, and over to the village in order to find the truck that would be not only delivering the food for the local market but providing us a way to get back to the civilization of Bandiagara, a land teaming with occasional electricity and hand-drawn well water.

The trip seemed to be taking its toll on me. Maybe it was all of the iodine I was putting in my canteen to purify the water, maybe it was a bad chicken, or maybe I was just getting tired of all of the dust and stench, but I was feeling a bit woozy at this stage of the trek. When Jos said that all we had to do was climb up another set of the cliffs to get back, I was more than willing.

However, the hike up the switchbacks proved challenging, and I was feeling quite light-headed. I knew we couldn't stop and rest at someone's hut, as we'd miss the market. Jos kept encouraging me to keep going. "The market! The market!" he kept shouting in French. "We're almost at the market! Keep going!" He could tell I was weakening and slowing down a bit, as each upward step was torture.

The market! What would be there? What kind of food awaited me there? Definitely mangos were on the horizon. All I could think about, all I could focus on to keep me motivated to take just one more step—and then another—was the prospect of peeling and biting into a juicy yellow mango. After all of the sickly tasting water I'd been drinking the past week, the promise of the sweetness of a hand-sized mango helped my parched body endure the dry foam surrounding my lips. I didn't have much water left, and it had to last until we arrived at the market. Only then could we get a refill of some semidrinkable water. Jos was already at the crest of the cliffs, and I was barely two-thirds of the way up. He was waving his arms and shouting down to me, "Let's go! The market!" Oh, those mangos that awaited me...

As I was finally reaching the crest of the cliffs, with Jos impatiently waiting and tapping his feet, I gave a glance back down at the base to see how much we had already hiked. Looking down through the haze, I could see huts seemingly glued to the side of the rocks, with people blithely going about their daily activities. Just what were their activities? Down in the flat valley were scattered huts, leafless trees with branches stretching out like something from a scary movie, and sand—lots of sand, with the huts barely visible through the dusty fog. Everyone down there was moving around in a fairly methodical manner. No one was in a rush, just going through the motions of existence like their previous generations had done for thousands of years. The timelessness of the place...had they ever heard about a God who loved them?

"Let's go! The market is ready for us!" Jos shouted at me as he pulled me along. By this time, I was feeling really weak, almost to the point of exhaustion. Slowly, trudging up the steps, I looked up about 150 feet to see Jos rapidly climbing up the trail, impatiently waiting for me and waving for me to catch up with him. Even just looking up to see my guide made my head spin with nausea. Oh boy, this was going to be a rough walk. I stopped to take a sip of water. It tasted like lukewarm, iodine-flavored liquid—nothing like normal water. It did nothing to increase my energy, but at least some of the cotton in my mouth started to go away. Because of my light-headedness, I lost my footing a couple of times, slipping and staggering on some of the stones. Better take tiny burro steps, I decided. Clip clop. Clip clop. I would make it, just for the sake of finally tasting some delicious fruit at the market that was going to be so wonderfully juicy. It would surely rejuvenate me for the trip back to Bandiagara.

Plodding along at a snail's pace, I finally reached the top crest of the cliff, feeling completely unemotional about the remainder of this hike—not worried, not scared, not excited. I just felt determined to make it, as this was market day, and there were no other options for me. There couldn't be any delay. It was kind of funny; here I was in the middle of nowhere, in a primitive society, and I was *in a rush to make an appointment!* Jos, having waited for me at the top for some time, looked at me with impatience, frustration, and, yet, cheerleading encouragement. "The market!" he continued shouting. "Keep walking! You'll feel better at the market!" This guy was trying to keep me motivated to hustle forward. I was trying to stay motivated to simply not lose my cookies...

A few more hours of hiking in the overcast heat went by, and we trudged forward as if we were in some scene from *Lawrence of Arabia*. There was no sign of anything; if there were a time *not* to trust my guide, this would be it, but he sure seemed to know where we were going. It was a good thing because, as I looked around, I realized there was absolutely *nothing* but rocks, sand, and bare trees. There were no reference points to even hallucinate about.

Jos was once again out in front of me by a good hundred yards. I could barely see him through the haze, but I could sure hear him. "Mr. George! There it is!" he shouted. "The market! Lots of food!" He enthusiastically ran toward me to grab my hand. Way out in the stark and open distance, I could barely make out a collection of mud huts, gathered in what looked like a traditional circle, with the village center being where that delicious market was located. Visions of juicy mangos filled my thoughts, giving me enough impetus to keep going. The structures were no hallucination or mirage; I could see them getting bigger and bigger with each step. Just in time, as I really felt like I couldn't go much further anyway, the market...the market!

Then, as I kept trudging forward, a strange sense of dread crept into the pit of my stomach. Was I going through some sort of food-deprived panic, or did I actually not see a market in the village? With each step closer to my mudded Xanadu, a knot grew inside. I could make out the huts in the distance, and maybe one or two people milling about, but there sure wasn't a truck—let alone any observable hustle and bustle normally associated with a farmer's market. In fact, as I kept getting closer, it started looking more and more like some deserted African ghost town!

We finally arrived, but as Jos and I trudged through the center and looked around, a feeling of dread enveloped us. Was this the wrong town? Where were we? How would we get back to semi-civilization?

I started feeling overwhelmingly weak and woozy. "Let's go to the chief's house. He'll tell us what to do," Jos said in a semipanicked tone, as he walked me over to a mud hut. Inside the cool and shady room was a tall, big-boned, mahogany-dark, and half-dressed woman sitting on her cot. She regally stood up to greet us. While Jos explained the situation to her, I plunged toward her bed for a few moments of cool repose. I immediately started uncontrollably shaking, as if I were having some sort of a seizure or chill. The woman blankly looked at me, went into another part of the hut, and came back with some water and beans for me to revive me. Grateful, I ingested the offering and immediately threw it all up on her dirt floor. Something was seriously wrong.

I fell back onto the cot while Jos and the lady talked. While still shaking, I glanced at him as he slowly walked over to me. "The market was yesterday," he explained. "We came a day too late. It won't be here for five more days."

With my head spinning from whatever ailed me, I tried to gather my thoughts. My mind was racing over our different options. I was definitely too weak to keep walking today. Maybe I could rest in one of the huts here for a day or two and then head back the way we came. My visa was getting close to expiring; it would be tight, but I could wait five more days and then wait for the truck again. Jos would find it for us, and then we could get back to Bandiagara, wherever it was. My head was throbbing and spinning from the news and from whatever bug, worm, or virus I had.

Jos interrupted my daze with a harsh, stentorian statement: "We must start walking back now!"

"There's no way I can keep walking today," I slurred. "I'm too weak!"

"We must leave *now*."

"Let's wait a day or two."

I couldn't believe this was happening. What was the rush? We were in a part of the country where its civilization would have to advance five hundred years just to be considered backward!

"Not today! I'm too sick!"

"Then pay me now."

Suddenly, I saw where I stood with this kid. I was only good to him as long as I was his bankroll. If I paid him, I figured he would have no motivation to stay with me and get me out of there. I had absolutely no concept of where we were. This kid was my passport to a return to health, as well as getting back to a normal life. I figured the money I was holding was all that stood between him being my loyal guide and leaving me literally high and dry.

"Our deal was that I'd pay you when we get back. You know that was our contract. As soon as we *both* get back, I will pay you."

"Pay me now!" he fiercely replied. "We go now!"

"I'm too sick! I'll pay you when we get back—"

"Then, I'm leaving you!"

And with that, Jos, my ten-year-old ticket back home, ran out of the hut.

CHAPTER 49

Stuck Inside of Mobile with the Memphis Blues Again

SUDDENLY, THE HUT WAS EERILY quiet. I was all alone, with just the memory of Jos's shadow leaving through the cloth-draped door. I was too weak to chase after him; I couldn't even raise my head. The chief's wife came back in, looking quite sympathetic. Behind her was her husband, the chief, wearing just a cloth robe—sort of resembling Fred Flintstone—looking at me with probably the same look I would've had if some sick stranger was lying in my bed. I could tell he was thinking, "How do I resolve this situation?" They both politely made it plain I couldn't stay in their hut, so they gently dragged me along the dusty floor and outside into their adjoining guesthouse, which was simply a fully functioning chicken coop.

Three of the walls and the roof were made of mud, and the front entrance consisted of a chicken-wire fence. The floor was a mix of dirt, sand, hay, chicken feed, and droppings, as well as about half a dozen chickens to serve as company. They all looked bemused and slightly inconvenienced at their new guest, just as the chief and his wife had merely a half hour ago.

Once they had plopped me inside, the wife tried to hand me one more bowl of water and beans, but they came right back up again. This was going to be a tough stay, to say the least. She must have decided the best thing for me at this juncture was to just leave me alone for a while and maybe I would recover on my own.

News travels fast in a twelve-hut village, however. Within a couple of hours, a pair of naked boys about seven or eight years old came up to the front of my cage and stared at me. Lying there, using my day pack as a pillow,

I figured I must be the entertainment for this town, since I hadn't seen any movie theaters or nightclubs. They seemed content to stare out me. Now I knew how it felt to be on exhibit at the San Diego Zoo...

One of them spoke up. "Bic?"

What was he saying?

"Bic? Bic?"

My mind was racing. What did he want? Was this a local word? Something in French?

I had been lying down for a few hours, and I had thought that maybe I could reach some sort of agreement with the chickens; they could have their part of the coop, and I could have mine. That idea didn't work out at all; as soon as I would lie still, they'd start walking over me, clucking away, and pecking at me like I had just come out of a bag from a feed store. I needed to keep moving, so I laboriously pulled myself into a sitting position. Whoa! I was a little light-headed, but I could do it, as long as I leaned against a mud wall. I figured I'd try to write something in my journal to pass the time, so I had taken out my booklet and pen...

"Bic! Bic!" the boys rapidly shouted while jumping up and down.

These leeches wanted my pen! The guy who brought the food in the truck on market day must have given these kids a taste of modern technology once in a while.

"No!"

"Bic! Bic!" They started opening the wire gate to the coop, reaching to take my day pack.

"No!" I weakly shouted, as I pushed them away. The boys immediately scurried out, closed the cage, and resumed their safe position, protected by the wire. The commotion got the chickens all stirred up, causing them to jump and fly all over the coop. Feathers and dust went in every direction.

"Bic? Bic?" My tormenters went back to their initial request. They were not going away for a while. Where did they have to go? Exhausted from this trial, I used my pack as a pillow to lie back down. I also tied one of the straps of the pack around my arm, so I could lie down to rest without fear of theft. There was a silent and oppressive stillness outside my coop. The only sounds interrupting the emptiness were the clucking of the chickens, returning to their daily activities, and the intermittent pleading of the boys saying, "Bic." Could this really be happening to me? There was no way I was getting up to do anything for a while. Maybe for days.

Lying there, with my head feeling like it was doubling as a punching bag, I realized my only hope—and I mean my *only* hope—of making it out of there was to stay alive for five days until the next market. Somehow, I could then find the guy with the truck that brought the supplies and have him take me to Bandiagara. From there, I would have to make my trek back to Mopti and, ultimately, to Bamako, where plumbing and electricity awaited me with open pipes and kilowatts. But first, I had to live.

I tried to write in my journal, but I was too weak to lift my pen. I had a book; maybe I could read that to pass the time and stay conscious. *The Razor's Edge* by Somerset Maugham. Hmm. I just didn't think that seemed right. I was dying, and my last deed would be reading a novel? I still had my Bible... much more appropriate.

I tried reading, but I was even too weak for that. I decided I would just work on a verse. I'd always wanted to memorize Isaiah 40:31, ever since I had seen it in a Norman Vincent Peale book.

But those who trust in the Lord shall renew their strength.
They will take their wings and fly like eagles.
They will walk and not grow tired.
They will run, and not grow weak.

So far on this trip around Africa, I had committed a couple little verses here and there to memory—nothing too long, as I was more interested in passing my time waiting for a bus or hitchhiking by memorizing songs from Tin Pan Alley or Tom Waits's catalog. Suddenly, here I was in this dire situation; those lyrics now seemed so trivial. Going over songs like "My Blue Heaven" or "Tennessee Waltz" was not going to save me now, but I felt that getting God's word inside my mind and soul could give me a fighting chance.

While the sun started to set on that first blistering day in the chicken coop, I simply repeated the words from Isaiah over and over—sometimes out loud, sometimes as a liturgical mumble—to pass the time. Too weak to eat, afraid to drink anything more than a swallow of putrid water every now and then, I put myself in the corner farthest from the wire gate, so the kids would have to wake me up by startling the chickens if they decided to pilfer my last worldly possessions.

And just what did I have that was so important anyway? Well, the kids probably just wanted the pens or some other trinkets, but I wondered if anyone there would try to roll me for my wallet. I had my passport hidden inside a secret pocket sewn in my pant leg, so that probably wouldn't be found unless I ended up dying here.

Dying. I just might do that. It was only the first night. Could I make it through five? Would I even be strong enough to find the truck, crawl over to it, and ultimately get back to Bamako? It was the only town in all of Mali with running water and electricity, and the thought of a nice, refreshing shower and a lukewarm Yukki Soda caressed my mind enough to let me sleep the first night.

At five o'clock, the sun rose, brightly shining in my face the next morning. I took roll call. My head was still splitting with dizziness and agony. I tried to get up, but the wooziness made me fall right back down again. The chief's wife came by to give me some food and water. I immediately wretched up the food again, but I managed to keep a bit of water inside. Back to lying down. I realized I was going to spend the whole day running the Bible verses in my mind.

Not too long ago, I had looked at a map of Africa and realized that no one on earth knew where I was, and I had reveled in the anonymity. Now, in this present predicament, I was in the same situation, but the conditions had changed totally: I was in the middle of absolutely nowhere, with no idea how to get anywhere, let alone the strength to do so, and without a friend, hired hand, or mercenary to get me back to some sense of security. With the chickens fairly quiet and docile this early in the morning, I lay there in complete silence. There were no background sounds, no breezes, footsteps, or outside conversations. Absolute silence was enveloping my existence. There was nothing to distract me to help me pass the time. All I had was myself and my innermost thoughts.

I had traveled by myself countless times the past few years while in college and chiropractic school in order to prepare myself for this trip and to see if I had the stomach for solitude. I had done well enough to convince myself to go on this two-year trek, and now, here I was, completely isolated from even a hint of civilization. I realized how often in my life I had used TV, the radio, tape players, newspapers, magazines, books, or even eating at a diner as ways of breaking up the silence of solitude. Lots of people I knew couldn't tolerate even five minutes by themselves, even with background music. I always enjoyed the role of a solo traveler, as I knew I could always link up with someone if I needed company. Well, here I was completely by myself, with simply the dark recesses of my mind as my only companion.

It's quite amazing what you can think about when you're *truly* alone—even more so when you think you might be living the final moments of your life. I thought of all the stories that appeared in newspapers, like "Body of American Traveler Found in Zimbabwe after Being Ambushed by Guerrillas." I started wondering just how long it would take for someone to find me. Let's see...

I had written my parents every week for the past two years, and I had numbered and dated each of the letters. How long would it be before they would realize I had stopped writing? Maybe four to six weeks? I had sent my last letter from Bamako about a week before, so I'd be dead and pillaged for quite some time before they'd even get suspicious. How would they start looking for me in Mali? Would they meet anyone who knew me or had met me? In a country like this that thrived on suspicion and fear, would there even be anyone who would admit they had seen me?

Who would identify me? American passports sold for a lot of money in the black market in Africa. That would probably be the first thing taken from me after I was dead, no doubt. My other identification cards would get into the hands of some smart dealer in no time flat for a few francs. I envisioned my mom and dad arriving in Mali without a single clue of what their next step would be.

And for what purpose would I have put them through this whole hellish misery? Just to see the world? And what end result had I accomplished? Had I made the world a better place? Started a family? Helped my fellow man? Not at all...it was all for myself.

Sometimes, when we start thinking seriously about our direction in life and what we've done with our time here on this planet, the self-evaluation can get quite discomforting. I remember someone once telling me that most people spend more time planning a two-week summer vacation than they spend charting their purpose on earth for their seventy-plus years. It was so true, and while I was lying there, I realized why. When our thoughts get too tough and harsh to handle, we tend to want to get out of that mental situation and change moods. So, we turn on a radio, clean a room, or watch a movie. We do something—anything—to prevent us from looking too deeply into who we really are, our purpose in life, and how to deal with the difficult issues in our mind and soul.

Well, stuck in this cage of mud and wire, I had absolutely nowhere to go in order to escape my thoughts. Every time I started thinking about my life and what I had done with it, I tried to divert my thoughts to something else. The problem was that there was nothing to distract me. I didn't have the luxury Scarlet O'Hara had to escape her thoughts by the blithe dismissal of "Oh, I can't think about that now; I'll just think about it tomorrow." There was nowhere to hide, and this wasn't Tara.

I reflected back on this trip and realized it had all been for myself—traveling experiences, just for myself; buying souvenirs, for yours truly as well;

seeing the world, meeting people, meeting up with various women, all for my own satisfaction and desires. Had I ever *really* done anything from completely altruistic motives…that wasn't at least partially tainted by self-interest?

Each morning, I woke up when the bright and merciless sun rose. Between episodes of repeating my Bible verses, I reflected back on periods of my life—working in Israel and Italy, traveling throughout the United States in my van, chiropractic college and undergrad school, high school—all the way back like a bad episode of *This Is Your Life*. All the sports I played, friends I had, girls I dated…everything I had done in my life—even going to church—had been pursued with selfish motives. The deeper I plunged into my heart, the blacker the inner recesses of my spiritual environment I reached. I would have done anything to turn away from the depths of my dark soul, but there was no other distraction.

I was ashamed of the shallowness of my life. What was the difference between me and someone like Pol Pot? Maybe the magnitude of the outcome was different, but our hearts were similarly tainted with the dark, ugly tar of sin. I felt that penetrating and addictive evilness within me, and I hated it. I couldn't deny it, and I was disgusted with what I had done with the life and salvation God had given me. This was the best I could do for Him? A life that ended with grief and sadness for my family and acquaintances?

I recalled that intense night at the missionaries' home in Kenya when I felt God's conviction of sin combined with an overwhelming sense of cleansing and forgiveness. Yet what had I done since then? I had still traveled, bought things, taken photos, and even met women all for myself. Nothing had really changed. Oh, maybe I was a bit less egregious in my wicked ways, or as an old non-Christian friend used to say, "I'm not that bad; I'm more of a vice follower." I wasn't different from him in kind, if perhaps in degree.

Now, I know a lot of people have made deathbed confessions. Some have done it in foxholes, and a famous one was recorded by a thief on the cross next to Jesus Himself. All I know is that I was truly sick and tired of my life up to that point, and I told God that if He got me out of that situation and back to safety, I would finally be serious and live for Him. I even told Him that both He and I knew that I was still going to blow it a lot more times, but it wouldn't be for a lack of trying anymore. In the past, I had worked on being godly for my own benefit. For the first time in my life, I was ready to commit to a steady path of living for His sake, pleasure, and glory.

A simple exclamation suddenly became illuminated to me. I had often heard the phrase "for God's sake." "For God's sake, clean your room!" or "Turn off the TV for God's sake!" It's a simple phrase that is mindlessly uttered to get people to do (or not to do) something; but that phrase is actually the most important motivation to live and exist. *For God's sake*, George, live *for God's sake*!

The evenings would mercifully come and break the oppressive heat. I'd fall asleep at sunset, and the bright-orange morning sun would greet me at dawn. Another day to survive. And that's what it simply was. "Yet those who trust…"

A couple more days passed. One morning, I looked at my watch (which I wore not so much to know what time it was, but—more important—what day it was, so I could take my malaria tablets on the same day each week to reduce the risk of getting the dreaded disease. According to my trusted horologic friend, tomorrow was the day. I was going to make it! The kids hadn't been trying to steal from me lately, and the chickens seemed to be taking fewer shifts of walking over me and pecking on my clothes and flesh. Since this was the fourth (or was it the fifth?) day, I felt pretty weak and listless. I hadn't moved in quite some time, let alone eaten; this was the ultimate diet plan.

I practiced crawling around a little bit to see if I had any strength left to get out of there. I figured that when the truck and driver came with supplies, he was not going to be looking for me; I had better be strong enough to crawl, hobble, or walk to his truck in order to get his attention to hitch a ride back to Bandiagara. Once there, I could recuperate for a few days before finding a taxi to take me either to Mopti or directly to Bamako. According to my visa, I had about twelve days to get this done. With the thought of a shower and soft drink within a week's time, I drifted into blissful sleep my last night in that sub-Saharan purgatory. I could feel the blessing of being given a second chance.

CHAPTER 50

Hit the Road, Jack!

⟶

LIKE A RELIABLE ALARM CLOCK, the sun shined like a flashlight in my face at five o'clock, preparing me for the most important travel day of these past two years.

I had my day pack slung around my shoulders as I crawled through the wire gate of the chicken coop to look around the village square. The chief's wife came over for her daily check on me, and I bid her a heartfelt thanks and adieu. I slowly glanced around the circle of mud huts. Where might the market and the truck be? I tried to slowly prop myself in order to stand up for the first time in a while—hey, not bad! I was a little wobbly, but I could walk around for a few steps. I practiced this for a couple of hours while waiting for my truck. I figured if I could bribe the driver, I could get a shotgun seat and rest inside while traveling back to Bandiagara.

I finally saw some commotion at the far edge of town, so I ever so slowly walked over, pausing to rest every ten to twenty steps. I was not used to being in a vertical position, and everything was spinning around from my head down to the pit of my stomach. Whew! This was like Marlon Brando in *On the Waterfront*!

There was the truck! Never did a vehicle look so glorious as did this shabby bucket of bolts and metal. I made my way over, and holding on to the truck for support, I stumbled to the cabin. No one was there. I asked around and got as many different answers about the driver's whereabouts as the number of people I asked. The most logical answer was a local eatery.

I managed to get to the place, and the driver was easy to spot, since he was the only white guy around and was wearing Western clothes. He was drinking his cup of something with a gruel-like breakfast. I hobbled over to him, and he gave me a quick glance before returning to his morning feed.

"What are you doing here?"

"Been waiting for you all week," I replied. "I'm really sick, and I need a lift back to Bandiagara. How much for a cabin seat?"

He looked straight ahead without pausing in his meal. "Sorry, would love to help you, but I've sold those seats already. Best I can do is put you on the truck."

I recalled the truck having a giant flatbed, but it was loaded up with tons of something or other, covered, and tied down with a giant sheet of burlap.

"Where on the truck?"

"*On* the truck, mate. You can ride on top of my stuff."

That didn't seem like a great choice, but the fact remained that my options were pretty limited. "I'm pretty sick and weak. How do I keep from falling off?"

"I'll figure something out. Just stay by the truck all day, and get ready to leave right away. No charge," he concluded as he finished off his meal, flipped the cook a couple coins, and headed off to some business destination with about as much thought for my travel needs as his concerns about fleas on a dog.

By midafternoon, market business was dying down, and the people started drifting back to their homes and daily grinds. I sat by the passenger door of the truck, hoping for some change in my transportation fortunes. I glanced up; the lucky stiffs who had gotten the cabin seats came sauntering over to the truck, gave a look and a smirk over in my direction, and slid into their luxurious bench. There were three of them; the seat only really held two people, so it would be a pretty tight fit. Besides, four to five hours sitting up might have been too rough for me anyhow; I was feeling pretty spaced out just sitting on the dirt waiting for the driver.

He finally arrived and strutted over with a getting-down-to-business look in his eye. He looked inside the cabin to check on his paying passengers, and then he gave me a glance. He called to a couple of locals, who climbed up the truck's carriage.

"Think you can make it up there?"

"Not sure. Pretty rough climb."

"Here," he said as he handed me a rope. "Put this around your waist."

"What for?"

"We'll use this to pull you up and then tie you to the top of the truck."

What else could I do? I dutifully obeyed. The assistants pulled me to the top of the baggage and tied me to the supporting cables on the burlap. They secured me pretty well, as I lay supine, with my day pack as my pillow.

"How's it feel up there?" my driver asked.

"I'll make it. Let's go."

The drive went smoothly and uneventfully until the tired sun started setting. Just at the approach of dusk, the truck stopped, and the three passengers got out and knelt, facing east for the evening prayers Muslims recite. What a sight—I was tied down on top of a truck, in the middle of absolutely nowhere in the desert, with the moon shining like a crescent, and the Muslims were dutifully worshipping their god. Everything definitely got put on hold for religion.

In the pitch-black of night, we arrive in Bandiagara. Step 1 was completed. The taxis and trucks departed for Mopti at various times of the day from there, so I could leave any time of the day (unlike the ride to Bamako from Mopti, which only left at one time—7:00 a.m., at the very latest).

I was untied from the truck and helped off. The driver took me to a place where I could get a bite to eat and spend the night before heading out the next day. Staggering over to the diner, I sat down with the driver in a daze at the community table. I couldn't believe I had made it that far, and yet I still had so far to go. Did I have the strength to do it?

Looking across the table, I couldn't believe my eyes; it was Jos! He was staring right at me with the most peculiar look. Was it guilt? Anger? Shame? In my half-hallucinogenic daze, I couldn't figure it out.

"That's the punk who left me for dead at the village," I said to the driver.

The driver said something in French to the kid, and Jos answered. "He said you still owe him for the tour."

I leaped across the table like a ravenous crocodile for the kill. I don't know what I would've done if I had grabbed him, but he ran into the night with all the speed of adrenaline, never to be seen again. I probably would have forgiven him if he had apologized, which was what I thought was going to transpire. His self-serving response had taken me by complete surprise. So, my first act after being saved was vengeance; I still had a lot to learn, and I felt that God was just at the starting blocks of teaching me.

The next day, I got a ride to Mopti without incident. Feeling unbelievably weak, I hobbled to town and found the place I had previously stayed. I had left my other belongings there, and—lo and behold—they were all intact! The kind manager told me where the bus station was. "But you have to get there very early," he warned, "as it's a twelve-hour journey."

I figured it would take me at least three to four days to build up the strength to wake up early enough in order to make it to the station on time. Since I was not vomiting anymore, I was able to eat and drink small portions of the daily fare, though not shaving or washing and drying my clothes on their three-day cycle anymore. Each day, I practiced getting out of bed and strolling over to the collection of taxis. The first day, I made it to the taxis at eleven o'clock. I had to do better than that. Ten o'clock…half past nine…I was getting there.

After about four days of practice, I felt my D-Day had arrived. The promise of running water and electricity was a powerful motivation. I had visions of sitting in a shower at the convent where I had previously resided and just letting the water pour over my squalid body. That and a semicool Yukki Soda were the promises of earthly paradise awaiting me as rewards for my odyssey. It amazed me what a powerful tool hope can be. I recalled a story told by the Russian novelist Solzhenitsyn in one of his gulag books. He had written that when the guards wanted to break their prisoners' hearts, they wouldn't give them difficult work to do. Instead, they would command the laborers to use a shovel to pile rocks in a wheelbarrow and dump them into a pile five hundred yards away. Then, they would be ordered to refill the wheelbarrow and dump the pile of rocks back in the original spot. They would repeat this procedure over and over again, breaking the prisoners' will by giving them not difficult tasks but *meaningless* ones. Hope, or the lack of it, was enough to influence just about any action.

On the appointed day, I was up at 6:30 a.m. and grabbed my pack. I was in my *On the Waterfront* mode again, and I wearily staggered to the taxi station, determined to find a ride for the next part of my trip. I looked at my watch and thought again how ironic it was that I needed to live by the clock in such a backward third-world country!

I arrived at the station by 7:30 a.m. It was deserted, except for one open-ended Toyota truck. I'd arrived too late to secure a comfortable car or station wagon. Since there was just one option, I went over to see about getting my ride. The cabin, once again, was already filled with passengers. The driver was indeed the last driver going to Bamako, so I had no choice. I crawled over the tailgate into the back and sat down in the corner. Eventually, the cabin bed filled with adult passengers destined to Bamako as well. They all looked at me quizzically—keeping to themselves but seemingly amused at me, as if I were some sort of entertainment for them.

Twelve hours to go. I just had to endure this ride for twelve hours, and I would be home free. I had endured five days in a cage, so this one should be doable.

We left Bandiagara on the corrugated dirt road, with a cloud of dust swirling around us. All the other passengers covered their mouths and faces with shawls and kerchiefs to protect themselves. I had no such luxury, so I just bowed my head and buried it in my hat.

The first hour passed slowly, and I was already feeling pretty rough and nauseous. The mix of the bumpy road, dry heat, and swirling dust started to get to me. I felt like if I could just throw up, maybe I would feel a bit better. All I could do was lean over the side of the moving truck and dry heave. I felt like my lungs were coming out of my mouth.

While I was going through all this misery, the other passengers started laughing at me! Was this some local way of showing pity, or was it mockery? It was beyond my comprehension to be laughed at while simultaneously feeling like I was about to die. This went on for about another hour. There was just no way I was going to make it for another ten hours. Something had to change, and I had no idea what that change could be in this West African no-man's-land.

Eventually, in the middle of nowhere, we arrived at a checkpoint, consisting of a crossing gate, a tiny station, and a cot. While we were stopped for the examination of our passports and papers, I got out of the truck's bed and lunged for the guards' couch, which was just past the blockade. Lying there, I started shaking uncontrollably. Every part of my body started trembling, and I felt like I was losing control of myself. My hands and toes started curling up. Was this the beginning of the end? The guard hovered over me, and the passengers circled like vultures, still laughing, as if they were waiting for me to die so they could get my documents and money. The guard looked at me and declared, "You have malaria." I was too weak to argue with the guy. Was this finally it? Would I go out, as T. S. Eliot wrote, not with a bang but with a whimper?

I have absolutely no definitive answer for what transpired next—and whether it was human or celestial in origin—but as I lay on what appeared to be my deathbed, I looked up and saw a cloud of dust arrive at our site from the distant background. As the dust settled, a station wagon appeared, and a stocky, bearded white guy—looking quite American—carrying a day pack, briskly walked through the crowd and leaned over me.

His eyes looked sparkling and intent, and he asked me seriously, "What's wrong?"

"Oh, just that I'm dying…" I tried to make light of the situation.

He took off his pack and pulled out a handful of small packets. They looked like high-tech sugar packs. He opened one of them and poured it into my canteen. "Here, try this."

Fluids never tasted so good, as they caressed my parched throat. There was something special in that water, and it felt life enhancing, almost like liquid forgiveness. Within seconds, my hands and feet started returning to normal. For the first time in weeks, I actually felt refreshed. *Wow*! I had been given some more time to live. But for how long?

"You just saved my life. Thanks."

"The weird thing is that I was supposed to be in Bamako yesterday, but I got delayed, so we had to leave today instead. Strange how that happened…"

I knew for certain I was on the last departing vehicle from Mopti, but I couldn't argue with the fact that there was another vehicle there that arrived after I had. Lying there, I felt God had just intervened in my destiny. My scruffy guardian angel, be he human or celestial, went over to the truck I had been traveling in. I could see him discussing something with the driver, and then he gave him some money. Was this some sort of bribe? He came back to check on me.

"There's a hospital about three hours away here. The driver is going to take you there. You'll be able to recover there and then make it to Bamako when you're a little stronger. You're gonna be all right."

His confidence inspired me, like I was getting a half-time pep talk from Vince Lombardi. He quietly got back in the wagon, and just as mysteriously as he arrived, he departed in a similar cloud of dust. Just who, or what, was he?

Rejuvenated from the magical potion, I returned to the back of the truck, but this time feeling a bit revived and hopeful, knowing I would be able to endure the ride to the hospital. The hours passed slowly on the dirt road, and I still had episodes of nausea from the dust. I finally collapsed in the corner of the truck bed, with the laughs of the bemused passengers still pelting me like a mocking Greek chorus.

We made a sharp hairpin turn, and up ahead, I saw a drab, run-down building, fronted by a circular driveway. It must be the hospital! We halted right in front, and the driver honked the horn, hopped out, grabbed me by the scruff of my shirt, and proceeded to plop me on the curb like a sack of potatoes. Then he drove off with the efficiency of a UPS carrier.

I lay there for a brief time, once again too weak to get up, while a group of apparent hospital workers came out to check on their delivered package.

CHAPTER 51

Hospitality on Parade

GRABBED LIKE A SACK OF fertilizer, I was half carried, half dragged into the hospital, or what pretended to be one. After entering through the front door, all I saw were metal frames of beds and springs lazily bending in various directions—some with stained, old, pockmarked foam mattresses haphazardly strewn over them. On top of just about every mattress and around and under each and every bed were cats of every size, shape, color, and creed. It didn't look like anyone had been a human patient here since the Scottish explorer Alexander Gordon Laing discovered Timbuktu back in 1826. I was going to recover in this place? I might have had better luck on the truck!

The uniformed aides placed me on a solid concrete slab that must have been used for cadavers or something. Lying on my back, with my pack as a pillow, I looked around to see that I was surrounded by a collection of local assistants.

"You've been bitten by a mosquito," one of them shouted at me above the rest of the murmuring audience. "They're getting a doctor," he enthusiastically told me.

"I don't have malaria; I just need some clean water to drink," I weakly told them in my fragile French.

"You were bit by a mosquito. Bzzzzzzzzzzzzzz," he repeated back, completely ignoring what I was saying.

"I'm dry! Bring me water." To think, I might just die in this stupid place, surrounded by people who couldn't understand what I was trying to tell them. Talk about frustrating! I knew what my problem was, and these people could have the power to help me, but they simply didn't want to or couldn't listen to me. "This morbid comedy scene doesn't have to be this way, but I'm trapped…"

In strolled the doctor—a Frenchman who was wearing a white coat, as well as a Nikon camera strung around his neck. I felt the slightest suspicion that he was not there on a completely altruistic humanitarian mission. He indifferently peered at me through the crowd and authoritatively announced, "He's been bit by a mosquito."

"*No!*" I told him. "I need clean water to drink. I drank something bad…"

"You have malaria," he calmly corrected with classic medical pomposity. "I'll give you something to help." He immediately called an assistant (I wouldn't insult the health profession by calling her a nurse), who brought him a syringe. "This will help you," he said, and he proceeded to assertively give me a shot in my rear end.

"What was that?"

"Vitamin C."

Great, a useless treatment for a disease that I didn't have. What was that supposed to do? Prevent my rear end from getting scurvy? When would the Marx Brothers pop into this act?

Uh-oh. Here I went again! I felt my feet and hands start curling up, just like before—sort of like a New Year's Eve blowout toy returning to its starting position. This was getting ridiculous; I definitely sensed a loss of control over my body this time, as I seemed to shrivel up for the last time, surrounded by a helpless and incompetent crew of strangers.

Once again, out of absolutely nowhere, another guest appeared. A tall, thin, bearded, American-looking guy about my age strutted in with a day pack on his shoulders. "Hey! Good-bye everyone!" he shouted as he looked around. He scanned the room and spotted me on the table. "Who are *you*? What are you doing here?"

"Oh, just waiting to die," I calmly replied. "Can you help me?"

"I can't, but I know someone who can," he eagerly replied. "There's a nurse who has lived here for two years, and she was supposed to go back to her home in Belgium today, but she missed her taxi, so she has to wait until later this week for the next ride. She's got a ton of medicine, and she'll be able to help you." He departed as mysteriously as he had come.

A few minutes passed, and my hands and feet curled tighter and tighter like a vise. A twentyish brunette, with a face filled with concern, competency, and compassion, came to my side. "I can help you," she calmly stated in French-accented English (I *love* that accent!), and she immediately ordered the workers around a bit. Meanwhile, she hung up a bottle of fluids and injected the IV needle into my arm. "If it's what I think it is, this will help," she said.

Immediately, my toes, fingers, palms, arches, arms, and hands slowly uncurled, responding just as if a dried leaf were getting a much-needed pitcher of water with Miracle-Gro. Ah! My body felt like it was breathing again!

"You saved my life. Thank you."

"It's very peculiar that I am here," she stated. "I was supposed to leave yesterday, but for reasons I couldn't control, I missed my taxi."

"Same here," replied the American. "I'm Paul. I've been working for the Peace Corps the past couple of years. I finished my assignment last week, and I was supposed to leave then, but I had some visa problems. I had to stay here for another couple of weeks to get it straightened out before I could go back home. I just popped back here to bid everyone one last farewell."

None of the people who saved my life were supposed to be where they were when they came at just the right time to intervene. Coincidence? Angels? People God had directed in order to protect me? Lying there, guarded by two people who lived thousands of miles away from each other—let alone from me—I realized that God wanted to save my life, for whatever reason, and nothing was going to stop Him. I knew I was going to make it. Even with the meowing of the dirty cats in the background, I felt a peace, knowing my life was out of my hands and in His.

"Look, George," the nurse calmly said, as she comfortingly held my arm, "I have to leave tonight to go back to my country. Paul here will take care of you. I've given him enough medicine to get you back on your feet. Good luck, and God bless you." And with that, she exited like the Ghost of Christmas Past.

"Was she real?" I asked Paul.

"Oh, yes." He chuckled. "Quite human. Hey, we've got to get you out of this dump before they kill you. I've got a place just down the block. Rest here for a bit, let the fluids fill you up, and I'll get a room and bed ready for you."

Within a couple of hours, Paul returned, lifted me off the concrete operating table, and walked me along the dirt path to his humble little house. It had concrete walls and ceiling, and while having the faucets and accoutrements of indoor plumbing, it relied on well water for the basics of drinking and hygiene.

A bed never felt so comfortable as it caressed this tired patient. It was nothing fancy at all—a couple of sheets on a foam mattress—but I felt safe and protected. I lay there the rest of the day. "Don't worry about feeding me, Paul," I groaned. "Just a bit of water with those powders, and I'll make it."

That was the last thing I remember before I woke up…two days later.

It was early to midmorning, and I slowly rolled out of bed to a semisitting position. I heard Paul fiddling in the kitchen, and he came by to tell me how long I'd been sleeping. Whew! No wonder I felt so well rested! I still felt pretty weak and wobbly from the whole ordeal, though. In fact, I didn't realize just how weak I was until I tried to stand up…and fell right back down again onto the bed.

"Let's try that one more time," he said as he lifted me up. "You want to try some breakfast?"

"Sure, but let me hit the head first. Two days is enough for anyone."

I slowly shuffled my feet to the bathroom. Wow. An actual toilet, sink, and…a mirror! I hadn't seen one of those in months! I was actually afraid to see how I looked after my ordeal. I didn't think I was ready to stare at myself yet, so I started at the entry level of self-examination by cautiously stepping onto the scale. The last time I had weighed myself was right before I had left Israel. I had arrived in Italy, two long years ago, weighing about 170 pounds. About a year later, before I headed to Egypt, I was in the high 170s.

I planted both feet on the scale, and the needle stopped at…150. Oh boy, had I lost some weight. At six feet four inches, I was a pretty skinny guy. Time to check the face. I felt like I was in that classic Harpo Marx scene where he's afraid to look at himself in the mirror.

Just who *was* that person in the reflection? White pasty complexion, hollow cheeks, dark circles under the eyes, vacant stare, unshaven for two weeks, hair in a million directions. "Hello, sucker," I greeted myself. "So, this

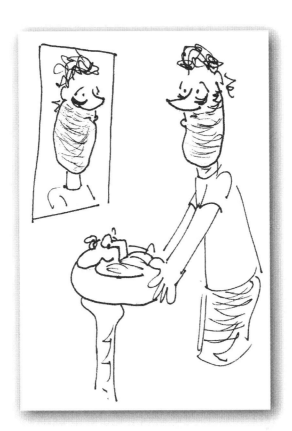

is where your glorious world travels have ended up." I felt like I was looking at a picture of Dorian Gray, staring at a specter of myself. Mixing fascination with bemused horror and disgust, I analyzed all the lines, sores, and marks on my face this trip had laid on me. It was almost like staring into my future. Or was it my past? I finally had to turn my head away, deciding not to look at that—or any other—mirror until I felt a good bit healthier. My face had given me a pretty rough welcome back to the real world.

Paul nursed me back to health for a few days. Both he and I had a limited number of days left on our visas (he had fewer than I), so we knew we had to get to Bamako at our earliest possibility. I finally felt strong enough after a few days, and Paul found us a taxi to take us on the nine remaining hours of the trip…in an actual car! I felt like royalty!

I could hardly believe it when we finally arrived at Bamako. Paul had the taxi drive up to the convent I had stayed at three long weeks before.

"I have to let you off here, my friend," he said, sticking out his hand. "I'm going straight to the airport to get home. Good luck."

And with that, he drove off. I've never seen him since. I never got a mailing address or any way to contact him. Did he really exist, or was he some strange illusion or specter? Sometimes, I wonder. It all happened in such a peculiar fashion. I couldn't argue with the fact, though, that I was back at the place I'd been dreaming about the whole while I was sick in the chicken coop: the land of running water and electricity.

My first shower felt so good. I just sat in the stall—still with my clothes on—with the water pouring over my head. It was my reward for enduring the journey. My enjoyment was short-lived, however, as I suddenly felt new rumblings of my illness…diarrhea! It continued for the rest of my trip, which was not a great thing to be endowed with in a part of the world where the public baths and "squatty potties" lacked toilet paper…and you never share a meal with a guy named Lefty, if you get my drift.

Suddenly, pages from my tour books became an essential part of my alimentary habits. I had about four days left on my visa to get my bowels in order, so as not to have some major international incident at the Bamako airport.

The next day, I purchased my plane ticket. The airplane left from Bamako to Dakar, Senegal, every Tuesday and Saturday. This was it. I would leave on Tuesday, and my visa expired the next day. I was all set, and boy, was I ready to feel the cool ocean breeze. I had been landlocked for four to five months, and the stillness of the air had been adversely affecting me and my attitude… or was it just that I was starting to get a bit travel crazy? John, my old traveling partner in Kenya, said you start "going troppo" when you travel for a long time. The dry climate never releases the needed precipitation, so you always feel barometric tension, which builds up into your system, causing you to go crazy. Is that what was happening? All I knew was I hadn't seen a cold, rainy, cleansing day for over a year, and I need the catharsis of a nice storm. Just as the Yukki Soda had enticed me and motivated me to make it to Bamako, so now I felt the calling of the breezes and misty airs of Dakar to revive me.

CHAPTER 52

Oh, Get Outta Town!

THERE WAS NOTHING LIKE THE exciting anticipation of a travel day that would take me to the paradise of ocean air. I had all my things together, and while I still felt weak and feeble, I knew I had no other option but to leave that very day, due to the visa situation. I made it to the airport nice and early in order to check in. Something about third-world airports exuded an air of vulnerability and uncertainty. You just never knew what might happen, so you had better get there with lots of time to spare just in case something went wrong—especially if you were booked on the country's notorious airline, Air Mali, derisively dubbed "Air Maybe" by the locals.

I took a break from reading Somerset Maugham's *The Razor's Edge* at the waiting station, and I looked around at the crowd. All the seats were taken. Well, that meant the flight would not, most likely, be canceled! Everyone was sitting in the usual third-world stupor when we heard a big commotion in the distance. A large entourage was headed our way, bursting its way through the passengers. A dozen or so really tall locals—wearing uniform basketball sweats, sunglasses, and wool caps—were surrounded by a support staff of coaches, families, and hangers-on, glistening with self-importance.

I went back to reading my book, but, a few minutes later, I heard something over the loudspeaker in French that I couldn't understand. However, I was easily able to figure out something was amiss, as all the people seated around me suddenly shot up out of their chairs and headed to a counter just beside the exit door that led to our designated twin-propeller airplane, waiting out on the tarmac. I figured it must have been the call to get on board, but there was too much urgency and agitation for that to be the cause. I headed over to the crowd.

"We're not getting on the plane today," one of the people told me. "That basketball team that came by took all our seats and bumped us off the flight. The man up there says we have to wait until the next flight, which is in four days."

I looked over the crowd and saw a diminutive, middle-aged, probably Indian man—or from somewhere else in Central Asia—wearing a semiofficial, semisafari khaki uniform. He had a harried look in his eye as he shouted over the crowd noise, telling us we would be getting our tickets returned. Submissively, the people started lining up to receive their punishment for being ordinary citizens and not some special celebrity.

This just couldn't be happening! My visa was running out, and I couldn't get it renewed! I was feeling absolutely nauseous and miserable, and I did not feel like I could survive in this air-stilted environment. I need that ocean breeze! I worked my way up through the crowd and told the bureaucratic clerk that I need to get on that plane.

"You can't get on," he sternly replied. "The flight is full."

"But I'm sick," I responded, coughing right in his face. "See? I need to leave this country now!"

"No room! You must get your ticket back," he dismissively answered as he held the box of tickets to begin handing them back to the sea of humanity, like a man feeding a school of fish in a koi pond.

"But I'm sick. I'm sick. *I'm sick!*" I continued to hack in his face, to extract some repentant pity, but it was to no avail.

How was I going to get on that plane? Suddenly, I had a flashback to my college days at CSUN registration. A sense of déjà vu overcame me; I had been in this situation before. It worked once; why not try it again?

I leaned over the counter, grabbed the astonished bureaucrat's box filled with airline tickets, and climbed on top of the counter. Looming over my uniformed adversary, I shouted at him, "If I don't get on that plane, no one is getting their tickets back. I'm holding this flight hostage."

Scanning the room, I saw a wave of passengers and their relatives. As if a switch were flipped, all of their eyes and angry outbursts turned from the airline attendant up about sixty degrees toward me. Over a hundred people were yelling and shouting at me; it was impossible to tell if they were yelling

for my victory or for my head. Regardless, while the attendant was yelling for me to give him back the tickets, I kept loudly answering that he would get them once I was on that plane.

I looked in the distance and saw a uniformed man (though too old and scrawny to be a soldier) work his way through the crowd to get my attention. "Please put down those tickets, sir!"

"Not until I get on that plane! I'm very sick, and I need to leave today!" I shouted, as I coughed to make my point.

"You will not get what you want unless you cooperate with us," he declared.

I had the dreadful feeling I was getting cornered into a difficult situation, but since this was a fairly safe country, I felt that I shouldn't push my demonstration. "If I give you the tickets, will you help me?"

"I cannot promise anything, but I will try to help."

He seemed sincere, so I handed the attendant the multitude of tickets. While the crowd refocused on their immediate transportation problem, the uniformed official led me to a corner of the airport. I explained my situation to him—how I needed to get on that plane, as my visa and health were both quickly running out. The din of the crowd had died down, and I could sense the eyes of the entire airport watching our animated exchange.

"But the plane is full!" he explained.

"I don't care where I sit or if I have to stand; please, just find something for me!" I gave as my final request, coughing in his face one more time as an exclamation point.

"I'll walk out to the plane to see what I can do. *Don't follow me!*" he firmly stated as he led me to the exit, where I could see him cross the tarmac and go up the steps to the plane. With a multitude of people following my steps and standing behind me, I felt like I was in some climactic scene in a Frank Capra movie!

I knew I was pushing its meaning—probably making it the most egregiously abusive application of a quote by Jesus of all time—but all I could think of was the most recent Bible verse I had memorized: "I am going to prepare a place for you."

After three or four minutes, the clerk popped his head out of the plane's doorway. With a look of defeated frustration, he gave me a wide, firm overhead wave of his hand to come onto the plane. As if signaled by that gesture, the entire airport exploded in joyous applause at the small but important victory of the little man over the powerful and favored.

My so-called seat on the airplane was a box in the luggage compartment, where I was firmly told I needed to sit and not move one inch one way or the other for the entire three-hour flight. They rigged some ropes as seat belts and said I needed to stay tied down until we landed in Dakar. I didn't care; I was finally exiting my last landlocked country and coming to the final round of my trip before heading home. Weak, hacking, suffering from diarrhea, and mentally beaten, I was ready for some rest and relaxation with a therapeutic ocean breeze before making it to Morocco, where I planned to build myself up before reuniting with Liz from Zimbabwe.

I was looking forward to traveling with someone who could lift my spirits. I had not anticipated the depth of desire I had to reunite with someone. Maybe, this could be the one I would marry! Lively, enthusiastic, honest, earthy, and moral, Liz suddenly seemed like the reason I had traveled across Europe, the Middle East, and Africa. What a great way to end a two-year trek!

CHAPTER 53

Don't Ya Know We're Ridin' on the Marrakech Express?

AFTER DETOXING IN SENEGAL WITH the ocean air and having some money wired to me from home, I headed to Morocco where I was told it would be easy to just take it slowly and live fairly cheaply, although still accompanied with my rebelling intestines. My sources were right on both accounts; my average spending was about three dollars a day, just as I had hoped.

I had a few weeks to kill while waiting for Liz, and I figured I'd see a few of the sights on my own. I'd heard Fez was a fairly easy place to travel, but I was also warned about the way the Arabs in that area treated Westerners.

"Don't get into close contact with anyone," a guy in a hostel warned me. "The people here will plant some drugs on you and then tell the police and get you arrested. Either that, or they'll sell you some hash and immediately tell the police. Consider yourself a target here."

I warily strolled around the market, with its narrow and winding streets, observing all the fascinating shops. The sights and smells were invigorating; I found a place that sold me some of the most delicious yogurt I'd ever tasted. It sure helped my poor, infected intestinal system.

A Muslim guy, looking maybe a couple of years younger than I was, came up to me. "Where are you from?" he asked.

Feeling a setup, I grunted, "America."

"I love America!" he joyfully responded. "Can I please spend the day with you? I can show you around town."

I was familiar with these self-appointed guides who would walk you through town and then set you up for some exorbitant fee for the tour. It was sort of a glamorized form of blackmail.

"No, thanks," I said as I walked away. "I'm fine."

He kept following me through the souk, trying to keep up a conversation with me. "I'm not one of those guys who's going to hustle you, like these other people here. I just want to get to know you. Don't you trust me?" He seemed genuinely hurt by my rejection.

What the heck? My passport and money were safely concealed in my pant-leg pocket; the most he'd get out of me would be the few dirhams I had in my front pockets. I had little to lose, and besides, since I'd gotten burned by that bratty kid in Mali, I had been fairly xenophobic. In fact, during the past few months, my communication with locals had been very limited. In Black Africa, I had stopped talking to people, as they had always ended up asking me for my money or possessions. Here in Arab Africa, I felt like a target.

Maybe it was time to get back to mingling with my fellow earthlings. "Not at all; I've just had some bad experiences with some people. Let's walk around the souk."

We had a fun time checking out the shops, and Ahmed showed me some really interesting parts of town I wouldn't have found on my own. I didn't mind buying lunch for him at all. Sure, it was an extra expense on my strict budget, but I figured I needed to build some goodwill and give this guy a break.

After a few hours, Ahmed and I had struck up a pretty cordial relationship. I really enjoyed his gentility and sincerity. "I'd like you to come to my house and meet my family. We can have some tea."

I was a bit suspicious, as well as a little tired from walking around. "Thanks, but I need to head back to my hostel."

"Please come. We Muslims love being hospitable. I would feel insulted if you didn't come and stay for just a little while. We're very close by."

Well, I felt that I sure could use some delicious mint tea to cool myself down, so I went along with him. Ahmed's family lived in a cozy, clean apartment near the center of town, through a myriad of zigzagging and winding narrow streets. As we entered the home, I met his parents, who were extremely cordial and warm. Ahmed spoke to his parents and had one of his sisters bring us some tea as he led me up to the roof, where we sat down and had an intriguing view of the city. Sipping the sweet drink, I felt a sense of relaxation for the first time in quite a while. Finally, I felt that I could at last start recuperating from my bug.

Ahmed finished his tea, paused for a second, and stared into my eyes. "Now, it's time to pay me."

"What are you talking about? You said you just wanted to be my friend!"

"Isn't my time as a friend worth anything to you?" He sternly glared at me. "I suggest very strongly that you pay me at least a couple hundred dirhams or twenty dollars *US*."

Staring at him, I felt like I was seeing an actual transformation of his character, demeanor, and facial expressions. He seemed not just a bit intimidating.

I immediately started taking roll call of my options. Could I just make a bolt down the stairs for the door? But how would I know how to get out of the maze of streets? If I gave him the money from my pockets, how could I guarantee it would be enough and he wouldn't keep me trapped here? Could I overpower him? But if others came, who would believe an American tourist in someone's house? He could say I barged in and tried to steal something.

"Look, Ahmed," I explained as coolly as possible, so as not to turn this into a major danger for myself, "all I've got is some money here in my pocket. I'll give you some of it. OK?"

Fiercely gazing right into my eyes, he sternly said, "What about the money you have hidden in your pant leg. Did you really think I wouldn't notice that?"

The blood quickly drained out of my face. I felt like I was in some sort of a chess game and was being checked at every move—one or two more, and I'd be checkmated. My options were limited.

"OK. I'll give you some American money; let's just get outside, and I'll pay you once we get out on the street."

As we slowly descended the stairs from the rooftop, I glanced at Ahmed's family, casually sitting around the television, watching something. Were they oblivious to the shakedown that I was undergoing, or were they tacit participants? I couldn't decide. We passed through the hallway to the steps. Once outside, I quickly scanned up and down the corridors that wound up and down in a myriad of directions, trying to figure some way of escape.

As we walked around a narrow corner, Ahmed sternly stated, "It's time to pay me now, if you want to know how to get out of this neighborhood."

I looked up and around and noticed a minaret I'd seen before. I had a landmark, so I felt secure in my next move.

I reached into my pocket, feeling lots of change with my fingertips. I grabbed as much as I could and, while still walking, said, "Here you go; this should be a good start." I threw the handful of coins at him, which distracted him for just enough time for me to briskly walk away and make my way through the side streets, losing my "friend" in the process.

Walking back to my hostel, some Arab leaning against the wall whispered to me, "Hey, want some hashish? Really good stuff!"

"No, thanks. I've been suckered by enough Muslims today."

CHAPTER 54

I Walk the Line

SAFELY BACK AT MY HOSTEL, I looked up while sitting in the lobby; checking in was an American (finally!) just about my age. We started up a conversation, and I found I liked the guy, who was named Peter. Like me, he was also on a sort of spiritual trek, but he was not planning on spending as long a time in Africa as I had.

"My goal is to check out every religion and cult out there and figure out what their weakest points are," he gently and matter-of-factly stated.

Fascinated, I picked his brain about the various groups he had met and what he had learned in the process. He shared humorous stories of spending nights with Hare Krishnas, who had thrown women at him so he would become romantically involved and join their group. He also told about accepting an invitation from a student on the streets of Berkeley to go to an EST (self-help) seminar, only to change his mind at the last minute, just as he was about to walk into the class.

"But you *have* to go in," the student told Peter.

"Why? I've changed my mind."

"Just *go in*! Having you go into the seminar fulfills my goal from my teacher. I don't care what you do in there. Just *go in*!" he shouted.

"Fine, just to make you happy."

As soon as Peter entered, the student leaped with joy. "I made someone do something!" he declared in victory.

"This is what I've noticed about most religions," Peter observed. "Most of them are just there for you to justify whatever you want to do anyway—sort of like finding a way to tell yourself that you're OK."

"Ever check out Christianity?" I asked.

"I've wanted to, but since I'm American, I figure that will be the easiest to sample once I get back into the States. I've been going for the wilder ones first. I do find it fascinating that all of them say they're the only one that's right."

"Well, they can all be wrong, or one can be right. But they can't all be right. That's the challenge of a lifetime. Or, as my brother-in-law would say, 'Ah, don't worry about it; it's just eternity.'"

He told me he'd been through Syria and Jordan, piquing my curiosity further. I had told him of my experience with Ahmed. "Tell me, Peter, what's your opinion of Islam?"

"Well," he soberly said, "you need to read the Koran to truly understand and get a grasp of their religion. It says that the highest honor for a Muslim is to die while killing an 'infidel,' which is essentially people like you and me. That gets you right into heaven. If you can't do that, the next best thing is to trick or screw a nonbeliever. That's why we're targets here."

I went to a local bookstore and bought a Koran. By the time I was about halfway done, all I could think was if a Christian was a hypocrite, it was because he was *not* obeying the Bible, and he was therefore doing harm to people. Here in the Koran, with so many verses talking about how to mistreat Christians and Jews, I was *hoping* that the Muslims would be hypocrites and *not* obey their scripture. What a contrast between this religion and Christianity! It seemed like Judaism just came short of the truth, in terms of Jesus. Christianity hit the center of Christ, and then Islam went one or two steps too far.

"One thing you have to say," I mentioned to Peter, "like you said, these three religions might be all wrong, but they sure can't all be right. They've got completely different opinions of Jesus."

We had a great time hiking, hitchhiking, and traveling together as he taught me scores of Johnny Cash songs while we rode the trains, but when Liz arrived in Casablanca, Peter knew it was time to graciously move on. It was wonderful seeing her again, and she was as effervescent as I had hoped. She was shocked at how thin I had become because of my illness and was fascinated by how God had protected me. The great thing about those first few hours together, getting reacquainted, was we both realized we would use this trip to see how well we would fit together as a couple. Amazingly, the physical part was never a major point of discussion. We both agreed that any physical intimacy should come as a celebration of our relationship, not as a starting point.

Having that lack of tension at the outset made life a lot easier for me because although Liz was a very attractive woman, within a few days of traveling, it became as plain as the nose on my face that we were not going to be the most compatible of couples. In all fairness to her, I had been hardened and aged by two and a half years of hard-core traveling and living in solitude— not to mention residing in vans, campsites, hostels, roofs, jails, brothels, and wide-open spaces. Liz had lived as a sheltered white girl in a country that was filled with black maids and servile housekeepers, subservient to her in act and attitude. She had never been out of a one-hundred-mile radius from her white-supremacist home, let alone on the road with a budget of three dollars a day.

Still suffering the effects of my illness, my worm-laden body was in no mood to travel with someone as inexperienced and as needy as Liz. Yes, we did a lot of hiking, sightseeing, and hanging out with the locals, but I now had to do the work for two people, as well as protecting her from Arab men continually harassing a white, seemingly Western woman. I even had to stand guard in front of the bathrooms each time she needed to relieve herself.

One time, on a particularly oppressive, heat-laden afternoon, Liz said she needed to go to the public toilet. "Can't you go just this one time by yourself?" I pleaded, as I was blithely taking in my morning soup and yogurt at the local diner. "I'm really feeling weak and tired."

Within two minutes of her departure, I heard yelling down the hallway, behind a door; someone was trying to break into the toilet, and I had to shoo him away. Poor, flustered Liz—we both realized she needed me as a bodyguard all the time, however weak I might be.

We survived our four weeks of Moroccan travels, and Liz continued on to vacation in Spain, while I limped onto a flight back to Rome, before finally heading home to the United States. After more than a year away, spent on two different continents, Rome felt like a completely different world to me. I had specifically planned the trip away from Rome to gradually travel to more primitive environments, so I wouldn't experience too much of the dreaded

culture shock. I hadn't anticipated my reaction to the return from the most primitive of third-world environments to the Eternal City.

The sophistication of the people, the hustle and bustle of a modern city, as well as the high-end fashion was a real jolt to my senses. During my whole trip through the Middle East and Africa, for example, I saw women dressed with all but their eyes covered—or simply topless, letting it all hang out. There was no sartorial middle ground until I returned to the Western world, with its teasing peek-a-boo approach to fashion and style. I felt like my visual senses were being mercilessly assaulted—with the assault to my ears a close second, with all of the sounds of traffic and urban hustle and bustle.

I grabbed a bus and went back to visit the old Centurion mission. Joan wasn't there anymore; after her nervous breakdown, she had gone back home to live in Colorado. Most of the other people I had initially befriended had finished their tour of duty and had returned to their pre-mission lives back in the United States. The ones who were still there did not give very encouraging news about how their whole evangelical adventure was going. No one seemed pleased with the results. It seemed the power of the Roman Empire was still hostile to the simple faith of the Son of a carpenter from Nazareth.

I felt like I was officially a stranger once back in Rome, and it wasn't my town anymore. I had no desire to see Rigel or any of the ladies I had dated. Like Dorothy in *The Wizard of Oz*, I just wanted to go home. No specific reason—I just knew this, or any place I had visited, was not where I was to live, so I might as well end up where I had started. Was it as a better man, or like a soldier from the Confederate army returning from Appomattox?

Through a circuitous route, I made it back to the United States—not before having missed the connecting plane to Los Angeles in New York City and being forced to spend the night in some fancy hotel downtown. I was bemused by the news when they relayed the information to us in the airport. In all the years I had traveled abroad, I never had missed a connection of any sort. Only in America! The bed that night in the hotel felt so peculiar. Sheets! A mattress! I had forgotten the sensations. I spotted a radio by the bed and turned it on; a very hip DJ with a deep voice was playing some jazz. I hadn't heard that in a while either. The next day the hotel gave me a voucher for breakfast. The orange juice was made from a concentrate, and the container of yogurt was some sweetened purple concoction. It was definitely going to take a while for me to adapt to the processed and sanitized modern society of 1980s America.

I finally arrived in LA. It was great reuniting with my family again at the airport. Yet, the amazing thing about the drive from the airport to home was no one really asked any penetrating questions about the entire two-year trip. My parents mostly talked about me finally finding a job and going to work, since I had now officially "gotten the traveling out of your system." My sister, Kathy, and brother-in-law, Warren, just went on about their own lives and their newborn daughter. Maybe they were trying to help me feel integrated back at home and didn't want to draw attention to how thin and sickly I looked. I was returning twenty pounds lighter than I had left, and as Kathy later said, "looking kind of wormy."

Warren (who was an MD) eventually did some tests on me and gave me some medicine to "kill the worm and anything else that might be in you by this time." It worked, and I started to feel a bit more human. Warren also took me to their ranch in Central California where I could look through the thousands of photos I had taken that had been developed from the film I had sent back home. I was really curious to see what the trip looked like in retrospect, and I figured the wide-open spaces of a pistachio farm just might be the best place for me to start getting reacclimated to American life.

On the way to the ranch, Warren pulled over at a tiny rural gas station to fill up his truck. I had to go to the bathroom, so as I had done so many times the past two years, I looked around a nearby field for someplace to relieve myself, forgetting that there were things like public restrooms. As I was standing out behind the station among the bushes and weeds in the open field, a small, gentle breeze brought a scent to me that I hadn't smelled in a few months. It smelled like Africa! A sense of nostalgia came over me. I felt like I was traveling again. I wondered what caused that glorious reminiscent aroma. It was sort of like when you smell something that reminds you of an old girlfriend...

"Excuse me, sir," I said to the gas-station attendant, "I was walking around the back and smelled something. Is there some type of tree or orchard around here?"

"No. Only thing back there is that big septic tank by the corner."

Sure enough, I walked over there and took a deep whiff, just to confirm. Yep, that was the Africa smell. No wonder I had never smelled that smell before my travels. America had been too clean for me!

CHAPTER 55

Home, Where My Thought's Escaping...Home, Where My Music's Playing

I SPENT THE FIRST FEW weeks back home sorting the photos from my excursion as well as sorting out and filing my thoughts. I was twenty-six years old and back from traveling for two and a half years. What did I have to show for it? A bunch of photos and some weird souvenirs, materials, and carvings. I showed these exotic knickknacks to some of my friends, but everyone just gave a dismissive glance. No one here could relate. No one I knew had ever done what I'd done or been where I had been. Understandably, they had lived their own lives by going to work, making friends, and trying to make something of themselves in the only way they knew how.

What was most ironic to me was the photos I had taken of Nehama were mostly out of focus, and the ones of Joan were so underexposed I could barely make her face out. Was God trying to tell me something?

I had seemingly burned all my romantic bridges in Europe and the Middle East. I had no desire to go back and live as an expatriate somewhere with a local wife and in-laws. I didn't feel I belonged there. But did I belong here? In middle-class, white suburbia? After all my traveling to figure out my life and direction, I seemed to have returned to my homeland with more questions than I had left with. I had no job, no idea of where to look for one, or even if I wanted to live here and begin a practice. Did I want to throw in my lot with this culture that, in one sense, was what I was used to yet, in another sense, was now completely foreign to me?

My dad repeatedly told me that since I was back, it was officially time to get to work. He seemed to be worried that after all of this sojourning in foreign lands, I was going to turn into one of those ne'er-do-well philosophers "like that guy in *The Razor's Edge* who goes off the deep end," as he would mutter every now and then to me. I had read that book by Somerset Maugham while traveling in Mali, and I don't think I reassured my dad when I told him I actually liked that guy. He just shook his head and told me to keep looking for work. "You'll learn more about God by working for someone," he'd say, while shaking his finger at me.

I wrote a few dozen letters to various local chiropractors, telling them of my desire to work in this area. While waiting for a reply, I started reading again. I went back to my old, friendly Christian author Josh McDowell, who had a bunch of newly written books at a local Christian bookstore. One was called *Answers to Tough Questions*. It looked right up my alley, so I started going through it with a fine-toothed comb.

What struck me more than anything inside the book was the little blurb on the back cover of the book. It mentioned that McDowell ran a training course for learning the basics of Christianity in the hills near San Diego. I thought maybe if I met him, I could get a few questions answered and be more encouraged with my lot in life. I put some food in my old, faithful van and drove four and a half hours to the tiny mountain town of Julian—population 1,495.

Ah! It was just like old times, with me at the wheel, heading to some obscure area, listening to the incessant puttering sound of the engine welcoming me back to the road.

Josh McDowell wasn't there, but a gent with a graying beard and gentle demeanor named Dick Day was. We talked for a while, and I felt that this was the first guy who seemed genuinely interested in my trip. "Did you find what you were looking for somewhere during that whole time?" No one had asked me that yet.

Stunned by the directness of his question and the piercing it caused as I reflected back on my pilgrimage, I burst into tears. "No," I weakly answered.

"You're obviously looking for truth," he calmly stated. "We've got a three-month residency here where I'll teach you how to look at the world from a Christian perspective. I think it will answer a lot of your questions."

Part of me wanted to jump in and go for it; however, I had just been gone for a long time. *Another adventure?* It really seemed like it might simply be another delay to the inevitability of joining the establishment of Western Civilization. If I decided to do it, breaking the news to my family was going to be a real test of nerves. As I drove home, I decided it was worth it. My mind spun with a myriad of scenarios as I drove back home to tell my folks about the next chapter of my life.

Sure enough, Mom was genuinely worried about my sanity, Kathy just laughed at me, and Dad exploded in anger. "You're going to be like one of those guys who never accomplishes anything!" he screamed at me for about two hours.

That day sure wasn't the end of it, even though I told them I sincerely felt that my entire trip would be in vain if I didn't get some more questions answered. I only had a few clothes, so I just threw them into the van, but my parents were adamant about going down with me to "see what kind of a nuthouse this place is." During my entire drive back to Julian, Dad sat in the seat right behind me, screaming and shouting at me about how I was running away from my responsibilities and was afraid to get a real job and life.

"I can't believe you're turning into one of those guys who just keeps search-ing for the meaning of life, just staring at your navel!" he yelled as we pulled into the gravel parking lot at the Julian Center.

He leaped out of the van and approached Dick Day, who sauntered over to greet us. "I'm not going to pay for this boondoggle," he warned. "And George has no money." I guess Dad figured if logic wasn't going to deter me, a financial burden would.

Day calmly responded, "That shouldn't be a problem. We have a scholar-ship program to help someone we feel is qualified for our center. George can pay it back at his own pace."

"It's up to him, as I'll *never* help him...or you!" he fumed as he stormed back to the van. By this time, I had gotten out of the front seat and had got-ten my pack full of clothes. I went to say good-bye to Dad, but he was already starting the engine to go back home.

"Aren't you going to say good-bye to me, Dad?"

"I thought I had a son," he angrily muttered, "but I now realize I don't even know you." With that parting shot, he drove off, out of the dusty parking lot in a cloud, with the sui generis puttering of the VW van getting fainter and fainter. I was all alone once again.

During those three months in the mountains of Julian, about twenty other people and I would meet together and go to classes and workshops, listen to lectures, read books, watch films by Frances Schaeffer, and have discussions about Christianity. Dick, patient as Job with me, showed me how the historic facts of Christ's life, death, and resurrection made Christianity objectively true, whether I believed it or not. Jesus's life on earth physically demonstrated what God thinks and acts like and what God's priorities are and, therefore, also served as an example for us to live by on this planet, in our own civilization and time. The beauty of Christianity, as Day pointed out, is that it is not a lifestyle I had to keep trying to work at; it was more of a matter of actually letting Christ live in me. What a difference *that* was to every other religion. This fact alone freed me up like nothing else.

The other people at the center were from a wide conglomeration of backgrounds. Among others, we had a dentist who was burned out from his practice, an army vet who was kind of angry at just about everything and everyone, a pastor's son who wanted to be a rock star, a daughter of missionaries from Morocco who had just come back to the United States with her parents, a gospel singer, a nurse whose husband had just left her, a married couple who had just left a Christian commune under bad terms, and an inner-city teenager who was angry at the world. Half of the education I got about Christianity while at the Julian Center was simply learning how to coexist with this disparate group of people. The fact that we were all united by a simple, and similar, faith in Christ fascinated me. There *had* to be something different about Christianity; nothing else could make this whole dynamic work. I gradually saw myself as part of something that had started two thousand years ago—a movement initiated by a sacrifice—dead to myself but alive in Christ.

The three months passed quickly. I was sad to leave, as living in those mountains in the fall was idyllic, but I also felt ready to return and launch into my calling. It was time to go back home. Back to work. I drove my van home, as I had taken it back up on a free weekend via a hitched ride—although I hadn't talked to Dad during that time. As I drove through the countryside, I thought about all of the events that had led me to this pastoral retreat, where my direction had finally focused.

Could I have saved myself a lot of time by discovering the Julian Center when I first got out of chiropractic college? No, it hadn't been formed yet. Why hadn't I learned these things while traveling or through some book? Why hadn't I learned any of this at all of the church-group meetings and studies I had been to before I left way back when?

The fact is, I just wasn't ready at the time. I recalled a story I had read about a young disciple asking an aged priest to teach him the truth and the meaning of life. The priest led the aspiring student to the beach and then slowly into the water. They were finally in about waist deep when the boy asked, "How can you teach me about life way out here?" Immediately, the priest grabbed the guy's head, shoved it underneath the water, and held the struggling youth there. Finally, the student broke free and shot up, gasping for air.

"Why did you do that to me?" he blurted to his master.

"When you fight for truth as intensely as you just struggled to breathe, then you're ready to learn," replied the wise man.

I realized I wouldn't have appreciated the teachings I had heard the past quarter of a year unless I had diligently sought out God during my long trek.

Like looking for a wife, you sometimes don't know what you're looking for, and she can be right in front of you, yet you aren't prepared to recognize her, so you let the opportunity pass by. Maybe you were looking for something else. "You will find Me," God promised, "if you search with all of your heart" (Jeremiah 29:13). Some people don't want to struggle underwater for the air. I praise God that I did.

EPILOGUE
DON'T YOU WORRY 'BOUT A THING

I won't say my family was initially impressed by the change in my life, but my tightfisted dad ultimately donated money to the Julian Center for as long as its doors were open.

Joan got married to the guy she went home for, had a bunch of kids, converted to Greek Orthodoxy, and wrote a book about her spiritual journey. Susan, continuing her pattern, unexpectedly dropped by my parents' house while I was away in Julian; I have never seen her since Texas. Liz, still single, is a motivational speaker for a New Age organization. Manuella, one of the Italian girls I dated, is a single mom and a high-powered businesswoman in Italy. I lost touch with all of my traveling partners. I assume John died of AIDS, as he got every other sexually transmitted disease known to human-kind. I never got the name of the guy who saved my life in Mali. I think about him almost every day and pray for him just as often.

Concerning the Emisarries (according to Wikipedia), after Martin Cecil died in 1988, about 2/3 of the people left the organization. Many had bitter departures with accusations being thrown around. Sort of like the parable about the house being built on sand that collapses once the storm comes. (Matthew 7:24-27)

As for myself, I finally met the right woman for me and got married (see appendix). We lost our first child at birth and then had two wonderful daugh-ters, who are fully grown. We go on medical mission trips to help persecuted church groups. I also teach Sunday school and have led high-school and col-lege small groups at our church. I have my own chiropractic office, and I also write for a jazz magazine and website.

The only reason I fill you in on all of this is because I've always been fasci-nated by people who go to fortune-tellers to learn about their future. When I look back on my life, if someone had told me everything I would eventually go through, I wouldn't have wanted to do it. It's the unknown future that makes life exciting and that gives you the strength to make it, day by day. "Each day's sufficient for its own trouble" (Matthew 6:34).

APPENDIX: HOW I MET YOUR MOTHER

After I finished writing about the spiritual and geographic parts of my journey, I felt I had comparatively ignored the relational discoveries and conclusions. This part didn't seem to flow well with the conclusion of my story, so I decided to add it here as a bonus for any of you who want to know a bit more about how I finally got around to finding someone to marry. Besides, my daughters think the story is so unique other people would enjoy reading it as well.

As you can well imagine, after spending three quarters of a year driving through the United States, about two years living and overlanding through Europe, the Middle East, and Africa, and then another third of a year in a Christian co-op, I was essentially out of circulation. I had not kept up with my friends, and most of them had moved somewhere else by the time I returned home. So, here I was, living in the same area where I had grown up all my life (not at my parents' home, but in an annex of my sister and brother-in-law's home) but not knowing a single soul. Where to begin this new phase?

Well, my first step after settling down and living at my sister and brother-in-law's house was to attend to my '71 VW van. My trusty ride was finally showing its miles, and it was not in perfect working order since it had been ignored for the two years I was abroad. I figured the best way to find someone to fix it would be to call some of the local churches and ask the pastors if they knew any good car mechanics to help me figure out the problem and give me a few tips for free.

I figured a Lutheran pastor should have a good connection with mechanics who could work on a German car like a Volkswagen, but the only pastor who took the time to call me back was one from a Presbyterian church, John Pound. He gave me the name and number of a guy who had a car-repair place, and he also invited me to his church. Since I had just finished my stint at the Julian Center and had nowhere else to go for a church service, I figured I'd give it a try.

The service was held in the gym of a middle school, and there were about 150 people in attendance, mostly middle-class WASPs in their midthirties to fifties. In fact, looking around, I might have been the only one there who hadn't grown up listening to radio instead of watching TV. I wasn't going to meet any women there to date; that was for sure. The service was fairly formal, or as my dad would say, "filled with stuffed shirts." After Pastor Pound's professorial sermon, a collection plate was passed around. As I saw it coming toward my row, I checked my wallet to see if I had any money to give. I had a lonely looking twenty-dollar bill that separated me from absolute poverty. During one of those quick flashes of internal gut checking, I figured, "What difference does it make if I give God part of this or all of it? I'm still going to be broke." I flipped the whole Jackson picture in. It actually felt pretty good to give my last buck to God; even in California, I could still be 100 percent dependent on Him.

While I was walking back to my trusty and tuned up van, I heard a woman calling me, in the way only older women can get away with: "Yoo-hoo!" A very well-heeled and coiffed woman in her forties nimbly came up to me. "Is this your first time here? I'm Joy Eden; my husband Neil is an elder here. Welcome to our church. What brings you here?"

I explained to her I had just arrived in town after being away for a while and that I was looking for a place to set up my office as a chiropractor.

"You're a chiropractor?" She beamed. "I've got a terrible back and would love to have you give me a treatment."

Her house was only a few blocks away from where I was staying with Kathy and Warren. I picked up my portable table—my trusty sidekick that had earned me so many jazz albums in earlier years—went over and introduced myself to Joy's avuncular husband. After the treatment, she thanked me, and as I was putting my portable adjusting table back in my VW, Joy gently grabbed my arm, looked me in the eye, and said, "You, of course, must be paid for your services."

"Forget it; it's Sunday. Consider it my ministry."

"I'll have none of that," she defiantly countered. "I'm a professional. You're a professional and should be paid like one." And with that, she gave me fifty bucks. "Hope to see you next week at church, young man." I liked this lady!

The next Sunday, and those after, I took Warren, Kathy, and my niece Faith to church with me. Warren had recently become a Christian, and he enjoyed the service a lot. My sister Kathy, who hadn't been to a church since growing up Greek Orthodox over a decade before, felt like she was coming home. Both Kathy and Warren actually knew a number of the people who attended Cal Pres—most notably Don Block, a local veterinarian who lived around the block from us. I had recently got a springer spaniel, and Don said he'd give the dog a onceover as a favor.

I took my dog, Velma, over to his office one Thursday morning. Velma had been given to me by my sister as a "welcome home" present. He looked her over, and with his calm Dr. Marcus Welby demeanor, he stated, "Well, I can give her something to de-worm her, put some stuff on her eyes to help her stop tearing up, clean out her ears with some spray and fluids, and bathe her with some special soap to help her skin and hair."

"Will that get her all back to normal?"

He patiently paused. "Let's put it this way. If we do all of those things for her, what you'll be basically left with is a dud of a dog."

After all of the time, effort, and medication, Block only charged me five bucks! I was getting the royal welcome at this church!

After a few more weeks, I finally found a place to start practicing chiropractic. I would rent out half of the office space from another DC who was just starting out as well, John Palmer. Between referrals from Warren, who was a medical doctor, and Joy, who was a realtor and seemed to know everybody, my fledging practice looked like it might survive the critical first year.

I was spending most of my time trying to build the practice, working every day except Thursday and Sunday, yet also trying to create some sort of a social life by visiting various churches that had singles groups where I might meet some people my age in this bedroom community. The area that I was living in—Agoura / Calabasas / Hidden Hills—was strictly upper-middle-class, white suburbia, and there was a dearth of nightlife for singles. Out of the handful of churches in the area, only one megachurch—West Community—had a social network of people my age.

This group met on Wednesday nights, and I attended their Bible studies and social events—essentially feeling like a complete alien outcast, not knowing anything about the current culture from having been away for so long. (To this very day, however, I praise God that I completely missed disco and Pac-Man.) I once had some of the singles group people over to show them photos of my trip, and the prevailing attitude was a mix of "I wouldn't do anything like that if you paid me all the money in the world," and "I'd give anything to be able to do something like that, but I'd never have the courage or the time" by about a ninety-ten split. At least I knew where I stood with my peers.

The lack of depth in the lessons taught by the "Singles Pastor" (There really is such a thing? What degree do you get to qualify?) at the West Community singles group made me wonder if these people were here to grow spiritually or if more carnal desires were the motivating factor. I figured it out pretty quickly when one girl, Maggie—a physical therapist no less—seemed interested when I talked to her about jazz and said she had some jazz albums (this was still pre-CD/digital days) at her apartment she'd like me to listen to.

I've always been a big believer that you can learn a lot about a person by examining that person's bookshelf and album collection. What he or she likes to read and listen to reveals volumes about his or her views on life, values, and culture. Arriving at Maggie's place, I glanced at her album collection...*George Winston*? This was background music for having your molars removed! I was definitely in White Bread, USA.

Maggie put one of the records on. "I just love his piano playing; it's so smooth." As the spacious and impressionistic music started filling the room, Maggie dimmed the lights.

"Let's see if you chiropractors can give a back rub as well as physical therapists." She winked as she lay flat on the floor, facedown, after doffing her top.

I did not like where this was going; yet, I was also thinking in the back of my mind that if I weren't a Christian, I *would* like where it was headed. Providing her a highly (but not thighly!) perfunctory massage, I gave her a "I think I hear my mom calling me" excuse and made an early end to the night.

Is this what the Christian single scene was going to be like?

I knew I had to do some deep soul-searching as to what I was looking for in a relationship and what this TBA relationship had to consist of. I talked to a number of Christian guys my age and asked them what their standards were in a dating relationship. How far did a relationship go before marriage? The responses I got ranged anywhere from sex "as long as there is a commitment" (always loved that one for the lack of definition of "commitment") to the just-as-nebulous answer "anything but sex." (What does that mean? Darts at fifty feet?)

TO TOUCH, OR NOT TO TOUCH?

After living in the Middle East, where I observed that couples sometimes didn't even touch before marriage; Saharan African countries; and Greece, where many marriages were arranged, I had to come to my own conclusion: just what was I going to have as a standard of where my boundaries were in various stages of a relationship with a woman? Any premarriage relationship that consisted of physical contact seemed to me to be a sign of commitment, so at what point was I promising something to a woman that I was not willing to fulfill?

Working backward from sex to foreplay to kissing to holding hands to signals between a catcher and pitcher, I came to the conclusion that anything after holding hands was stimulating an attitude in a woman that I didn't want to falsely promise I would reciprocate. Then and there, sitting in my van while driving home from Maggie's apartment, I decided I was never going to even kiss a girl again unless I felt she was the one I was definitely going to marry. Anything else would be false advertising.

You must remember that this was 1983—before the concept of courtship and Joshua Harris's "kissing dating good-bye" became major paradigm shifts. When I told my single male friends my epiphany and its implications, I felt I might as well have told them I was radioactive; I probably would have received the same reaction.

While the dating action was clearly at the local megachurch, after visiting several churches, I felt I could be most helpful at the tiny, local Presbyterian church I had first attended, Cal Pres, where I essentially made up the entire singles group. I also looked around for opportunities to meet with other serious Christian men for encouragement. One day, I called all the local churches to inquire as to whether any of them had a group of men who got together regularly for a Bible study or prayer time. Much to my disbelief, I found out that only one church had such a thing, and that group of three was comprised of gents from three different churches; if I attended, I'd be the fourth. I decided to check it out.

Ray Garcia (we called him Father Ray) was a soft-spoken bear of a man, with thick glasses, a gentle spirit, and a love of witty puns. He led this group that met at 6:00 a.m. each Tuesday, and he felt called to serve as a spiritual guide to the motley group of guys (consisting of an ex-alcoholic painter, an ex-cocaine-snorting ex-Mormon, a workaholic ex-baseball player, and a forest ranger) who were trying to figure out how to live a consistent life in modern suburbia.

I attended the group for the first time one predawn morning and was up front with them from day one. "I'll be perfectly frank with you," I confided. "I'm here to grow as a Christian, but most of all, I want you guys to be praying for me every day to find a woman to marry." These men—all of whom were at least ten years older than I—restrained their smirking smiles and accepted the responsibility with vigor. Each Tuesday morning we met, they'd read over the list of prayers they'd been giving to God and they would check with me to see if there were any new intercessions for working out my salvation or my marriage.

In the same vein, I included a note to pray for my ability to find a wife to every ministry or charity that I was donating money to (following the biblical directive to give at least 10 percent to God's work). In return, I would get newsletters and magazines from these various organizations.

My attention was piqued when one of the newsletters from these para-church ministries included an editorial entitled "Fasting." In it, the author wrote of how the Pharisees (religious leaders in the first century) had been praying and fasting for the coming of their own Messiah. The only problem was that when He finally came (in the form of Jesus Christ), they were too blind to see the answer to their own supplications, and they ended up crucifying Him.

"That is how it is with so many people in this present generation," wrote the author. "Every now and then I get letters from pitiful single men, agonizingly requesting for God to provide them a wife. I have absolutely no pity for them, as God is sending these weak-kneed underachievers perfectly suitable women every day of their lives, but they are too blind to notice and appreciate them. What they should petition God for is the same thing the Pharisees should have done; they should ask God to *open their eyes* to give them wisdom and discernment, so they will recognize the right woman when she comes into their lives."

This little article blindsided me like Muhammed Ali's right hook. OK, I didn't like getting chastised by someone I was sending money to, but I had to agree he was absolutely right. Like so many single guys, I had comprised a list of what I was looking for in a wife.

Doesn't everyone have a list of must-haves in a mate? I sure did before I finally came to my senses and chucked it. Mine had to be a woman who was the following:

1. *Not* a doctor—talk about egos colliding all the time!
2. Of a unique ethnic background—I figured a Mediterranean, African, or Middle Eastern woman would have the right temperament for me, after having traveled for so long. I might as well have put a sticker on my VW that read "No WASPs." That was going to be a tough one, though, having moved back to white suburbia.
3. A strong believer—hopefully from the mission field. I'd had enough spiritual battles with women.
4. Tall—I remembered my five-foot-eight and five-foot-nine aunts harassing me during my teenage years: "Don't you dare date short

girls. They get the pick of every guy. Give the tall girls a break, and go out with them. It's tough for us tall girls to find a guy!" Besides, raising tall kids would be fun!

5. Musical—I couldn't imagine being married to someone who was not as excited about music as I was.
6. Younger than I was—less baggage to deal with.

I realized that instead of looking for the right person, I needed to *be* the right person, so I could be ready to appreciate the woman God would send me as a life mate.

It reminded me of a conversation I had had with some of the guys from the West Community megachurch singles group. About five of us were hanging around in the parking lot after a meeting one night, and we had just learned that one of the girls in the church, Sophie, had become engaged.

"Funny, I thought she looked a bit different lately," one guy commented.

"Yeah, she actually looked really nice," replied another.

"Do you guys ever notice that when a girl first comes into the singles group, we all check her out, and usually she seems a bit plain and unattractive to us. Then, she gets into a serious relationship with some guy, gets engaged, and suddenly she starts looking pretty good!"

"Yeah!" we all agreed. "What's with that?"

"I don't really know. All I can tell you is that once they have a guy committed to them, they give off this really attractive glow. I can't tell you how many times I've looked at girls like Sophie and wouldn't give her a second glance. Now, she looks fantastic, with this alluring glow about her."

"Yeah, like this guy just woke something up in her."

That was it. I realized it was my job to find the right woman to give that glow to. Forget my wish list. I needed someone to pour my life into…not to take from.

This Is It?

AFTER A FEW MONTHS OF being in the singles scene, I started hanging around a nice young lady named Cindy. She was a sweetheart of a girl, and we had a great time together. Was I in love with her? No, but she and I had some really wonderful times together, and I told her my standards of dating. I'm still not sure to this day, but I think she appreciated them, as she hung in there with me. Maybe, like the old song said, "Until the real thing comes along."

After a particularly uninspiring Sunday service at Cal Pres, my vet friend Don Block—who'd nursed Velma, the springer spaniel, back to mediocrity—came over to speak to me. He looked intently into my eyes.

"Hey, George, are you seeing anyone right now?"

Without a moment's hesitation, I said, "Nothing serious at all. Who have you got for me?"

Now looking a bit sheepish, he admitted, "I've got this fairly new vet at my office, Rita Gorton. She's been working for me for about half a year. She's a great lady and a smart vet, but she's got the mouth of a sailor and it turns the patients off. I've been getting some complaints about it. She's a fantastic doctor, but I just can't have that in my office.

"I was wondering…how about if my wife, Michelle, and I double date with you and Rita a few times, and you can talk to her about becoming a Christian?"

"Don! You've got to be kidding! I have absolutely no desire to do any missionary dating!" I pleaded. "Don't do this to me! I'll be more than happy to meet with her and share my faith, but the last thing I want is to get involved with someone I have no intention of marrying."

Don reluctantly agreed. "OK, let's just all go out for a dinner. It won't be a romantic setup or anything like that. She still doesn't have many friends out here, so we'll just tell her it's a get-together with another professional. I've tried sharing my faith with her, but she just shoots me down with her sharp tongue."

That left me completely nonplussed. "You figure out the place and the time, and I'll be there. *You're paying!*"

About a week later, I came home from my office after having a very difficult morning: uncooperative patients, not much money coming in, difficulty with the secretary. Nothing seemed to be easy. At least I was only scheduled to work a half day and could collapse back at my sister's house—where I was still living—and just soak in some music on my stereo and try to recuperate for tomorrow's challenges.

The couch felt invitingly comfortable as I flopped onto it, letting the back of my wrist cover my eyes like Greta Garbo in *Grand Hotel*, "vanting to be alone." After two deep breaths of relaxation, my peace was disrupted as Kathy came running into the house.

"Velma just got stung on the nose by a bee!" she shouted. "You've got to take her to the vet right now, or she'll suffocate from the swelling."

I was so exhausted, I initially didn't even care if the dog died. "Fine! The end of a perfect day."

By the time I put Velma into my van, she looked like she was wearing a Donald Duck mask. Her top lip was swollen about four times its normal size. The secretary couldn't control her laughter when she saw me carry her in. Somehow, between hysterical guffaws, she contacted the vet through the intercom to announce that I had arrived.

"Dr. Block isn't in today, but his associate, Dr. Gorton, is. You'll like her; she's real smart," she managed between her giggles and chortles.

Great. What a way to be introduced to this lady I was supposed to present the joys of Christianity to.

I was ushered into the treatment room, and after about five minutes of waiting with my beaked spaniel, in walked a professional woman—very businesslike, with a trim hairstyle that shouted, *"Professional single woman"* from the rafters.

"Hi. I'm Doctor Gorton," she stated in a way that seemed both nervous and professional.

Was she nervous because she knew I was the guy Block was setting her up with? I wasn't sure, but there was no way I was going to bring *that* topic up. I curiously checked this lady out.

Hmm. She sure was short! Maybe five feet. Going to a dance was definitely *out*!

She had very WASPy features. A day out in the sun would burn this lady to a crisp! *This* was the woman they wanted to set me up with? Who were they kidding?

She walked over to Velma and methodically and thoroughly examined her mouth. As I looked on, I noticed her hands as she took her gloves off and started explaining the diagnosis and treatment to me in professional lingo. (Was that to impress me, or was that also a sign of being a single female professional?) Her hands looked like they belonged to someone who worked hard, very hard. They had the look of what I imagined O-Lan's hands from *The Good Earth* had: the hands of a laborer. I liked that. Whenever I hired a secretary, I always checked her hands and nails to see if the person was afraid of manual labor. This lady wasn't afraid of hard work. I was impressed!

"You did a great job!" I told her afterward. "Thanks."

"You can pay on the way out." With that, she whooshed professionally out of the room.

I went up to the desk to say good-bye and thank them for getting me in so quickly. The secretary had finally stopped laughing, and she looked at me straight-faced and with her hand out. "That will be thirty-five dollars, please."

"Are you kidding? Block charges me almost nothing!"

"That's between you and Dr. Block. Dr. Gorton charges full price. Thirty-five dollars, please."

If I was going to see this chick, even on a simple social level, there had definitely better be a cheaper way. For thirty-five bucks, I could take her on at least five dates. Expensive vet visits with this lady were definitely out of the picture until further notice.

CHAPTER B

A Blip on the Radar

TIME PASSED, AND I WENT on merrily trying to build up my fledging practice. Block kept trying to work out a date for all four of us to get together for a show, an evening out, or just a dinner at his family's house. Every time he called me to see if I was free for an evening, something would come up at the last minute that would cancel the get-together.

Bemusedly frustrated by all the failed planning, I got to the point where I figured, "What the heck? Just go over and see her." So, one Saturday about noon, after working that morning, I drove over to Block's vet clinic, where I knew Rita was working that day.

"Hi!" Joyce, the receptionist, beamed. "No bee-bitten dogs today?"

"No, smarty-pants. Not for *thirty-five bucks*! I just wanted to see if Dr. Gorton was here. Could I please talk to her?"

Giving that look that only a woman who is setting someone up can give, Joyce pointed me to an office, and there Rita sat, turning to see me, and looking a bit self-conscious by the surprise. She looked pretty cute as she greeted me with her bright eyes. Hmm. I hadn't noticed them before.

"Hey, I was wondering," I blurted out. "The Blocks have been trying to get us all together to go out for the past month or so. How about just the two of us going out to lunch right now?"

Turning a bit red, Rita looked pleasantly surprised. "Sure. What have you got in mind?"

"Something cheaper than a vet visit! There's a great sub sandwich place down the road. Wanna meet there or take one car?"

"Actually, I got a ride today from Joyce, so why don't you just drive us there and we can pick up the food and eat at my house?"

We arrived at her cozy apartment, and I put the sandwiches on the table as Rita went to get some plates, water, and chips. While she was setting things up, I decided to check out her place, once again adhering to my belief that you can tell a lot about a person by the book and record shelves. (I don't know how this could be accomplished in this present day of Kindles and iPods, but it was of great help to me back then.) By perusing a person's books and music, I could see what kind of life intrigued him or her. Was the person artsy? Outdoorsy? Intellectual? Religious?

I felt a sinking feeling as I scanned her literature: *The World According to Garp*, Kurt Vonnegut, *Shogun*, Robin Cook...pretty trendy. I checked out her albums...Donna Summer? Loggins and Messina? Huey Lewis and the News? *Ambrosia*? Oh boy. This was going to be a short conversation!

Wait a minute! What was this? I saw an interesting album: *Only Visiting This Planet* by Larry Norman. I used to listen to that record with Ron Galpin at the old Baptist church! This guy was the first one to play what was then called "Jesus music" and was now called "Christian rock". Seeing a Christian recording artist among the stack of pop pablum was akin to watching a foreign film and suddenly seeing the word "Pepsi-Cola" pop onto the screen. What kind of blip on the screen was going on here?

"Hey, why do you have this album?"

"Oh," she said as she started setting the table, "he's a client of mine and gave it to me. It's actually not bad."

I couldn't help but stare at the record album. Hmm. Someone else was working on this lady. I wasn't alone. That was a good sign!

After a bit of small talk, she told me she liked hiking and invited me to hike a local trail with her and a vet friend of hers.

The next Saturday, Rita, her friend Shawna, and I walked around some lovely hills just outside of town. We talked about various things, and we seemed to have a fun time. I decided to pull a trigger.

"Hey, why don't you guys come to church with me tomorrow?"

"Don't go shoving religion down my throat!" heaved Shawna.

Coming to my rescue, Rita defended me by saying, "Hey, he was just inviting us to something he likes. What's the big deal?"

That was sure nice of her!

"Thanks for the invite," she replied. "I don't think I need to go there. I can communicate with God just by walking around here in the hills."

"But how do you objectively know you're talking to God and not to the devil?"

Rita stopped in midstride. "I'd never thought of that. I guess I really don't!"

This Is Dinner and a Movie?

I DROVE RITA AND SHAWNA back to Rita's place, and I asked Rita if she wanted to go out sometime. In my mind, it wasn't a date, as I had no intention of anything more than fulfilling my promise to Block.

"Sure."

"What do you like to do, besides hiking?"

"I love movies!" She beamed.

Dinner and a flick? Could anything be less original? What the heck? It wasn't like we would be on a date or anything. This lady only had *one* of the qualities I had on my wife list: she was female.

One evening, as I perused this mental list, I reflected on the fasting article that had taught me, "Don't look for the right person; rather, *be* the right person." That hit me hard. Here I still was, looking for someone to fit my needs instead of looking for someone to pour my life into. I still obviously had work to do on myself—or rather, God still obviously had work to do on me.

So…she liked movies. I was not a big modern-movie fan…and to me, something modern was a movie that was in color. After being spoiled from immersing myself in films from the 1930s through to the 1950s, I found most of the newer movies devoid of intricate plots and characters, with an over-reliance on violence, foul language, and sex. As a friend of mine used to say, "People swear when they've run out of ideas."

At church, Pastor Pound mentioned that the evangelist Billy Graham had just released a new movie called *The Prodigal*. It was one of those Christian movies—the kind that told the story of someone who eventually struggles with life until finally becoming a believer. I'd never seen one before, but I had heard from friends that they tended to be very tacky.

Block said he had seen this one, and it wasn't bad. I called Rita up and threw the option at her, and she seemed fine with it. Besides, this wasn't some major date. Rita knew I was still seeing Cindy pretty casually, and I had just met another nice girl at my aerobics class. (I *told* you this was the eighties!)

The movie was fairly heavy-handed, but the story line was actually pretty cute. It ended up with Billy Graham preaching at a giant crusade (i.e., baseball park with a preacher instead of a pitcher on the mound) and the protagonist walking down an aisle to ask Jesus into his heart. It was a bit predictable and contrived, but hey, at least Rita somewhat knew where I stood in life!

The drive home from the theater was filled with simple small talk. The movie's message was so up front and blatant that to follow up with any kind of spiritual discussion would have seemed like waterboarding.

As we sat inside her place, I sipped on the glass of water she gave me.

"So, what did you think?"

She looked at me very politely but with a touch of dismissiveness in her light-blue eyes. "Your religion is fine for you, and I'm really glad for you that it makes you happy. I just don't think it's right for me, and I really don't need it."

"That's fine," I replied. "It's your life, after all. I'm not here to force you to believe anything. That is a big turnoff for me. I just want you to think about something. If you're right and I'm wrong and this life is all there is, then we both end up the same way: dead and in the ground, with nothing afterward. If that's the case, you have absolutely nothing to worry about. If we're both wrong, we still will end up the same way, so it really makes no difference, and again, there's nothing for you to worry about."

She looked at me with a comfortable smile.

"*But*…if I'm right and *you're* wrong, then after you die you are going to be separated from God forever in hell, while I'll be with Him in heaven. Then, you have *everything* to worry about."

Her expression switched to deadpan. With that, I turned to the door and smiled back at her.

"Good night. Thanks for the fun time. See you sometime soon."

I drove back home in my van, assuring myself, "I'm never going to see *that* chick again!"

The next morning was Sunday, and I woke up all excited, as I had a date to take Luanne—the girl I had met at an aerobics class—to church. After I had answered Block's inquiry about if I was seriously dating someone, I realized I had to go over to Cindy's place and tell her that I felt that our relationship was really not going anywhere very seriously and I saw no future for us. So, what does every guy do who ends a relationship? He starts a new one with an aerobics teacher, of course!

Anyway, since I felt that my Presbyterian church was a bit too stuffy for a newcomer, I figured I'd take Luanne to the local megachurch, West Community, to make life a little more comfortable for her. Music from a familiar century, more of an uplifting sermon than a scholastic lecture, and with a few more people in the range of our general Social Security numbers should make the service easier on her.

I was whistling while getting dressed when my phone rang. Could I actually be getting stood up for a church service? No—much to my shock, it was Rita on the other end!

"Hi, George. Can you take me to church today?"

She had *gotta* be kidding! I just wrote her off a good ten hours ago! Besides, now I was going to take *two* ladies to church? Wouldn't *that* look wonderful, walking arm in arm with two young things, like something from a Fred Astaire movie...

"Well, sure. You should know, though, that I'm also taking another girl to church," I warned her, just to let her know what the situation was.

"I don't care. Do whatever you want. I just want to go to church!"

With a mixture of relief and deflation of my ego, I hung up and immediately called Luanne to explain the situation. What would any lady do, except be a good sport about the whole thing and acquiesce?

I first pulled in to pick up Rita from in front of her apartment. She looked pretty cute, all primed for a church service in a white peasant dress topped with a blue vest—sort of a Greek gypsy look. She was scoring points! My next stop was Luanne's house, where I once again explained the whole scenario.

She answered politely, but her true feelings were betrayed by her look of being sucker-punched in the stomach. Even though Rita offered her the front seat next to me, Luanne plopped herself way back in the passenger seat of the van, stewing in secluded solitude.

The sermon was a classic, nonthreatening megachurch lesson on love. Actually, it was perfect for someone like Rita. I offered to take them both out to lunch afterward, but Luanne wanted to get home as quickly as possible. I never did go back to that aerobics class again.

As I drove Rita home, I asked her what she had thought about the whole thing.

"I actually liked it, much to my surprise. What should we do next?" This didn't come off as a pickup line but more as the query of an honest seeker of truth.

"Probably, you should look at a Bible, so I'll get you one. Start with the book of Matthew."

I dropped a Bible off at her place, and then I didn't see her for a couple of weeks. That was fine because I felt I needed to check on Cindy to see how she was holding up. I went to her place, and she seemed fine with the dead end. At least I thought so, as much as a single guy in his twenties can tell from reading a woman. I left a bit down and sorry for her. Maybe I would check on Rita, another one of my failures, and see how she was doing.

I knocked on the door that evening and heard, "Let yourself in." Entering her tiny apartment, I looked to the left, and there she was, sitting on the couch reading the Bible! The gentle celestial glow from the lamp hovering over her as she sat there so peacefully actually made my heart skip a beat. I felt a jolt; she looked absolutely lovely right there, like someone I could be with forever!

Wait a minute, buddy. There was *no way* I was going to date a non-Christian. The path of my romantic life was strewn with female casualties by the side of the road from all of the mistakes I had made by being the spiritually wrong guy for the spiritually wrong girl. I had to make sure I was only interested in her salvation, making sure I stayed a healthy distance away from her so nothing would cloud either her—or my—decisions about God.

"How's the Bible reading going so far?"

"I finished Matthew. I really liked it. Now, I'm in John."

"What do you think?"

"Well, it's pretty clear that he's claiming to be God. Like you said, you've got three choices with His claim: He's either a real bad man and is trying to deceive everyone, He's just plain nuts, or He really was who He claimed to be, God in the flesh."

"So, what do you think?"

"I'm still working on it. There's a lot to process."

"Ready to try church again?"

"Maybe in a couple of weeks. I'm going away skiing, and then I'll let you know."

She was going with some guy she knew. Perfect—there was no sexual tension between us.

Sometime later, Rita called me. "Hey, my sister, Mary, is visiting from San Diego. How'd you like to take two women to church again? That seems to be your style!"

"Very funny. No problem."

We went to West Community again, and once again, I walked in escorting two short beauties. The sermon this time was decidedly different in tone, as the pastor talked about the temptation of Christ in the desert. Then, in front of the packed congregation of about twelve hundred attendees, he did something I'd never seen someone as slick as him do before: an actual altar call. Just like the one in the Billy Graham movie.

"If anyone here wants to make Jesus Christ your Lord and Savior, you need to do it in front of other people as your first step of faith and obedience. He says if you confess Him before the world, He will confess you before His Father in heaven. So, if you want to make this the day you start to follow Christ, make that step right now, and stand up in front of us all."

Oh boy, was *this* going to make Rita feel uncomfortable! I looked around, and *no one* in this well-heeled, upper-class church was going to do something as unsophisticated and lowbrow as confess that he or she was a sinner in front of that person's real-estate agents and investment planners. There was complete, library-like stillness, until…*Rita stood up*! What was she doing? She had tears rolling down her face and was shaking like a leaf. Her sister then stood up to join her, seemingly more for moral support than making a statement herself. (I had no idea where her sister stood in terms of beliefs.)

The pastor looked dumbfounded. He seemed pleasantly surprised that someone here actually acknowledged her need for salvation. Immediately after the service, some ushers hurried up to Rita and took her into some room.

Mary and I stood outside the church while people were milling about and going back to their Mercedes-Benzes and BMWs. A few minutes later, Rita came out looking pretty calm and collected.

"What went on in there?" I asked.

"Oh, they just wanted to make sure if I was sincere or not—whether it was some emotional thing or actually a meaningful choice. After I convinced them I meant it, they invited me to something called a beginner's Bible study. I think I'll go to it."

"Great idea! What clicked with you? Why did you make this decision?"

"Well, I told you I was going skiing with this guy, Bruce. He was some guy I'd met and had been seeing for a while, but since reading the Bible, I just wasn't interested in dating him anymore. Still, I love to ski, so I decided to still go with him just to ski. And I do mean *just* to ski!

"Anyway, one morning at the condo we were staying in, I heard something like one of those air-raid alarms going off. Instinctively, I turned on the TV to see if there was some news or directions on what to do. The channel had a religious program on with this guy Josh-something-or-other speaking."

"Josh McDowell! I know of him! He's written some great books."

"Well, anyway, he brought up that when he decided to follow Christ, he didn't get some one-time jolt, but over a slow period of time, he just started feeling this peace that transcended understanding. While he was saying this, I said to myself, 'That's what's happening to me! I'm feeling like a different person.' I read more of the Bible while up there and have finished the book of John. I realized God was changing me. My standing up just now simply seemed like the next thing to do!"

My mind was filled with hundreds of thoughts from a myriad of directions. Great! The pressure was off me to be this lady's spiritual caretaker. But was she really sincere? Was she doing it because she liked me? I didn't think so. Was she now open game for dating? Did I even want to date someone who was so new to the faith? Could this actually be a good thing, as she didn't have any Christian hypocrisy or religious baggage yet? Would she associate Christianity with me? Was that a good or a bad thing?

All these thoughts bounced between my ears as I took Rita and Mary back home.

"See you soon!" she cheerily said as she went into her condo.

See me? In what capacity?

Within a few weeks, Rita got involved with the beginner's Bible study, which consisted of a group of around eight to twelve people who were fairly new to the Christian faith, led by someone in leadership at West Community Church. They met once a week to go over the basics of what the Bible teaches about God, Jesus, the Bible, and what it means to be a Christian.

I was glad Rita was going to this, as it took a burden off me that I did not want to have: namely, to work on the spiritual life of someone I barely knew and to whom I was gradually being attracted. I really liked her attitude about life; she was able to balance being really serious with time to be fun loving.

This was important to me, as I had gotten into a pattern of dating someone who was outgoing and adventurous but who had no spiritual depth. I'd then break up with that person and date someone the complete opposite—deep and thoughtful but veering toward a melancholia that would make one need to stay away from sharp objects. I had never seemed to find the right balance until Rita came along. Also, she seemed determined to try her hardest at everything she attempted, and I saw that as a real character strength. Drive and self-discipline were things that just couldn't be taught as an adult; you either had it or you didn't, and those special qualities drew me to her.

Still, I kept things pretty safe and sane, taking her to things I liked to do to see how she'd respond. She fit in with my friends at West Community and even enjoyed the more staid Cal Pres where I regularly attended. The Blocks were overjoyed when they saw Rita at church and overwhelmed by the news of her new spiritual direction.

"I knew something had happened," explained Don. "I haven't heard her cuss at all in weeks!"

I took her to meet Kathy and Warren; both knew her a bit, since they took their dogs to Block's clinic. We went horseback riding one day on trails around Kathy's property, and after we finished, Rita went back to her place.

"What do you think of her?" I asked my sister.

"In all honesty, if you don't marry her, you're probably a homosexual," she answered, as only an older sister is able, mixing counsel with sibling nastiness.

CHAPTER D

Why Don't Ya Just Kiss Her?

I FIGURED IT WAS TIME to see how Rita would react to the kind of music I liked, so I took her to an African rock concert, featuring some singer from Zaire. Waiting at our table for the show to start, we had such a heated political discussion that she started to cry. Rita got up from where we were sitting and ran to the bathroom. When she came back to the table, I gave her a consoling hug and kiss. *A kiss! I had kissed a girl again!*

My mind was swirling with thoughts and emotions. I had promised God I wouldn't kiss anyone until I knew she was *the one*. Did this mean Rita was it? Or was this just one more of my impulsive moves that returned me to my dead-end cycle of relationships? Could my impulsive gesture be a sign from God that Rita *was* it? All these thoughts ran through my head while we were in a major lip-lock.

We left after the concert and kissed more at her front door. What now? We talked about it for a while. My biggest concern was that Rita would associate her spiritual walk with God with a relationship with me, so I told her that.

"Don't worry about that," she reassured me. "If we break up, I'm still going through with all of this. It doesn't depend on you; it depends on Jesus."

Never did being put in my place feel so good.

A few days later, during another kissing session, I gently approached the topic uppermost on my mind. "Ever think you could marry someone like me?" I volleyed in her direction.

"Sure!"

That was too easy! I hadn't expected an answer so direct; in fact, as soon as she said that, I felt as if cameramen with a lighting crew were about to jump out of her closet and yell, "We've got you on TV!" I had cowardly tiptoed into the subject of marriage, and I was caught by surprise that someone really wanted to be with me. Was this what success felt like? I guess we were engaged!

We went out a few more times and talked about our future together. It was April, and we talked about dating through the summer, and if things worked out, maybe getting some marriage counseling in September or October to figure out if we should go through with the whole thing. To a twenty-eight-year-old bachelor, who had never had a relationship last longer than nine months, this sounded both thrilling and scary. This could be the end of my loneliness but also the end of my selfish freedom! The finality of marriage seemed quite intimidating, but I reassured myself that a nice, healthy summer of dating would answer a lot of those questions.

Having become unofficially engaged, I decided the time was right for Rita to meet my parents. I rarely introduced my dates to them, as there is nothing as bothersome as having a Greek mother constantly ask you, "Whatever happened to that nice girl you brought by last year?" or "Are you still going out with *that* girl?" Those kind of open-ended questions do nothing for family bonding.

I explained to Rita what to expect when meeting my parents and the difference between Greek families like mine and WASP families like hers. She told me her ancestors had even come over on the *Mayflower* in 1620. Mine came over on the Ellis Island Express before World War II!

Driving through my old neighborhood, Rita suddenly declared, "Look, George. We're getting along really well, and we know we're right for each other. These necking sessions aren't making our lives any easier, since we're not going to sleep together. Dating like this during a long, hot summer is going to be torture for both of us. Why don't we just start the process of getting married by June and get it over with?"

I was so stunned by the thought that I honestly don't remember a single word that was said the rest of the evening. I remember she met my parents; she gave Dad a big hug that caught him off guard, and she held her own during our evening discussions about every topic known to humankind.

Marriage in two months? After being on the road for almost three years, I still couldn't believe that when it came to things like this, I was not very good at change—especially when it was a big shocker like this one! Could this really be it? The drive home was eerily quiet.

"I scared you, didn't I?" asked Rita.

"Why would you say something like that?" I replied in a voice that resembled a singer from the Vienna Boys' Choir.

"Fine. I get your point. Look…you know what you should do? Get away from me for a few days. Go camping—just you and God—and figure out what you want to do. If you come back and decide I'm not the one, I'll be fine. I'm thirty-two years old! I know how to be single! If you decide we should be together, then we'll go for it."

"What if I don't get a decision one way or another?"

"Do it again next week again, buster!"

This girl was smart! I took her advice and went away to Tehachapi for a few days, just me, God, the Bible, and lots of open space. Here I was, with an opportunity I seemed to have wanted all my life, but I could feel myself hesitating. Maybe it was (*once again*) like that old Groucho Marx joke, "I refuse to join a club that would have me as a member."

I sat by my old, faithful VW, just thinking about all of my disastrous relationships. They had been failures because I had done them all "my way" as Frankie Boy so poignantly sang. Finally, as I was approaching thirty, I had tried it God's way, and it seemed to be working out fantastically. Could I actually be a success in a relationship? I couldn't get over a verse in Genesis 2:18: "It is not good for man to be alone." I had done a lot with my life, but I had done all of it alone, and the Bible said that wasn't good. I needed someone to share my life with and, more important, to pour my life into. As Rocky Balboa so correctly said in the movie *Rocky*, "It fills gaps." I needed to fill her gaps, and she would fill mine. I was ready, and Rita could tell by the look in my eye when I saw her once I returned from my monastic trip.

We decided the next step was to visit her parents in San Diego—not to put any pressure on me or anything, but Rita and I both realized this meeting was going to be a combination of meet the family and ask for permission to marry the daughter. How's that for a one-two punch introduction? Rita had warned me that they were alcoholics; I had never known any before, so I didn't know what to expect.

Marigold and Bob Gorton seemed like fine, upstanding people. They were short like Rita. What did I expect, Masai warriors? We had a bit of small talk over dinner, and I realized the time to pull the trigger had arrived.

"Well," I said as I wiped my mouth after the dessert, "I've come here for a couple of reasons. The first was to finally have the honor of meeting both of you." I sat right across from Rita's father as he looked me in the eye. "The other reason I've come here is to let you know I've had the honor of getting to know your daughter, and she has impressed me so much with her character that I believe she's the one I want to spend the rest of my life with. I'd like to ask your permission to marry her."

The room got awfully quiet. Marigold was all aflutter, just like Mrs. Bennett in *Pride and Prejudice*. Bob looked at me and then flipped his wrist, looked away, and muttered, "I don't give a damn."

Not exactly what I expected, but as they say in football, sometimes you win ugly.

The next Tuesday morning, I went to my weekly men's Bible study with "Father" Ray Garcia. We soberly opened our notebooks, and Garcia asked each of us how we were progressing with presenting the gospel to the people within our social circle. When my turn came, he looked through his list of names and turned to me. "We haven't talked about Rita lately. What's the latest on her since you took her to the Billy Graham movie?"

"Good question. After that, I took her to church. Three weeks ago, I gave her a Bible. She read John and Matthew, and I answered her questions. Two weeks ago, we went to church again. She received Christ as her Savior at an altar call and is now a follower of Jesus. Last week, we got engaged."

The usually groggy, six-in-the-morning faces woke up as if injected with a hypodermic of Cuban coffee. "Just like that?" Breaking into a grin, Garcia shook my hand, and he said with his understated charm, "That's what I call 'relational evangelism'!"

Next on the list of things to do was to get some marriage counseling. During these weeks, Rita and I decided that if we were going to embark on this path, we needed to pray for something to happen that would make us break up if God didn't want us to be together. Pastor Pound of Cal Pres

Church was a pretty sober and straitlaced guy, so if he thought there was a problem with our getting hitched, he'd be sure to let us know.

We set up a time to get together and arrived in his cozy church office on the appointed day. Our church didn't actually have a building, since we had our services in the gymnasium of the local middle school. So, the church office was located in one of those strip malls. We sat in our seats and eagerly faced the man who had the ability to sanction or break our plans.

Sitting right in front of us on a folding chair, the genial pastor smiled as he handed both of us some papers. "Here are a few things for you to fill out—nothing really out of the ordinary, just a few questions to flesh out your opinion on things like family, faith, money, responsibility, and sex."

"What do we do with this?" I asked as I fumbled through the sheets of questions.

"Why don't you two just fill these out this week and give them back to me? I've learned that most marriages get into trouble over a few basic things, and if you get the conversation started on those topics, the counseling basically takes care of itself. I figure we'll be meeting for four to five times, unless some red flag comes up."

Four weeks! I couldn't help but laugh to myself. To become a member of this church, it took *twelve* weeks of attending classes before being considered acceptable! No wonder this church had stayed so small!

"Don't you think we might need a bit more counseling, since we've only known each other for two months?" I asked, not looking for an escape hatch but more for some sage advice from an older man.

"Look," he replied with a sardonic grin, "you're almost thirty, and Rita's older than you are. You've both been around the block enough times to know what is right for you. Neither one of you has any major baggage from previous marriages, and no matter what, you're going to have arguments during your marriage. My goal is to flesh out the major pitfalls, offer some solutions, and then set you on your way."

Somehow, this made a lot of sense to me and Rita. My parents had always told me that marriage doesn't solve problems but creates them. Also, at one of the classes at the Julian Center, Dick Day had been speaking about family and had said, "No matter what, one day, you're going to wake up in the morning with your spouse and simply not be able to stand her. That's when you decide that love is a choice. You don't marry the one you love; you love the one you marry."

I wanted to have a Greek service, but the priest at my old Orthodox church said Rita would have to convert in order to have a service there. That put the kibosh on that idea, but the priest was acquiescent enough to give us a script of the service, which Pastor Pound was glad to use as a template for our more Protestant service. He had us meet four times for "premarital counseling," but the gist of that was that we'd both been around the block enough times to know what we wanted and as long as we were both trying to be better Christians together, the unavoidable future problems and conflicts could be worked out. "Love is a choice," he said. "When a couple comes to me and says, 'We're not in love anymore,' I say, 'Good. Now you can start choosing to love each other.'" With both of us having so many failed relationships, this simple fact seemed like the key we'd needed to open the door to a long-lasting relationship in a trusting marriage.

We set our wedding date by picking when my favorite Greek band had a free night to play at our reception. We invited all our friends, family, and acquaintances. Many of Rita's professional female friends were aghast when she said during the ceremony that she would "submit" to her husband, ignoring my part about giving my life for her. Rita wore my mom's wedding dress and definitely had "that glow" that our singles group of guys had talked about. It was a truly joyful occasion, combining relatives with friends from all parts of my sojourn. It was a hint of the heavenly reunion that I had anticipated since my Sunday School teacher introduced the heavenly city back in my childhood. We finished the evening by cutting a wedding cake (with a sword that my father-in-law got as a Shriner) that had the husband and wife symbolized on top by a five-inch model of a spinal cord and a Milk Bone dog treat, displaying to the world, once and for all, this glorious union of a chiropractor and a vet.

ABOUT THE AUTHOR

George Harris grew up in California and attended California State University, Northridge, and Los Angeles College of Chiropractic. He now lives in Southern California and is married with two daughters and a granddaughter. He has been a contributor to *Africa on the Cheap* and the associate editor of *All About Jazz* magazine and is presently the editor of the website www.jazz-weekly.com. He and his wife, Rita, have led high school and college groups for over twenty-five years, and George has created a two-year curriculum that he has taught in fifth- and sixth-grade Sunday school for over twenty years. He still practices as a doctor of chiropractic in Agoura Hills, California, and still practices his tenor sax and clarinet—to the regret of his coworkers.

Made in the USA
San Bernardino, CA
18 April 2017